OECD Business and Finance Outlook 2020

SUSTAINABLE AND RESILIENT FINANCE

OECD
BETTER POLICIES FOR BETTER LIVES

Please cite this publication as:
OECD (2020), *OECD Business and Finance Outlook 2020: Sustainable and Resilient Finance*, OECD Publishing, Paris, *https://doi.org/10.1787/eb61fd29-en*.

ISBN 978-92-64-38456-9 (print)
ISBN 978-92-64-54453-6 (pdf)

OECD Business and Finance Outlook
ISSN 2617-2569 (print)
ISSN 2617-2577 (online)

Photo credits: Cover © JM_Image Factory/Gettyimages.com.

Corrigenda to publications may be found on line at: *www.oecd.org/about/publishing/corrigenda.htm*.

Foreword

This is the sixth edition of the *OECD Business and Finance Outlook*, an annual publication that presents unique data and analysis on the trends, both positive and negative, that are shaping tomorrow's world of business, finance and investment.

The COVID-19 pandemic has highlighted an urgent need to consider resilience in finance, both in the financial system itself and in the role played by capital and investors in making economic and social systems more dynamic and able to withstand external shocks. Using analysis from a wide range of perspectives, this year's edition focuses on the environmental, social and governance (ESG) factors that are rapidly becoming a part of mainstream finance. It evaluates current ESG practices, and identifies priorities and actions to better align investments with sustainable, long-term value – in particular, the need for more consistent, comparable and verifiable data on ESG performance.

The publication was prepared under the supervision of Antonio Gomes and Mats Isaksson, based on contributions from Robert Patalano and Riccardo Boffo (Chapter 1), Robert Patalano and Catriona Marshall (Chapter 2), Mats Isaksson (Chapter 3), Mamiko Yoko-Arai, Elsa Favre-Baron and Yael Regev (Chapter 4), Barbara Bijelic and Denis Bravenec (Chapter 5), Hans Christiansen and Sara Sultan (Chapter 6), and Raffaele Della Croce (Chapter 7). The following colleagues from the Directorate for Financial and Enterprise provided comments: Pablo Antolin, Winfrid Blaschke, Timothy Bishop, Tihana Bule, Jingjing Chen, Thomas Dannequin, Pamela Duffin, Oliver Garrett-Jones, Tyler Gillard, Shivani Kannabhiran, Fatos Koc, André Laboul, Flore-Anne Messy, Gary Mills, and Cristina Tebar-Less. The chapters also benefited from useful comments from the OECD Economics Department, Environment Directorate, Directorate for Public Governance, Directorate for Science, Technology and Innovation, and Trade and Agriculture Directorate.

Table of contents

FIGURES

TABLES

Follow OECD Publications on:

- http://twitter.com/OECD_Pubs
- http://www.facebook.com/OECDPublications
- http://www.linkedin.com/groups/OECD-Publications-4645871
- http://www.youtube.com/oecdilibrary
- OECD Alerts http://www.oecd.org/oecddirect/

Editorial

Environmental, Social and Governance (ESG) investing has grown considerably and is fast becoming mainstream. Yet market participants across the board are missing the relevant, comparable ESG data they need to properly inform decisions, manage risks, measure outcomes, and align investments with sustainable, long-term value.

The funds flowing into sustainable investment have grown steadily in recent years, with over USD 30 trillion of assets worldwide incorporating some level environmental, social and governance (ESG) consideration. This growth has been spurred by shifts in demand from across the finance ecosystem, driven both by the pursuit of traditional financial value, and by the pursuit for non-financial, values-driven outcomes.

From a *value* perspective, asset managers and institutional investors increasingly recognise that non-financial ESG risks can have a material impact on risk-adjusted returns and long-term value. From a *values* perspective, we have seen the rise of 'social investing' as financial consumers become more attuned with how their savings are invested, with a growing share looking to avoid supporting activities that do not align with their values. More widely, the social license to operate has also moved, with an expectation from some governments and citizens that private finance helps meet global challenges like climate change adaptation and mitigation or delivering on the United Nations Sustainable Development Goals, which may mean reputational risk for investors and institutions that do not keep up.

At the same time, the COVID-19 pandemic has highlighted an urgent need to consider resilience in finance – not just in the financial system itself, but the role of capital and investors in making economic and social systems more dynamic and able to withstand external shocks. Beyond the pandemic, physical and transition risks associated with climate change, including for financial stability, are perhaps the most pressing challenges to resilience.

This year's *OECD Business and Finance Outlook*, with its focus on sustainable and resilient finance, comes at a time when ESG considerations are rapidly becoming a part of mainstream finance. And yet, as our analysis shows, there is little common understanding within the market – from retail consumers and asset managers to financial service providers, market regulators and other stakeholders – on what the goals of ESG investing are or should be.

For the vast majority of investors, incorporating ESG factors has the stated objective of enhancing management of material risks to improve long-term risk-adjusted returns. However, as the original research in this Outlook shows, in practice market participants often lack the tools they need, such as consistent data, comparable metrics, and transparent methodologies, to properly inform value-based decision-making through a sustainability risk lens. This is despite a proliferation of ratings, methodologies and metrics on ESG performance.

This lack of comparability of ESG metrics, ratings, and investing approaches makes it difficult for regulators, consumers and fiduciaries to draw the line between managing material ESG risks within their investment mandates, and pursuing ESG outcomes that might require a trade-off in financial performance. It makes it difficult for lenders to carry out appropriate due diligence on the activities they are financing. It makes it difficult to compare infrastructure projects across sustainability metrics. And it makes it difficult for those who *are* prepared to make a trade-off between returns and social outcomes to do so with the confidence that the outcomes they are investing in are actually being achieved.

The growth and development of ESG and other sustainable finance products is promising, and evolving regulatory frameworks and international principles are beginning to form a more solid foundation. But much more needs to be done for ESG practices to support market efficiency and integrity. We cannot rely on finance to deliver better environmental, social or governance outcomes if investors do not have the tools and information to price related risks and direct investments accordingly.

This year's *Business and Finance Outlook* is a call to action for governments and market participants to make ESG investing fairer, more transparent and more efficient. It provides a comprehensive map of fiduciary duties and the extent to which ESG can be incorporated into investment decisions under current legal frameworks, and the challenges in doing so. It sets out priorities for policymakers to help markets deliver the data needed to identify and manage material sustainability risks. It lays out existing areas for governments to drive better ESG approaches, for example as owners of companies and as infrastructure investors, or through existing international policy standards and guidelines.

Critically, this Outlook helps governments take stock of what markets can reasonably deliver in terms of ESG impact, where alignment is – and isn't – between private and public objectives, what can be left to market forces and what must be taken up by public policy. This is particularly important where markets have difficulty connecting the management of short and medium-term risks with long-term material consequences, such as the eventual impacts of today's carbon emissions. To this end, governments can usefully help business and investors to better price longer-term ESG risks by providing consistent and reliable forward guidance on the timing, character and extent of forthcoming reforms that will influence the viability of assets, to provide certainty and incentivise the necessary adjustments in investment patterns.

None of these efforts can happen in a vacuum; financial markets are inherently global, and so demand global solutions. Governments and regulators will need to work together internationally to pursue the priorities outlined in these pages and ensure a level playing field. Close engagement with the industry, including institutional investors and lenders, ratings and index providers, and international standard setters, will be critical. Together, we can drive positive change in financial markets towards better sustainability and resilience, and ensure finance meets the needs of investors, our economies and of society now and in the decades to come.

Greg Medcraft

Director, OECD Directorate for Financial and Enterprise Affairs

Abbreviations and acronyms

ACI	Anti-corruption and integrity
ACSI	Australia Council of Super Annuation Investors
ACWI	All Countries World Index
AUM	Assets Under Management
CBAs	Cost benefit analyses
CCAs	Community choice aggregators
CDP	Carbon Disclosure Project
CDP	Carbon Disclosure Project
CO2	Carbon dioxide
COP21	21st Conference of the Parties
COVID-19	Novel Coronavirus Disease of 2019
CRR-2	Capital Requirements Regulation
CSR	corporate social responsibility
E	Environnemental
E&S	Environmental and Social Risk
EBA	European Banking Authority
EC	European Commission
EEA	European Economic Area
EIOPA	European Insurance and Occupational Pensions Authority
EP	Equator Principles
EPFI	Equator Principles Financial Institution
ESCOs	Energy Service Company
ESG	Environmental, social and governance
ESIA	Environmental and Social Impact Assessment
ESMA	European Securities and Markets Authority
ESR	Environmental Social Risk
ETF	Exchange-traded Fund
EU	European Union
FTSE	Financial Times Stock Exchange
G20 (IWG)	G20 Infrastructure Working Group
G20 IDI	G20 Infrastructure Data Initiative
G20/OECD Principles	G20/OECD Principles of Corporate Governance
GDP	Gross Domestic Product
GHG	Green House Gas
GI Hub	Global Infrastructure Hub

GRI	Global Reporting Initiative
GSIA	Global Sustainable Investment Alliance
GSSB	Global Sustainability Standards Board
IASB	International Accounting Standards Boar
IEA	International Energy Agency
IFC	International Finance
IFRS	International Financial Reporting Standard
IIRC	International Integrated Reporting Council
ILO	International Labour Organisation
IMF	International Monetary Fund
IOPS	International Organisation of Pension Supervisors
IPO	Initial Public Offering
IR	International Framework for Integrated Reporting
ISO	International Organization for Standardization
JFSA	Japan Financial Services Agency
KPI	Key Performance Indicator
LMA	Loan Markets Association
LPFs	Large Pension Funds
MNE	multinational enterprise
MSCI	Morgan Stanley Capital International
NASDAQ	National Association of Securities Dealers Automated Quotations exchange
NCP	National Contact Points
NFRD	Non-Financial Reporting Directive
NGFS	Network for Greening the Financial System
NPL	Non-performing loan
OECD	Organisation for Economic Co-operation and Development
OECD ESG Survey	OECD survey on ESG integration by insurance companies and pension funds
Paris Agreement	Paris Agreement on Climate Action
PPRFs	Public Pension Reserve Funds
R&D	research and development
RBC	Responsible Business Conduct
ROE	return on equity
S&P	Standard & Poor's
S&P	Standard & Poor's Composite Index
SASB	Sustainability Accounting Standards Board
SDGs	Sustainable Development Goals
SDIs	Sustainable Development Investments
SEC	Securities and Exchange Commission
SFDR	Regulation on sustainability-related disclosures in the financial services sector
SLLP	Sustainability Linked Loan Principles
SME	Small and Medium Enterprises
SOE	State owned enterprise
SPV	Special purpose vehicle
SRI	Socially Responsible Investment

STP	Sustainability performance targets
TCFD	Task Force on Climate-Related Financial Disclosures
TCFD	Task Force on Climate Related Disclosures
UN	United Nations
UN PRI	United Nations Principles for Responsible Investment
UN SDGs	United Nations Sustainable Development Goals
UNEP FI	United Nations Environment Programme Finance Initiative
UNFCC	United Nations Framework Convention on Climate Change
UNPRI	United Nations Principles of Responsible Investment
US GAAP	United States Generally Accepted Accounting Principle
US SEC	United States Securities and Exchange Commission

Executive summary

This edition of the OECD Business and Finance Outlook analyses current tools and practices with an emphasis on private finance and investment towards long-term value creation. It highlights the progress made to better incorporate ESG considerations in investment decisions, as well as challenges to effective implementation of ESG-based investment and finance strategies. It puts forward priorities and actions for market participants and policymakers to address such shortcomings, particularly around the urgent need for consistent, comparable, and verifiable ESG data.

Current market practices, from ratings to disclosures and individual metrics, present a fragmented and inconsistent view of ESG risks and performance. ESG ratings and investment approaches are constructive in concept, and potentially useful in driving the disclosure of valuable information on how companies are managed and operated in reference to long-term value creation. To this end, investors looking to manage ESG factors, particularly large diversified institutions, typically rely on external service providers of indices and ratings as a cost-effective means to guide the composition of ESG portfolios. However, the lack of standardised reporting practices and low transparency in ESG rating methodologies limit comparability and the integration of sustainability factors into the investment decision process. The link between ESG performance and financial materiality is also ill-defined, with little evidence of superior risk-adjusted returns of ESG investments over the past decade.

This fragmentation and incomparability may not serve investors in assessing performance against general ESG goals, or targeted objectives such as enhanced management of climate risks. The relationship between Environmental ("E") scores and carbon emission exposures is highly variable within and between ratings. In some cases high "E" scores correlate positively with high carbon emissions, due to the multitude of diverse metrics on different environmental factors and the weighting of those factors. This illustrates the broad challenges in ESG investing, but also the specific difficulties facing investors looking to consider both financial and environmental materiality. It also underlines how current ESG tools cannot be relied on to manage various climate risks, or to green the financial system, at a time when these are rising priorities for investors and policymakers alike.

Fiduciaries such as asset managers and boards should be managing material ESG risks in a way that supports long-term value creation – but are not necessarily getting the data and information they need to do so. The OECD's global survey of pension funds and insurers reveals the growing consideration of ESG risk factors in portfolios, the extent to which such institutional investors rely on external ESG data and service providers, and reiterates the challenges mentioned above in reference to investor experiences. These challenges extend to infrastructure financing, where the investment horizons of institutional investors and the nature of the assets increase exposure to longer-term sustainability risks. For corporations, managing and disclosing ESG performance and related risks is no different from their interest in managing and disclosing other material information as a key function of corporate governance.

Effective disclosures are important to the communication of forward-looking, financially material information, but practices remain at an early stage. Inconsistent disclosure requirements and fragmented ESG frameworks mean both institutional investors and corporates encounter difficulties when communicating ESG-related decisions, strategies and performance criteria to beneficiaries and shareholders respectively. This in turn makes it hard for beneficiaries to assess how their savings are used, and for companies to attract financing at a competitive cost that fully considers ESG factors. There is also an implicit ESG scoring bias in favour of larger companies and larger, advanced markets, which could affect the relative cost of capital and corporate reputation of companies outside of these groups, which is due in part to the high cost of ESG disclosure.

Banks are also looking to scale up ESG integration in lending transactions, but also face capacity, competition and data challenges. Given the scale and significance of lending and underwriting activities globally, stronger due diligence in reference to ESG risks would help align global capital with activities that avoid negative impacts on society and the environment, and enhance resilience in the financial sector, including to climate-related risks. To this end, banks would benefit from enhanced ESG risk management practices and sustainability reporting in their lending activities, and the development of metrics and methodologies to facilitate meaningful measurement of ESG risk.

Governments have levers available to drive better ESG outcomes as both enterprise owners and as investors. Around one-fourth of the largest global companies are entirely or largely state-owned enterprises (SOEs), and these companies can and should serve not only long-term value but also the fulfilment of widely held public policy priorities, including on sustainability measures. SOEs tend to have higher ESG scores than private companies, but this is not a given and depends in part on state ownership policy. A case study into the energy sector demonstrates how state ownership has sometimes been an obstacle to sustainability goals, such as the low-carbon transition, because of political concerns over the value of energy assets.

If left unaddressed, challenges in ESG investing could undermine investor confidence in ESG scores, indices, and portfolios. Developments and progress in ESG practices to date are promising, and they have the potential to be valuable, mainstream tools to manage risk, to align incentives and prices with long-term value, and to lessen the impact of future shocks like climate impacts or future pandemics. They can also be a valuable input into policymaking, by better articulating what the market can and should deliver in terms public outcomes, and what kind of further government intervention is needed to meet stated policy objectives. Taken together, the chapters of this Outlook conclude more needs to be done to fully harness this potential.

There are clear priority areas for policy action in facilitating fit-for-purpose data and disclosures in ESG investing. Greater attention and efforts are needed by regulators and authorities – including through guidance and regulatory requirements – to improve transparency, international consistency, alignment with materiality, and clarity in strategies as they relate to sustainable finance. This extends to the appropriate labelling of ESG products, with information that delineates the financial and social investing aspects of ESG investing.

At the same time, existing frameworks and policy instruments can drive better ESG outcomes and provide a solid foundation for reform. Closer adherence to, and wider implementation of, OECD standards, policy guidance and international best practices can already address some of the challenges described in this Outlook, especially around the assessment of risk and disclosure of material information. Key examples include the G20/OECD Principles of Corporate Governance, the OECD Guidelines on Corporate Governance of State Owned Enterprises, and the Guidelines for Multinational Enterprises and accompanying guidance, with specific guidance on Responsible Business Conduct for Institutional Investors and Due Diligence for Responsible Corporate Lending and Securities Underwriting.

Close engagement and cooperation between jurisdictions and with the financial industry is needed to strengthen the policy environment and drive better outcomes in ESG investing. Regulators of large jurisdictions with developed financial markets are already engaging on these very topics, and making good progress. However, capital markets are global in reach, as are many of the environmental, social and governance factors ESG practices seek to assess and manage. Therefore, global principles are needed to help establish good practices that acknowledge regional and national differences, while ensuring a constructive level of consistency, transparency, and trust.

1. Environmental, social and governance (ESG) investing

ESG investing is attracting growing attention from investors and policy makers over its promise of utilising a range of non-financial information to better align finance with long-term value and societal values. ESG practices, however, remain at an early stage of development, with challenges around consistency, comparability, and financial materiality. This chapter assesses current market developments, as well as the financial ecosystem and the key stakeholders shaping ESG practices related to disclosure, consistency of metrics, comparability of rating methodologies, and alignment with financial materiality. It scrutinises the performance of ESG approaches by exploring different ESG investment strategies of portfolios and investment funds, and their returns relative to traditional market benchmarks. The chapter concludes with a set of global recommendations to improve market confidence and integrity, so that sustainable finance can more effectively support resilient and inclusive economic growth.

1.1. Introduction

In the past decade, forms of sustainable finance have grown substantially due to an increasing demand by institutional and retail investors to better reflect sustainability issues in their investment choices. In particular, the use of environmental, social and governance (ESG) investment approaches has been driven by increased investor demand to make better use of non-financial information to guide asset allocation decisions to improve long-term value, while also better aligning portfolios with societal values. In this respect, growing concerns over the impact of climate change and the consequences of pandemics have drawn greater attention to environmental and social risks, combined with policy signals that the financial sector should be a driving force in advancing global sustainability.

In recent years, investors and financial intermediaries have been increasingly factoring ESG assessments into investment decisions. As of 2018, the number of signatories of the UN Principles of Responsible Investment (UN PRI) – an instrument that calls for the integration of ESG factors - had grown to over 2,300, managing over USD 80 trillion in assets.[1] Surveys of professional investors suggest that they consider ESG-related information increasingly important to determine whether a company is adequately managing risk and aligning its strategy to achieve long-term returns. However, even within the investments made by actors integrating ESG factors, insufficient distinction has been made between ESG assessments and related approaches such as socially responsible investing, suggesting that even a basic characterisation and measurement of the ESG market is a challenge.

Despite the mainstreaming of forms of sustainable finance, the terminology and practices vary considerably. One reason is that while ESG investing stems from investment philosophies such as Socially Responsible Investing (SRI), it has since evolved into a distinct form of investing. While earlier approaches used exclusionary screening and value judgments to improve their investment decisions, ESG Investing now looks to find long-term value in companies, beyond supporting a set of values.[2]

ESG disclosures and ratings represent an increasingly important tool for integrating sustainability considerations into the investment process, in several ways. First, ESG practices help financial investors who seek to evaluate the financial materiality of non-financial reporting about conditions, practices and strategies related to environmental, social and governance issues over the medium term. For example, they could relate to risk management practices to reduce the impact of climate change on corporate performance, or renewables strategies for new growth opportunities. Second, ESG ratings and metrics are also being used by social investors to monitor and assess the impact from their investments, such as to reduce carbon emissions or to better adhere to human rights standards. Moreover, certain investors may use these metrics to incorporate a blend of both factors, depending on the investment strategy and objectives. For each of these purposes, ESG criteria provide a useful framework for investors to assess how these prominent non-financial factors in the short-term could affect firm performance and impact its external environment over the long term. Thus, in concept, the ESG disclosures, metrics, and rates should serve to support investors to make more informed decisions and value judgments.

Despite substantial efforts to improve ESG disclosure in recent years, concerns arise over the current lack of standardised reporting practices and transparency at the international level. In particular, the absence of a universally accepted global set of principles and guidelines for consistent and meaningful reporting, creates a barrier to the effective comparability and integration of sustainable factors into the investment decision process.

In addition, consistency and comparability of ESG ratings could be hindered by the vast amounts of ESG related data that are disclosed using divergent core metrics and methodologies. This could be further compounded given the relatively early stage of development of ESG practices and the differences in methodologies adopted by ESG rating providers, including the incorporation and transformation of determined aspects, such as materiality. At the current stage, outputs across providers show a low degree of correlation as to what constitutes a high or low-scoring ESG rating, due to differences in subcategories, number of metrics, weighting and scope.

While market research of loosely defined sustainable metrics seem to show superior returns, a more in depth analysis suggests that financial performance based on ESG ratings is mixed and there is little evidence of consistent over-performance in recent years. Challenges in assessing ESG performance arise, in part due to the wide variance in ESG practices, such as negative and positive screening, proprietary ESG scoring, and rebalancing portfolios toward entities with higher ESG scores. Also, ESG practices are combined with other investment strategies that may include thematic focus, or an investment style, such that it is difficult to determine the extent to which particular ESG approaches are gaining success in generating long-term value.

Importantly, these identified challenges do not negate the benefits, in principle, of considering ESG criteria in the investment process. The additional information provided by ESG criteria offers further valuable insights on how companies are managed and operated to support long-term investing. Nonetheless, current approaches to ESG assessments and ratings appear highly inconsistent and incomparable, and risk undermining their potential value. While ESG ratings are constructive in concept and potentially useful in driving the disclosure of valuable information, a number of current challenges need to be addressed before investors can trust the integrity of such instruments in financial markets.

This means that, notwithstanding the potential for ESG investing to unlock value and align with societal values, the extent to which *current* ESG practices sufficiently unlock material information to deliver on value and values remains uncertain. What is clear, however, is that strengthening ESG practices at a global level would be needed to help ensure that disclosure and rating are transparent, consistent and comparable, which would improve outcomes both financial and social investors.

In light of these growing questions surrounding ESG investing, this chapter explores a number of key issues that are shaping ESG practices; the materiality of ESG disclosures; the current usefulness of ESG ratings; and, performance of ESG indices and funds. In addition, challenges that relate to transparency, consistency, materiality, and the ability of financial consumers to understand both the loose taxonomy and how it relates to portfolio composition, returns and risks are also reviewed. This is particularly relevant where investors have an expectation that they can use ESG factors to improve financial returns while aligning with societal values related to ESG practices.

The **first section** provides an overview of the size and composition of the ESG market, in terms of issuers and assets under management, while offering working definitions of ESG investing within the investment spectrum. In addition, it maps the ESG financial ecosystem, in terms of various market participants and other stakeholders involved in providing ESG information, ratings, indices, and investment products. Findings suggest that many organisations are now involved in coordinating the reporting of more consistent forward-looking information into issuer disclosures, setting principles and standards aligned with societal values, or establishing good practices on ESG reporting and analysis.

The **second section** reviews the challenges associated with ESG rating outputs and methodologies. The section observes that there remains fundamental distinctions between different approaches, including the wide range of categorisation and weighing of publicly available information, in part compounded by the subjective judgments of rating providers. While some key criteria are the same across providers, important aspects of the methodologies can differ, undermining the usefulness of the results.

The **third section** offers an assessment of ESG scoring, as well as benchmark and fund performance based on several prominent industry databases. The assessment builds on several strands of portfolio theory, including Markowitz modern portfolio theory, Fama-French factor models and an analysis of ESG funds. The aim of the assessment is to understand how the integration of ESG factors in the investment process affects performance and volatility when compared to traditional investments.

The **fourth section** introduces the main policy implications of the chapter, highlighting that greater transparency and consistency of core metrics and methodologies in the rating process is needed to improve the reliability of ESG ratings and investment approaches.

1.2. Dimensions of ESG investing and the financial ecosystem

1.2.1. Dimensions of ESG investing

The sustainable market size has grown considerably in the past decade and was estimated to exceed USD 30 trillion in total assets in the five major markets[3] at end-2019, an increase of more than 30% compared to 2016. Globally, almost USD 1 trillion of assets were held in sustainable funds at end-2019. Of these, around 75% were held by institutional investors and the remaining 25% by retail investors. The majority of sustainable investments are allocated in public equities (51%) and fixed income (36%) assets, with the remaining share divided among real estate, private equities and other types of assets (Global Sustainable Investment Alliance, 2018[1]). In this regard, it is important to understand the difficulties related to the differentiation between ESG investing and impact investing. ESG investing generally applies ESG ratings to the investment process (even though some of the strategies, such as exclusionary screening, may rely on product or norms-based information), while impact investing is focused on solving social or environmental issues through targeted investments. For the latter and according to the Global Impact Investing Network, the estimated current size of the global impact investing market is USD 715 billion.

With respect to sustainable investments, the European Union leads in total assets committed, with the total estimated amount higher than USD 14 trillion (Global Sustainable Investment Alliance, 2018[1]). The United States follows with more than USD 12 trillion of assets under management (AUM). The majority of this is held by asset managers and investment institutions. The data for the United States also suggests that USD 2.6 trillion (around 20% of total AUM) is managed through mutual funds, exchange traded funds and closed-end funds. Japan is the third largest centre for sustainable investing, showing strong growth potential, despite a more modest AUM of around USD 2 trillion.

Figure 1.1. Share of market coverage by ESG scoring companies by region, 2012-2019

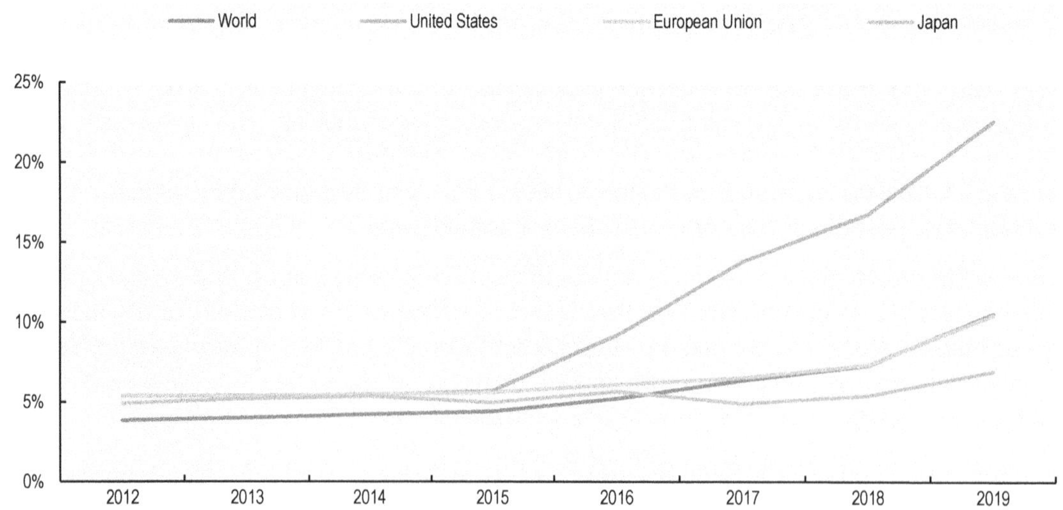

Note: Calculated as the number of public companies with an ESG score over the total number of public companies, in each year for the different areas.
Source: Refinitiv, OECD calculations

OECD analysis using Refinitiv ESG data yields similar findings when focused exclusively on ESG ratings. Findings illustrate disparate ESG market coverage across economic regions when analysing the following markets: World, United States, European Union, and Japan. Notably, market coverage is low in markets outside the United States, despite significantly increasing in recent years (see Figure 1.1). In the United States, market coverage has reached an all-time-high of almost 25% of public companies while in Europe and worldwide it remains just over 10%. Japan lags behind with just over 5%.

When analysing market capitalisation, however, a different pattern emerges: The market capitalisation of total ESG scoring companies (companies for which Refinitiv has calculated an ESG score based on the information reported by the company) represents 78% of the total global market capitalisation, representing around 95% in the US, 89% in the EU, and 78% in Japan (see Figure 1.2).

Figure 1.2. Share of market capitalisation by ESG scoring companies by region, 2019

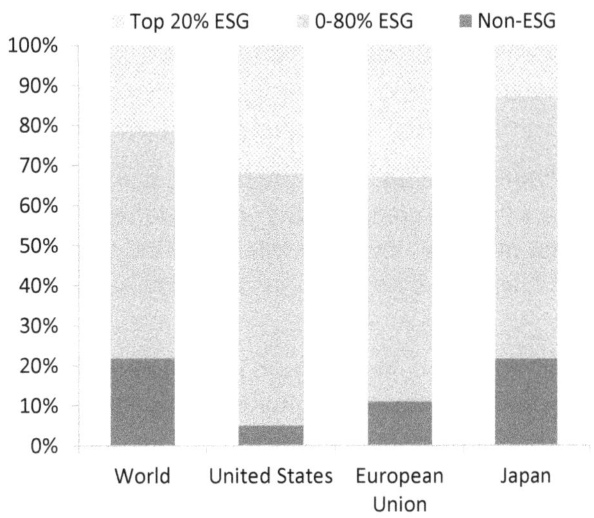

Source: Refinitiv, OECD calculations

Of total assets under management in sustainable funds, the majority are currently held by institutional investors, even though retail investors are increasing at a higher rate. Evidently, investor interest in ESG products is growing, yet concerns remain that, if ESG products are not clearly labelled with transparent methodologies, this could contribute to misaligned expectations when compared to actual outcomes.

ESG investing can fall within a broader spectrum of investing based on financial and social impact. At one end of the spectrum, pure social investing, such as philanthropy for example, seeks only social return. At the other end, pure financial investment pursues the objective of maximising financial returns based on a given investment strategy, risk parameters or constraints. Additionally, impact investing[4] seeks a social return, in addition to financial returns – but the balance of social and financial returns depends greatly on the chosen investment objective and strategy. As such, the delineation between what constitutes these different approaches and their anticipated impact on long-term value is not obvious.

In contrast, ESG investing incorporates different meanings depending on the motivation of the investor that uses it. When used by impact investors who want to better align capital allocation with environmental and social causes, what matters the most is how the sustainable practices of the company are reflected in the ESG rating. Yet, investors who have pledged ESG integration broadly see it as a necessity for long-term value creation, which will reward long-term investments, such as those that reduce exposure to reputational risks. Anecdotal evidence from surveys of institutional and retail investors suggest that investors are increasingly seeking both enhanced financial returns over time, and the societal alignment of their investments, to maximise financial and social returns. While such alignment may be possible in concept as environmental and social factors become more material,[5] in practice the returns of ESG have yet to show such evidence.

In this regard, ESG investment approaches may include some or all of five distinct forms. On one side, the least amount of complexity is through excluding certain firms categorically (e.g. based on moral or risk-related considerations), and on the other side is full ESG integration such that it becomes an integrate part of the investment processes, governance and decisions.

To this end, three broad investment approaches can be identified. The first form is **"exclusion" or "avoidance"** which signifies the exclusion of corporates and governments whose behaviours do not align with societal values. This is the largest sustainable investment strategy globally, with almost USD 20 trillion of AUM. Causes for exclusion commonly include:

- manufacturing controversial weapons;
- violation of global compact principles;[6]
- countries systematically violating compact principles; and,
- companies with more than a certain percentage of revenues from coal extraction, tobacco production or similarly activities with a negative impact on society.

This category can also include **"norms-based" or "inclusionary screening"** which pursues the inclusion or higher representation of issuers that are compliant with international norms, such as those by the OECD and UN.[7] This can include **"best in class"** investing whereby firms achieving above a pre-defined ESG score thresholds are included. This form of investment approach is applied to roughly USD 5 trillion in assets.

The second form, which in many cases is a step following exclusion, is the realignment of the remaining assets by ESG scores, with **greater tilting toward higher ESG and away from lower ESG scores**. Funds can chose to align with an ESG type of index for passive investing, or engage in active investment through a selected approach relative to an index. One derivation of this approach is a reweighting by which index providers or investors rebalance initial ESG ratings of "best in class" companies in each sector to ensure that there are high ESG scores per industry.

The third form is the pursuit of a **thematic ESG focus** within at least one of the ESG areas. These types of funds may or may not exclude or rebalance, in line with the approaches set out above. The thematic focus could include low-carbon funds, or good governance funds, which explicitly search for better-rated issuers in these areas in at least one of the environmental, social or governance areas, using particular expertise to assess the submetrics that drive the pillar score (see Chapter 2). The amount managed under thematic focuses is around USD 1 trillion.

Funds can also employ an **impact focus**, which in this case would suggest investing in *lower ESG companies* that show some propensity to transition to higher ESG, and/or where the *fund engages in some form of shareholder activism through share voting or bilateral communications to change company behaviour and practices*. This approach can be generalised across ESG, or can be thematic in focus, where fund managers may have expertise in one area of ESG, such as green finance or good governance.

Lastly, **ESG integration,** which refers to systematic and explicit inclusion of ESG risks and opportunities in investment analysis. Unlike the best-in-class method, ESG integration does not necessarily require peer group benchmarking or overweighting (underweighting) the leaders (laggards). Similarly, ESG integration does not require any *ex ante* criteria for inclusion or exclusion. The integration of ESG risks and opportunities into investment analysis is relevant for most, if not all, investors. Signs of ESG integration often include dedicated governance to oversee ESG integration; substantial resources given to the assessment of ESG considerations; explicit exclusion policies to avoid certain companies with very low scores and engagement policies to improve impact for those with relatively low scores but opportunities for improvement; and quantitative research and tools to assess performance. It is the second largest strategy, with more than USD 17 trillion of assets under management.

Within these rebalancing and thematic approaches, ESG can be used to pursue certain strategies that can be superimposed on the ESG investing approach. These strategies can include momentum, shorting, alpha investing, factor investing, carbon transition strategies, exploiting ESG rating inefficiencies in emerging markets, and alignment with Sustainable Development Goals (SDGs). Certain strategies seek to overweight high-ESG issuers, and others seek to overweight low-scoring ESG issuers with the intention that they will improve over time, either due to market pressures or direct investor engagement with company management. While these represent only some of the strategies adopted, their use illustrates that the resulting portfolio composition of an ESG fund can vary widely, and the wide range of approaches may mean that there can be little difference between the ESG portfolio choice to traditional funds.

1.2.2. The financial ecosystem

In light of the various assessment and portfolio construction practices, it is important to understand the financial intermediation chain that converts sustainable finance concepts into ESG practices, identifying subsequent implications for the end investor. This ecosystem is illustrated in the diagram below, and includes issuers and investors who disclose and use information related to environmental, social and governance issues. Many players are now involved in the ESG ecosystem, which is becoming increasingly complex, as the methodologies are different with a continual growth in the number and type of investment products. This in turn, puts pressure on regulators and framework providers to be more and more involved, trying to determine how data should be reported and used as well as how best to provide greater transparency for retail investors and asset managers.

Figure 1.3. The structure of the ESG financial ecosystem

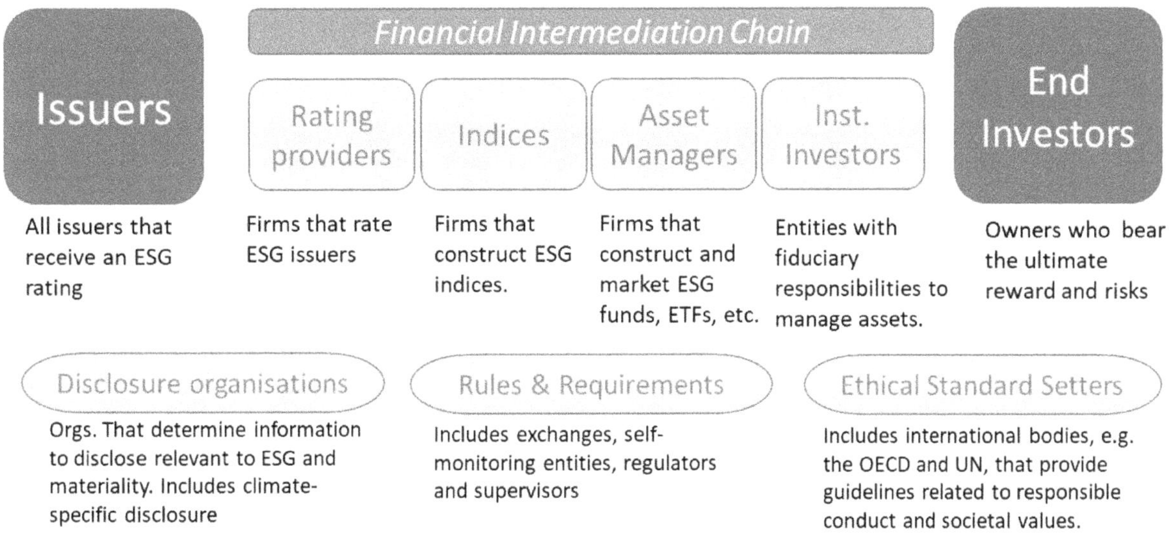

Financial Issuers. In short, financial issuers are any issuers that supply equity or debt to the financial market, through either public or private channels. ESG information is also being provided by sovereign bond issuers, as well as by SME equity issuers, and other types of issuers. In concept, all issuers belong in some part of the ESG ecosystem, as ESG assessment is being demanded by a growing number of investors, who are seeking to analyse information that comes from issuers directly, and other sources including financial and social media.

ESG ratings and index providers. ESG ratings and index providers include firms that (i) provide assessments of equity and debt issuers based on their disclosures that explicitly or implicitly offer metrics and information that help determine ESG scores, and (ii) index providers that convert ratings into market indices by reweighting market portfolios in accordance with some or all of the approaches described above. Some of these ratings are highly quantitative, by using and weighing numerous subcategory metrics based on identified quantitative data, either offered by corporate issuers or pulled from other sources such as financial media.[8] A number of rating providers are also index providers. The use of such indices is growing rapidly as a means to benchmark relative performance. These providers offer a range of stylised benchmarks that in turn allow for fund products to be developed for passive or active investment, and also for portfolio managers to utilise as a benchmark to compare their ability to generate risk-adjusted returns. By virtue of their growing use as benchmarks for ESG investing, the way in which indices are created, including exclusion, extent of tilting toward higher ESG scores, and other forms such as thematic indices (e.g. high "S" issuers), is highly influential in guiding overall ESG portfolio management.

ESG users: asset managers, institutional investors, and public authorities including central banks. The users of ESG ratings and information include, at the very least, types of investors across private and public entities. Asset managers that create investment products such as investment funds and ETFs use ESG ratings to either inform portfolio composition decisions, or to contribute to the portfolio managers' own ESG ratings. Institutional investors (e.g. insurance and pension plans) may incorporate ESG ratings for portfolio management, and to align with their fiduciary duty to incorporate forward-looking material information in their investment process (see Chapter 4).[9] Public sector institutions, including central banks and public debt issuers, have begun to consider the importance and need for ESG integration. A key reason is that central bank reserve managers increasingly seek long-term financial sustainability of their portfolios, and are striving to assess climate transition risks and the market impact of investors' shift toward lower carbon-intense industries.

ESG framing, guidance and oversight. ESG framing, guidance and oversight includes an array of actors that help define forward-looking, non-financial reporting to help ensure long-term sustainability as well as alignment with societal values. Many are **disclosure bodies** that assess and determine appropriate issuer information at national and international levels, including exchanges, self-regulating bodies, and related industry associations. In addition, a host of other bodies set **rules and requirements**, or influence them. These include oversight authorities such as markets regulators and bank and pensions supervisors. Lastly, **standard setters** for responsible conduct include international organisations that set standards and guidelines regarding responsible investing and sustainability goals. Given the number of regional and global organisations that seek to coordinate the reporting of forward-looking information in issuer disclosures, the integration of consistent and material reporting of ESG information remains work in progress.[10]

Different framework providers attempt to map and measure key criteria to help issuers provide consistent, meaningful ESG ratings to investors. A host of organisations have contributed to this wave of increased ESG transparency, ranging from the Sustainability Accounting Standards Board (SASB) and Global Reporting Initiative (GRI) to the Task Force on Climate-related Financial Disclosures (TCFD), including stock exchanges such as NASDAQ and the World Exchange Council. In addition, regulators from around the world are getting more involved in the supervision and understanding of how ESG metrics are created and measured, in order to create a clear framework for investors.

Box 1.1. Regulatory interventions to clarify ESG practices

Regulators are taking action to provide more clarity around sustainable finance ESG practices

Specific bodies such as the FASB, TCFD and GRI have already taken steps on sustainable finance and ESG, in order to develop common standards on how basic data are gathered, how metrics should be created and the way in which materiality should be incorporated.

In light of the rapid growth of assets under management by asset managers utilising forms of ESG practices, national financial regulators have begun to assess a range of practices associated with forms of sustainable finance, with an increasing focus on ESG taxonomies, approaches, and marketing to investors.

This follows actions by the EU, as part of its commitment to achieve the United Nation's 2030 Agenda and Sustainable Development Goals and to comply with various international agreements, such as the Paris Climate Agreement, to move ahead on ESG disclosures and benchmarks trough the EU Action Plan on Sustainable Finance, with the aim of providing a regulatory framework to support and promote sustainable investment in the EU. The European Commission's Technical Expert Group on Sustainable Finance has published its final Taxonomy report for screening environmentally sustainable activities. The taxonomy is expected to facilitate a pan-European ecolabel for financial products The Commission will conduct a consultation of the first draft of the screening criteria for the taxonomy shortly. Moreover, mid-2020, three European supervisory bodies – ESMA, EIOPA and EBA - issued a Consultation Paper seeking input on proposed environmental, social and governance (ESG) disclosure standards for financial market participants, advisers and products. These standards were developed under the EU Regulation on sustainability-related disclosures in the financial services sector (SFDR), with the aim of strengthening protection for end-investors; improving the disclosures to investors from a broad range of financial market participants and financial advisers; and improving the disclosures to investors regarding financial products.

The US SEC has launched an initiative to scrutinise ESG investing strategies of regulated investment products. The review will consider the potential risks associated with inconsistent ESG disclosure, including with respect to investor protection and breach of fiduciary duties. One objective is to provide investors with the "material, comparable, consistent information they need to make investment and voting decisions" by developing a framework to disclose material in order to reduce reliance on third-party ESG data providers or disclosures. ["Recommendation from the Investor-as-Owner Subcommittee of the SEC Investor Advisory Committee Relating to ESG Disclosure, 14 May 2020, https://corpgov.law.harvard.edu/2020/05/28/recommendation-from-the-investor-as-owner-subcommittee-of-the-sec-investor-advisory-committee-relating-to-esg-disclosure/]

In Japan, the Financial Services Agency revised its code of conduct for institutional investors in March 2020 to encourage institutional investors to focus on ESG when making investments. The revisions call on institutional investors to engage in dialogue with investee companies and clearly state how they will incorporate ESG into their investment strategies. ["Finalization of Japan's Stewardship Code", FSA, 24 March 2020, www.fsa.go.jp/en/refer/councils/stewardship/20200324.html]

On this matter, a number of additional jurisdictions are taking steps to address perceived concerns about the clarity of ESG among asset managers, retail investors and other market participants, to help strengthen market resilience and integrity.

1.3. ESG rating outputs and methodological challenges

The sustainable finance transition is currently under way and as such ESG ratings are an evolving instrument being shaped by industry and expectations. In this regard, the analysis of ESG ratings and related outputs underlines the difficulties faced by investors and how fundamentally different these ratings can be depending on the provider. This is mainly due to methodological differences in structuring the ratings and also on how materiality is incorporated. This section explores potential possibilities to overcome bias and increase transparency to improve the usefulness of and trust in ESG ratings.

1.3.1. ESG rating outputs

Scoring approaches begin with the consideration and identification of relevant criteria within each of the E, S, and G factors. Environmental factors can include natural resource use, carbon emissions, energy efficiency, pollution and sustainability initiatives. Social factors can include workforce related issues (health, diversity, training), and broader societal issues such as human rights, data privacy, and community engagement. Governance factors can include corporate governance and corporate behaviour, ranging from shareholders' rights to executive compensations.

Different providers use different metrics and submetrics, aggregated and translated in different ways to create the overall ESG scores. Every provider ranks different aspects of the sustainability of the companies it assesses. These metrics and aspects are then aggregated to create a key pillar score, which usually defines one of the elements supporting the pillars (E, S and G).

Both MSCI and Sustainalytics state that their services are designed to help investors identify and understand financially material ESG risks and opportunities, in order to integrate these factors into their portfolio construction and management process. Thomson Reuters and Bloomberg provide an ESG reporting score, which focuses on how and what type of information is reported by companies.

Even though the users of ESG information largely retrieve information directly from issuer disclosures, with third party analysis and scores largely developed using the same base of information, ESG scores can still vary widely from one ESG provider to another.[11] ESG scoring can be criticised because the adoption of different methodologies by rating providers can lead to wide variance in results. This implies that if investors are using and relying on different service providers, the inputs of the scores that shape securities selection and weighting could be driven by the choice of rating provider.

The metrics used by companies and data providers are affected by the lack of consistency and varying levels of transparency between stakeholders in the ESG ecosystem. Among the major market data providers such as Bloomberg, Thomson Reuters, FTSE, MSCI and Sustainalytics, the methodologies vary significantly. While variation in analytical practices and judgment can bring additional insights to investors, the correlation is low between the scores they assign to the same companies (see Figure 1.4).

OECD analysis assesses different rating providers, namely Bloomberg, MSCI and Refinitiv in order to understand how their ratings vary when analysing specific indices, such as the S&P500. The results illustrate wide differences in the ESG ratings assigned, with an average correlation of 0.4.

This highlights how some companies ranked top by one provider get much lower scores from others. This depends on what is measured, and how the measurement is affected by company disclosure.[12] Research by (Berg, Kölbel and Rigobon, 2019[2]) investigates the differences in ESG ratings of five providers. It decomposes the differences in ratings into three sources and finds that different scores among providers are mostly driven by the scope and the measurement of categories, explaining more than 50% of results, while the weight assigned has a limited impact. This assessment substantiates concerns over the meaning of current ESG scores and their value to investors.

OECD analysis then compared ESG ratings with the issuer credit rating by major providers and found that credit scores for selected issuers vary much less, in part because they are based on a clear set of financial metrics that drive ratings results, while qualitative judgments tend to influence decisions that most affect notches (see Figure 1.5). These differences raise important questions on the reliance of ESG ratings to make investment decisions, including for structuring investment portfolios that are considered to have a tilt toward higher ESG scores. In short, if high ESG scores are simply a judgment that varies significantly across firms, the extent to which investors can be assured that this approach either provides enhanced returns or aligns with particular societal values merits further scrutiny by policy makers and the investment community.

Figure 1.4. Correlation of S&P 500 ESG ratings by different ESG score providers, 2019

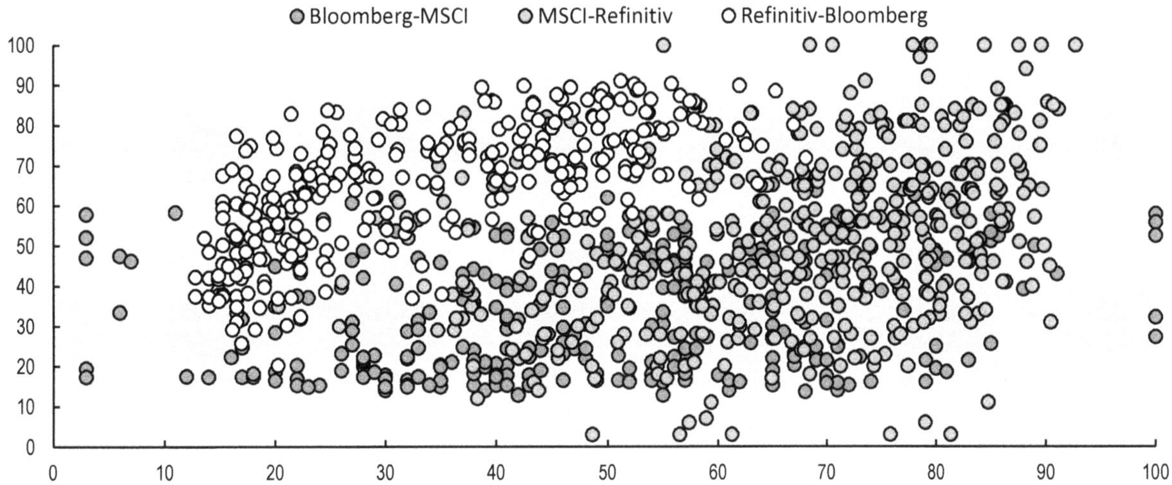

Note: Providers' names in the legend correspond to the Y axis when at the left and to the X axis when at the right.
Source: Bloomberg, MSCI, Refinitiv, OECD Staff calculations

Figure 1.5. Selected ESG ratings and issuer credit ratings by sector in the United States, 2019

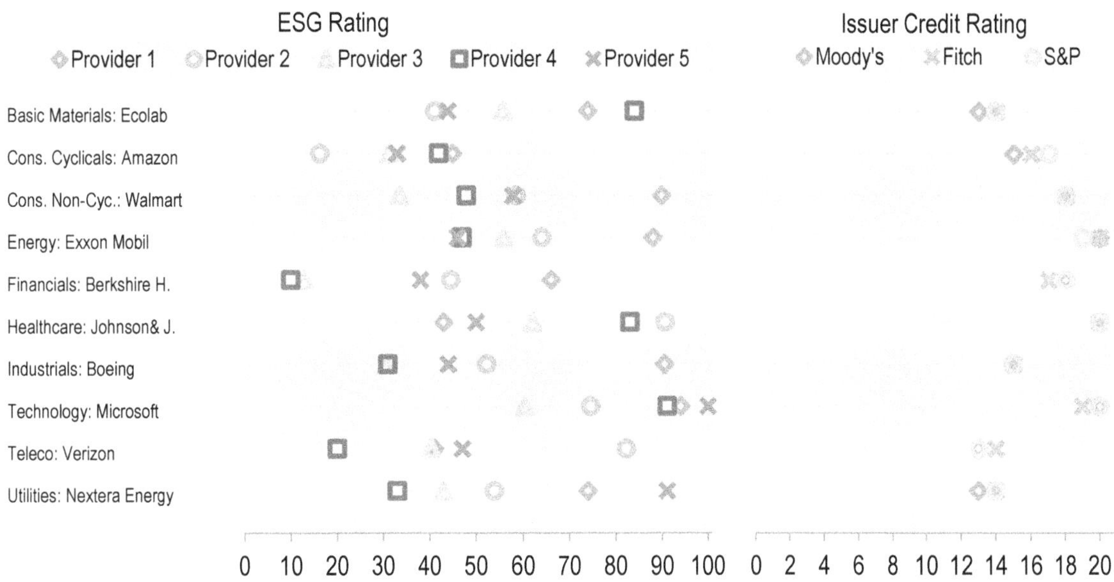

Note: Sample of public companies selected by largest market capitalisation to represent different industries in the United States. The issuer credit ratings are transformed using a projection to the scale from 0 to 20, where 0 represents the lowest rating (C/D) and 20 the highest rating (Aaa/AAA).
Source: Refinitiv, Bloomberg, MSCI, Yahoo finance, Moody's, Fitch, S&P; OECD calculations.

1.3.2. Methodological challenges

ESG rating methodologies are still evolving following demand from investors and regulators. Therefore, the methodologies of different providers have been analysed to understand how the underlying data is transformed. As discussed earlier, ESG scoring methodologies include both quantitative and qualitative elements, which include different weight factors for each industry and a highly subjective judgment of each company based on disclosures and a host of other public information used to arrive at scoring results.

Nonetheless, concerns arise over methodology and metrics issues in ESG ratings. In particular, industry participants have noted that a lack of consistent corporate disclosure regimes at the international level hinders information available to investors. There is a poor understanding of ESG rating agency approaches, in part due to the opacity of detailed rating methodologies and specific metrics, highlighting difficulties in assessing the rating results and the wide differences across key providers. Many organisations report difficulties in obtaining specific guidance on the ESG information reviewed by each ESG rating agency and how they analyse data and qualitative information. Disparate rating outputs by different agencies can create confusion in the market, both for investors and issuers. Moreover, the mixed ratings results and mixed evidence on financial performance raise the need for more thorough assessment of how financial materiality and values alignment are captured. In particular, the assessment of each industry to determine the relative importance of each factor and sub-factor depending on the external environment and business model is extremely important to have a clear view of what ESG ratings reflect.

The mixed results regarding the final ESG score of different providers raise the need for more thorough assessment of how financial materiality is captured in ESG data and ratings. Currently, the various ESG reporting and ratings approaches generally do not sufficiently clarify either financial materiality or non-financial materiality (e.g. social impact), so investors are not currently able to get a clear picture of whether the measurements suggest a net positive or negative effect on financial performance. An example of a financial material framework for ESG reporting is the materiality map developed by SASB, which emphasises the importance of materiality and embeds its importance at the industry level. SASB notes that it prioritises and maps issues that are reasonably likely to directly impact the financial condition or operating performance of a company and therefore are most important to investors. Financial materiality may be influenced by societal values related to environment, governance and social issues and these factors can change over time, creating the need to constantly improve and adapt materiality.

Figure 1.6. Comparison of company ESG scores by different ESG score providers, 2019

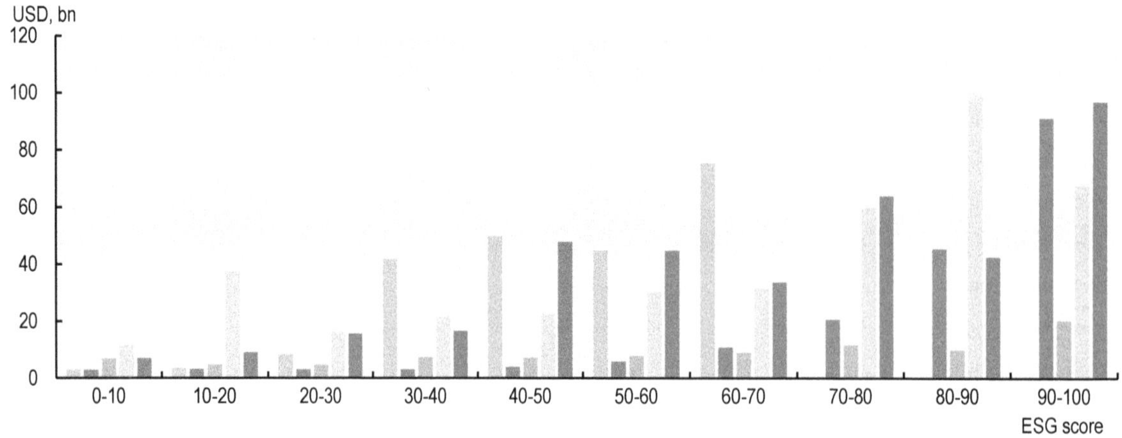

Note: Comparison of five different providers of ESG scores (shown in different colours) in terms of average market capitalisation.
Source: Bloomberg, MSCI, Refinitiv, OECD calculations

Methodological concerns also arise when looking at the final ESG product. External research and OECD analysis indicates an implicit ESG scoring bias in favour of large-cap companies and against SMEs. This is reflected in the OECD analysis of ESG ratings compared to market capitalisation and may be due to the fact that SMEs do not have the resources to invest in non-financial disclosure, as the costs may outweigh the investment gains in the near term. However, this bias, and the hurdle of unlocking useful ESG information from smaller companies, creates a market inefficiency that affects both the relative cost of capital and corporate reputation.

There is some evidence that this bias also exists with respect to ESG scores among Emerging Market issuers. As there is lower ESG disclosure practice in parts of EMEs, some companies with sound practices with respect to environmental, social and governance issues could be penalised because they do not yet disclose their assessment of ESG risks and opportunities in a manner consistent with emerging good practices.

1.3.3. Transparency of ESG products alignment with investors' sustainable finance objectives related to financial and social returns

Where expectation gaps exist between investor objectives, between impact and regular financial investing, such gaps need to be addressed to ensure market integrity and trust in financial markets. OECD analysis shows that methodological issues, differences between providers, and biases raise concerns with respect to investors' expectations. Recalling the investment spectrum between social and financial investing, investors should be able to ascertain sufficient information from investment funds or institutional investors as to how, and the extent to which, they would be expected to sacrifice financial returns for social returns. Put differently, if a fund excludes certain companies due to values (e.g. tobacco), or rebalances portfolios due to the incorporation of socially relevant information then there are potential impacts to absolute and risk adjusted returns relative to a similar traditional index (same constituents, but without an ESG scoring tilt). At least, such historical attribution analysis is entirely feasible, but communicating such variations in returns and risk does not appear to be the norm.

On a related matter, the trends in using ESG scoring illustrate that a substantial portion of those who pursue ESG investing are doing so, at least partly, for ethical reasons and may have expectations of what their investments will and will not support. Yet, much of ESG scoping and fund offerings illustrate that rebalancing based on "best in class" shifts investments within industries. In this manner, some investors may not realise that their ESG funds are even more heavily weighted toward very large carbon-intensive oil companies or BigTechs that face data privacy scrutiny, or behave in a manner that is not aligned with societal values.

More transparency is therefore needed to ensure that funds disclose the full spectrum of performance criteria in terms of past returns and risks, and the extent to which this is due to portfolio decisions that could compromise absolute or risk-adjusted returns relative to a suitable traditional index, based at least on past performance.

1.4. Critique and empirical assessment

Given the current market size dimensions of ESG investing and the methodological challenges faced by investors, an analysis of the financial performance of portfolios integrating ESG strategies is conducted, in order to provide a broader view of what ESG really means. Different methodologies have been applied, ranging from classical portfolios theory to funds analysis, to different rating providers.

The review of academic and industry literature reveals a wide range of approaches and results, which are largely inconsistent with one another. The research highlights the difficulty of identifying the real impact of ESG on investment performance. While some show a positive impact, improving the overall performance of investments, others do not show any meaningful effect. The inconclusiveness of research may be caused by problems with different providers, methodologies, investment strategies, geographical selection, sample selection and timeframes.

A considerable amount of research has been conducted over the past decade on socially responsible and sustainable investing, including the impact of corporate social responsibility and good governance on market-based and financial statement measures of financial performance. These studies analyse Corporate Social Responsibility comprehensively but do not directly relate to ESG ratings and their impact on shareholders returns.

The financial industry has in recent years turned its attention to the extent to which ESG investing can achieve superior returns, or at least avoid inferior returns, relative to traditional investing that does not incorporate sustainability considerations beyond immediate financial performance and corporate strategy to further enhance future performance. It has pursued several forms of analysis: (i) academic studies of performance using ESG or other related sustainability metrics; (ii) financial industry studies using established ESG ratings; (iii) megastudies that assess various forms of prior studies of corporate social responsibility and good governance, and impact on performance.

This chapter seeks to answer some important questions that have arisen from the review of practices. They include:

Composition and bias. To what extent have ESG scores penetrated firm coverage by count and market capitalisation? Are there biases in ESG scores that favour or penalise certain types of firms? This question has been already been addressed to some extent in the previous section, focusing on the methodology and the biases underlying the ratings.

Portfolio performance. How do ESG portfolios and funds perform; do they show clear signs of superior performance over the past decade? To answer this question different classical financial analysis methodologies have been used to enable a broad view on the subject.

Concentration. Does tilting of portfolios lead to higher concentration and volatility for a given return? Classical financial theory indicates that an increase in returns depends on the level of risk that investors are willing to take. Therefore, analysis is conducted to assess the extent to which the volatility of ESG portfolios and indices change with respect to traditional indices.

OECD analysis of ESG scores and performance using different providers aims to answer these questions. The analytical approach focuses on portfolio optimisation and efficient frontier portfolios, using Markowitz's portfolio theory and the Fama and French factor model, which are widely used in financial analysis. Markowitz's methodology is used to create the best portfolio based on different assumptions and based on expected risk and return. The Fama and French model instead aims to understand the return of a portfolio after taking into account the variables underlying the risks of the market and of the portfolio itself. Tail risks and maximum drawdowns are analysed in order to have a comprehensive view on the subject.

In testing for the Markowitz efficient frontier, it can be observed that, depending on the ESG index analysed, risk adjusted performances vary. In particular, risk analysis shows a varying volatility, but a lower maximum drawdown for ESG indices.

The findings are based on the analysis of ESG indices and ratings, which do not necessarily represent firms with current strong environmental and social performance, given the integration of multiple forward looking factors. The findings are meant to provide clarity over the performance of ESG ratings and not a broader sustainable framework. To compute the Markowitz efficient frontier, both ESG indices and non-ESG indices are included from a selection of indices from MSCI, to assess whether ESG criteria influences risk-adjusted performance. A framework in which every index is treated as if it was a single asset has been adopted, to understand the difference in risk adjusted returns and drawdown risk.

The drawdown risk is widely used as an indicator of tail risk over a specified time period, which helps to understand downside risk in the event of extreme conditions. It is calculated by comparing the value of a cumulative return with a previous peak that is the maximum cumulative return, in a pre-specified period of time. One example of extreme drawdown refers to the S&P500, which dropped by 48% in 2008 during the financial crisis.

Within this context, a total of nine MSCI indices are analysed, in which 6 are ESG indices, to assess returns and risk-adjusted returns (see Figure 1.7). These indices are considered using the same approach, even though they are built using different methodologies and with different objectives in mind in terms of sustainability and risk management.

The Minimum Variance Portfolio is computed and the efficient frontier of risky assets selected. The results show that different ESG indices have varying risk and performances depending on how they are built. For example, the ACWI minimum volatility performs slightly better than its ESG counterpart, even though the latter has a lower drawdown risk (-7.83% against -8.56%), with that being true for most ESG indices. For instance, the ACWI Quality ESG reduces the volatility of the benchmark while maintaining the same return. This could show that investors are willing to renounce a part of returns in order to achieve higher security, namely through a lower drawdown risk. When looking at the other indices, they are treated as inefficient according to the efficient frontier. This might be due to the different nature of the indices analysed and the fact that they are treated as single assets when in reality they are not.

Figure 1.7. Comparison of ESG and non-ESG MSCI indices by risk-adjusted performance

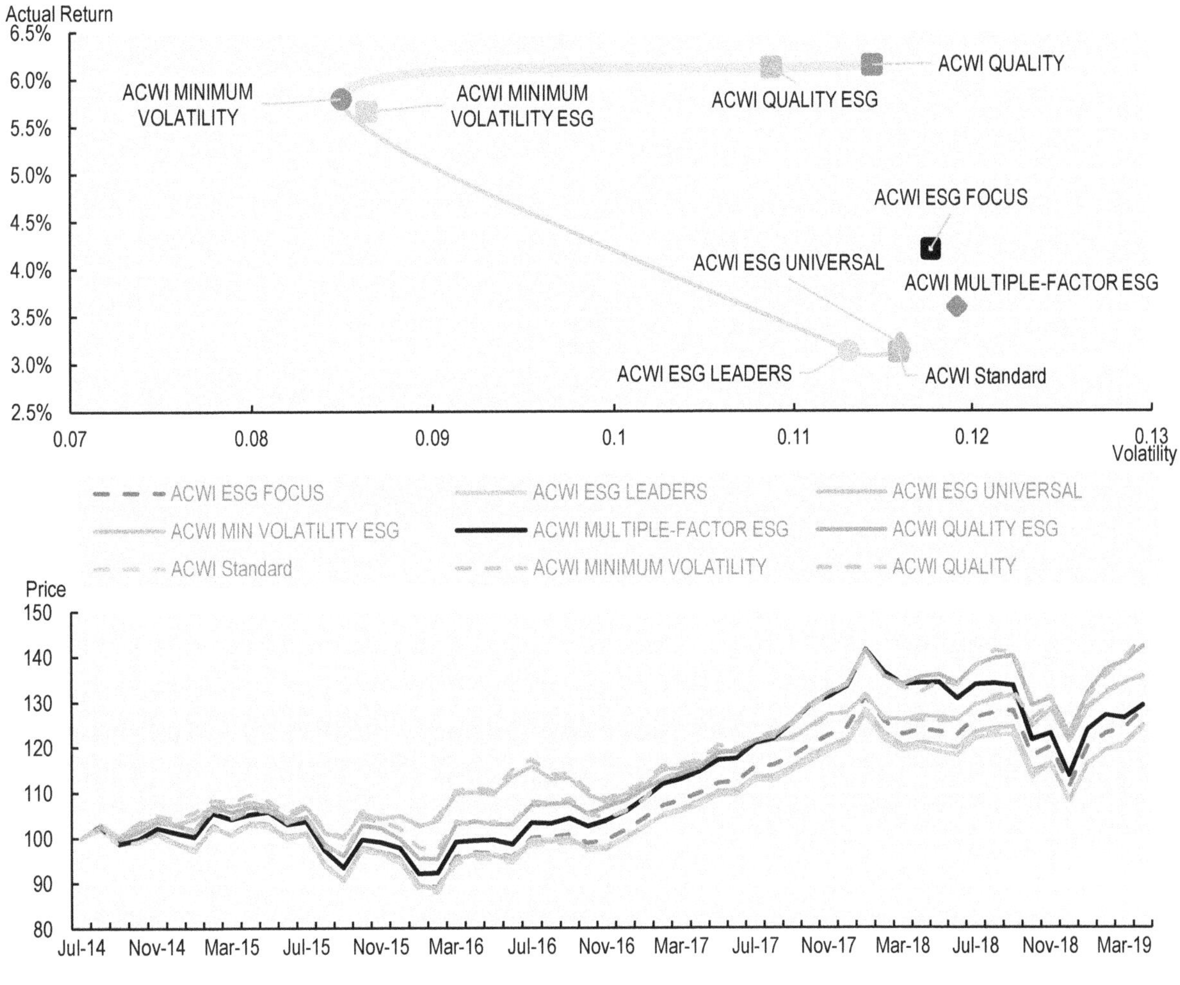

Source: MSCI, OECD calculations

Using Fama and French portfolio analysis, **it can be observed that the excess return generated depends on the provider chosen to build the portfolio, even though low scoring portfolios generally perform better than the market.**

Using this hypothesis, OECD analysis examines how ESG scores perform in comparison to the market, and in particular to assess whether high ESG scoring stocks outperform low ESG scoring stocks using the Fama and French 5 factor model. A similar pattern for each provider is observed, except for one, which shows positive alpha on the best scoring ESG portfolio.

The results of the analysis are adjusted for different risk factors, excluding systemic risks, which cannot be captured by the Fama and French 5 factors model methodology.

The model aims to price assets taking into account risk factors such as systematic market risk,[13] size of companies and book-to-market ratio. The risk-adjusted alpha extracted from the model measures the excess return of an investment relative to the return of a benchmark index. In this case the benchmark index is provided by Fama and French and is a proxy for the market.[14] This result was obtained by running a regression between a portfolio of securities and the 5 factors provided by Fama and French.

Figure 1.8. ESG top and bottom quintile Alpha by different providers in the United States, 2009-2019

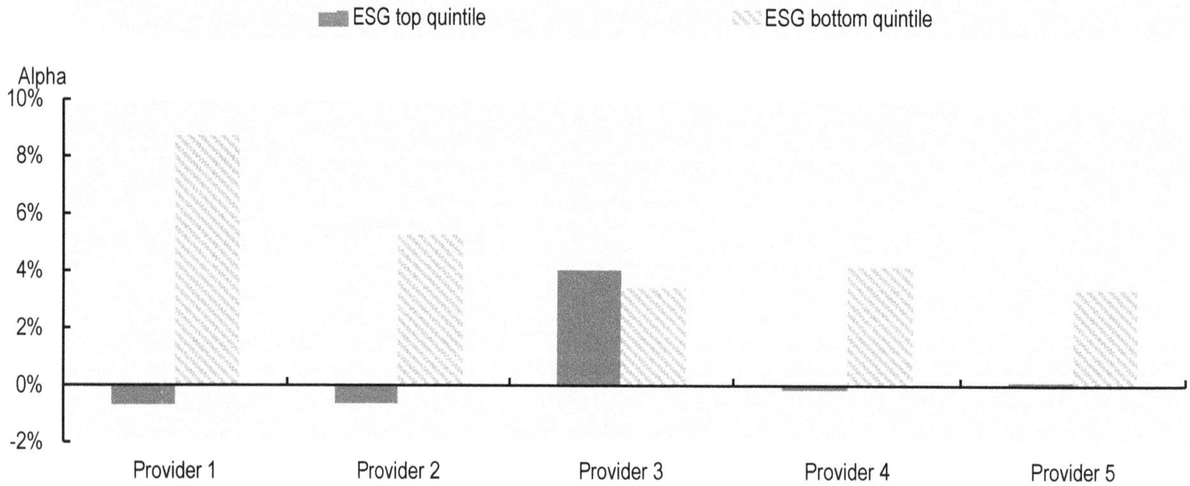

Source: Bloomberg, Fama and French, MSCI, Refinitiv, OECD calculations

Moreover, the assessment of ESG funds considers how they perform when compared to traditional funds based on several prominent industry databases. The assessment builds on several strands.

Distinct from indices and portfolios, the analysis assesses the extent to which actual investment funds holding high-ESG issuers outperformed funds which benefit from investment management strategies and decisions on ESG investments.[15] To do this, a sample of funds from Morningstar is analysed to understand how ESG ratings affect fund performance.

The results of the analysis, focusing on the best and worst rated funds, provide a framework which shows that the distribution of the returns has similar ranges for both categories, except for some outliers in the lower rated funds. In particular, while the distribution of the funds look similar, when focusing on the low scoring funds there is a higher likelihood that these funds will suffer from downside risk, with some funds performing well below -20%. This reflects the findings of Markowitz's Minimum Variance portfolio, showing that ESG assets imply a lower systemic risk, for example during unexpected events. This was evident during the COVID-19 pandemic, where some ESG indices appeared to provide a better choice than standard indices, with lower underperformance (see Box 1.2).

Figure 1.9. Distribution of the performance of 300 sustainable funds (5 stars), 2019

Note: Analysis of the 150 best and worst funds with a 5 star sustainability rating by Morningstar. The returns are 5 years annualised.
Source: Morningstar, OECD calculations

Figure 1.10. Distribution of the performance of 300 low sustainability funds (1 and 2 stars), 2019

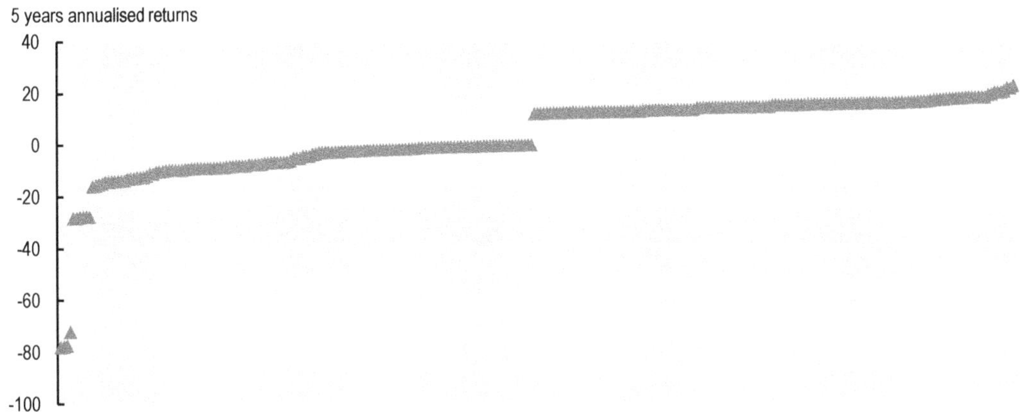

Note: Analysis of the 150 best and worst funds with 1 and 2 stars sustainability rating by Morningstar. The returns are 5 years annualised.
Source: Morningstar, OECD calculations

Box 1.2. ESG funds and indices during the COVID-19 pandemic

Following the spread of the COVID-19 pandemic in Q1 2020 which put downward pressure on financial markets, sustainable finance market participants observed that ESG funds and indices outperformed traditional investments. This box provides a brief analysis of the main ESG indices to help understand the magnitude of this outperformance and whether ESG considerations can actually improve portfolios' resilience against tail risks. Different market actors such as Bloomberg, Morningstar and MSCI showed a relative outperformance of ESG funds and indices over standard ones, with these instruments losing less value than traditional indices during the downturn. The findings are consistent with OECD analysis showing a lower drawdown risk for some ESG indices.

To understand the extent of this outperform (illustrated by lower underperformance), different indices from MSCI have been analysed to see how they compare. Figure 1.11 represents the MSCI ACWI Standard Index with value 100. This is done in order to compare MSCI ESG indices with the MSCI standard index.

The results show that almost all MSCI ESG indices had lower underperformance than the ACWI standard index during this period. The only standard index that performed better than its ESG counterpart is the MSCI Minimum Volatility Index, which performed better than the ESG counterpart until end-April as it served as a hedge against the high uncertainty regarding the extent of the economic consequences of the pandemic.

Given the rapidity with which markets change and the unpredictability of how measures to address COVID-19 will evolve, further analysis will be needed to assess the genuine differences between the returns and volatility of ESG and non-ESG indices and funds, and the factors that contribute to these differences.

Figure 1.11. Comparison of ESG and non-ESG MSCI indices since the COVID-19 pandemic

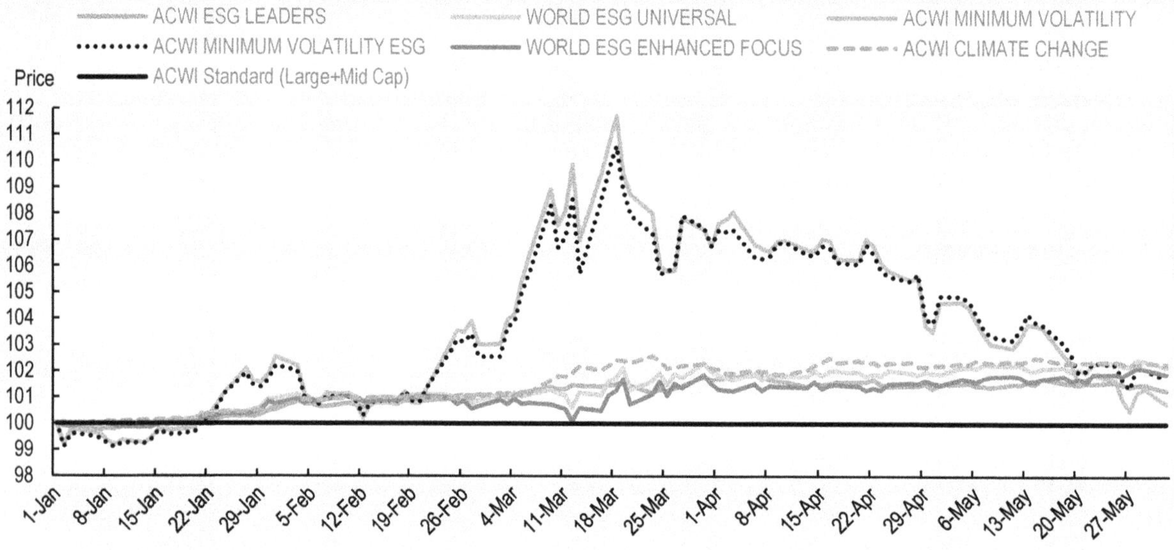

Note: This figure compares selected MSCI ESG indices with the MSCI standard index
Source: MSCI, OECD calculations

1.5. Policy considerations and conclusions

The results of the analysis show a wide range of financial performance of ESG investments between indices, portfolios, and investment funds. OECD analysis generally finds little outperformance, and some underperformance of ESG-tilted indices and portfolios relative to traditional (ESG neutral) market portfolios. Where there is some evidence of superior absolute return performance, this is often accompanied by higher levels of risk, such as volatility, that dampens risk-adjusted returns, but also with a lower tail risk, namely a lower maximum drawdown. While OECD analysis is based on commercially available ESG ratings from major providers, there are a plethora of ESG portfolios and proprietary ratings that could exhibit superior risk-adjusted returns, just as a portion of active managers are able to achieve such returns against traditional market indices.

These results, however, do not call into question the fundamental purpose and potential benefits of ESG investing. In principle, and supported by some evidence, ESG investing can improve returns where knowledge of policies and certain strategies, such as momentum investing, can capture benefits of companies that are improving practices with respect to environmental, social and governance policies. In turn, new forms of disclosure to help investors and other stakeholders make decisions about financial and social returns can empower them to have a longer-term view of sustainable investing through the cycle, rather than from one reporting period to another.

More work is needed to understand the drivers of the individual Environmental, Social and Governance pillars. In this regard, the second chapter of the BFO analyses more closely the E pillar, to understand the link between environmental practices and scoring. The social pillar remains to be further analysed to acknowledge which social aspects are rating agencies taking into account, having received less attention than environmental and governance factors.

There are clearly benefits of reporting additional information that can be useful to investors willing to act upon some drawbacks in the ratings, allowing them to incorporate new data on sustainability to understand if a company is implementing more sustainable investments. As ESG investing matures, it has the potential to effectively capture forward-looking information about environmental, social, and governance issues that enhance investors' decision-making about long-term risks and sustainability of financial performance. However, more work is needed to ensure that the ESG disclosure, rating, investment, and investment communications processes are consistent, transparent, and effective, in the following areas:

- **Overcoming the disclosure bias to improve fairness of issuer ESG assessments**. External and OECD research indicates that there is an ESG scoring bias in favour of large-cap companies at the expense of SMEs. This phenomenon may unfairly penalise SME issuers with higher cost of capital, and could also distort the performance results of ESG vs traditional portfolios, by underrepresenting the growth dynamics of many smaller firms. As this may be due to the fact that the current costs of appropriate ESG disclosure may be perceived to be excessive by at least a portion of smaller issuers, more clarity and international standardisation of disclosures could help reduce reporting costs and incentivise adequate ESG disclosure.
- **Ensuring relevance and clarity in reporting frameworks for ESG disclosure.** Notwithstanding progress to date, the reporting of ESG factors still suffers from considerable shortcomings with respect to consistency, comparability and quality that undermine its usefulness to investors. There is still more to be done to ensure that issuers can rely on core criteria and metrics for E, S and G disclosures that are relevant to a wide body of equity and debt investors, and are supported by stock exchanges and disclosure organisations. A universally accepted global set of principles and guidelines for consistent and meaningful reporting across ESG will help build scalable expertise for issuers, and improve consistency, comparability and reliability for investors and analysts. Moreover, it will then help all users assess the meaningfulness of such disclosures over time so that they can be further refined.
- **Improve transparency and standardisation of core elements of ESG ratings methodologies to ensure that metrics and methodologies of ratings outcomes are widely available to investors.** Widely different outputs across major ESG rating providers – in contrast to that of credit ratings -- can create confusion in the market among institutional investors, fund managers, and retail investors as to what constitutes a high ESG-rated company. If left unaddressed, this persistent opacity could undermine investor confidence in the ESG scores, major ESG indices, and portfolios built upon these products. There is need for clarity on how E, S and G subcategory factors and metrics, their weighting, and subjective assessment contribute to final ESG scores. This would allow users and issuers to understand and compare methodologies and results. Such transparency is particularly warranted if the scores among ratings providers continue to differ widely. Also, where ESG ratings are combined with other traditional financial approaches, from credit ratings to investment strategies, the impact or output of the ESG element of the approach should be

communicated distinct from the traditional approaches. Otherwise, investors will not be able to judge the effect and value of the ESG approach on portfolio construction and financial results.

- **Strengthening the link between ESG ratings and financial materiality over the medium to long-term.** There is mixed evidence thus far about the prospect of ESG investing meeting or exceeding the performance of traditional investment indices, which suggests the benefits of ESG disclosures to unlock forward-looking information that is financially material is still at an early stage of development. As such, it raises the need for more thorough assessment of how *financial materiality* is and should be captured in ESG ratings, benchmarks and portfolios. The industry and policy makers need to address two issues: first, to better define financial materiality over the medium- to long-term, to overcome short-termism that might otherwise underrepresent slower moving environmental and social risks. Second, to isolate the effects of financial materiality from alignment with social investing, which may strive for societal impact even if not aligned with financial materiality. As both are relevant to sets of market participants, more research and communication is needed in this area to make ESG investment meaningful for long-term value and values investing.
- **Ensure the appropriate labelling and disclosure of ESG products to assure their exposures, risks, and other traits are sufficiently material, comparable, and consistent to allow investors to make investment and voting decisions in line with their investing objectives and risk tolerance**. While this chapter focuses on materiality and financial value derived from ESG investing, it also acknowledges that the motivation for end-investors – from retail investors to central banks -- is also to align their investment portfolios with societal values related to environment, social and governance issues. Therefore, the clarity with which ESG products across ratings, benchmarks, and funds explicitly delineates the financial and social investing aspects of ESG investing is of high importance. In particular, where product features are meant to align with social investing rather than financial returns, such choices should be made abundantly clear to investors. Likewise, when funds portray a positive alignment with environmental concerns, exposures to carbon-intense industries and the rationale for this exposure should be made explicitly clear. In sum, there is a greater need for consistent taxonomy of sustainable finance investing that is meaningful and reliable across global markets.

Strengthening the regulatory environment is an important step to support consistency and resilience in major markets and within jurisdictions, but more is needed to strengthen good practices across global markets. An underlying theme throughout the report is that greater engagement between the financial industry and the public sector is needed to strengthen practices as they relate to investor protection and market integrity related to disclosures, data, ratings, indices, and investment vehicles. Certainly, regulators of large jurisdictions with developed financial markets are already engaging on these very topics, and making good progress. However, capital markets and sustainable finance are global in reach, as are the societal issues they seek to assess. Therefore, global principles may be needed to help establish good practices that acknowledge regional and national differences, while ensuring a constructive level of consistency, transparency, and trust. In sum, to unlock the potential benefits of ESG investing for long-term sustainable finance, greater attention and efforts are needed to improve transparency, international consistency, alignment with materiality, and clarity in fund strategies as they relate to sustainable finance. Doing so will help strengthen transparency, confidence, and integrity of sustainable finance through global financial markets, so as to contribute to resilient and inclusive economic growth.

References

Bannier, C., Y. Bofinger and B. Rock (2019), *Doing safe by doing good : ESG investing and corporate social responsibility in the U.S. and Europe*, https://ssrn.com/abstract=3387073. [16]

Berg, F., J. Kölbel and R. Rigobon (2019), "Aggregate Confusion: The Divergence of ESG Ratings", *SSRN Electronic Journal*, http://dx.doi.org/10.2139/ssrn.3438533. [2]

BNP (2018), *Investing for tomorrow: applying ESG principles to emerging market debt.*. [9]

Cerulli and UN PRI (2019), *Survey: Responsible Investment in Hedge Funds -The Growing Importance of Impact and Legacy.*. [13]

Climate Disclosure Standards Board (2012), *Climate Change Reporting Framework Advancing and aligning disclosure of climate change- related information in mainstream reports.*. [5]

Dolvin, S., J. Fulkerson and A. Krukover (2017), "Do 'Good Guys' Finish Last? The Relationship between Morningstar Sustainability Ratings and Mutual Fund Performance", *SSRN Electronic Journal*, http://dx.doi.org/10.2139/ssrn.3019403. [3]

European Commission (2018), *Feedback Statement: Feedback Statement Public Consultation on Institutional Investors' and Asset Managers' Duties regarding Sustainability.*. [7]

Fama, E. and K. French (2013), "A Four-Factor Model for the Size, Value, and Profitability Patterns in Stock Returns", *SSRN Electronic Journal*, http://dx.doi.org/10.2139/ssrn.2287202. [17]

Global Sustainable Investment Alliance (2018), *Global Sustainable Investment Review*, Global Sustainable Investment Alliance. [1]

GRI (2018), *The Materiality Principle: The Deep Dive.*. [14]

J.P. Morgan (2016), *ESG, Environmental, Social and Governance Investing.*. [6]

Markowitz, H. (1952), "PORTFOLIO SELECTION*", *The Journal of Finance*, Vol. 7/1, pp. 77-91, http://dx.doi.org/10.1111/j.1540-6261.1952.tb01525.x. [18]

OECD (2019), *Social Impact Investment 2019: The Impact Imperative for Sustainable Development.*. [20]

OECD (2017), *Investment governance and the integration of environmental, social and governance factors.*, https://www.oecd.org/.../Investment-Governance-Integration-ESG-Factors. pdf. [19]

Task Force on Climate-related Financial Disclosures (2017), *Final Report: Recommendations by the Task Force on Climate-related Financial Disclosures.*. [10]

Taskforce on Climate-related Financial Disclosures (2017), *Recommendations of the TCFD.* [11]

UN PRI and ICGN (2018), *A Discussion Paper By Global Investor Organisations On Corporate ESG Reporting.*. [4]

UN Principles for Responsible Investment, (2019), *What is Responsible Investment.* [15]

World Economic Forum (2019), *Seeking Return on ESG.* [12]

World Economic Forum, I. (2019), *Seeking Return on ESG: Advancing the Reporting Ecosystem to Unlock Impact for Business and Society.*. [8]

Notes

[1] While the overall AUM of the signatories is USD 80 trillion, the portion of assets overseen is materially lower than this amount, as explained in the following paragraphs.

[2] CFA Institute: https://www.cfainstitute.org/en/research/esg-investing

[3] Australia and New Zealand, Canada, Europe, Japan and the United States.

[4] The (OECD, 2019[20]) explores more in detail Social Impact Investments, providing guidance and recommendations to stakeholders.

[5] Should society's demand for socially-aligned consumption progress, consumers would in theory align with companies that adhere to high ESG standards, providing such companies higher revenues from consumption and brand loyalty, which can translate over time into higher capital returns.

[6] United Nations Global Compact: "The Global Compact asks companies to embrace, support and enact, within their sphere of influence, a set of core values in the areas of human rights, labour and environmental standards, and the fight against corruption.

[7] (J.P. Morgan, 2016[6]), "ESG, Environmental, Social and Governance Investing."; makes a particular distinction between exclusion and norms-based investing.

[8] Large ESG providers include MSCI, Sustainalytics, Bloomberg, Thomson Reuters, and RobecoSAM. In addition, traditional ratings agencies such as Moody's and S&P now also provide forms of ESG ratings. Index providers include, for example, MSCI, FTSE Russell, Bloomberg, Thomson Reuters, and Vigeo Eiris.

[9] The OECD has conducted work on ESG investing and fiduciary duties, particularly with respect to pension plans, and includes guidance by the International Organisation of Pensions Supervisors (IOPS). See IOPS (2019), "Supervisory guidelines on the integration of ESG factors in the investment and risk management of pension funds." Fiduciary duty is discussed in other parts of this publication.

[10] Given the difficulty in reporting metrics related to sustainability, different stakeholders have called for more standardised reporting guidelines. Eighty exchanges have published their own ESG reporting guidelines and many more are willing to do so. NASDAQ, for example, issued a report to help companies to report on ESG criteria using 30 metrics, 10 for each pillar.

[11] See https://morphicasset.com/esg-ratings-no-quick-fixes/, referring to Investment bank CLSA and Japan's Government Pension Investment Fund (GPIF).

[12] See https://www.wsj.com/articles/is-tesla-or-exxon-more-sustainable-it-depends-whom-you-ask-1537199931.

[13] Systemic risk describes an event that can spark a major collapse in a specific industry or the broader economy. Systematic risk is the overall, day-to-day, ongoing risk that can be caused by a combination of factors, including interest rates, geopolitical issues, and corporate health, among others.

[14] Fama and French provide five different factors, including the market factor. This factor represents a proxy of the market. When adding the others factors, the result is a risk-weighted performance measure.

[15] Previous research by (Dolvin, Fulkerson and Krukover, 2017[3]) focused on the efficiency of sustainable funds and how they perform using Morningstar sustainable metrics. The analysis found no difference in risk adjusted returns of ESG against non ESG funds returns. However, it did find a relevant difference in risk profile, with high sustainability scores largely confined to large cap funds.

2. Making sense of the environmental pillar in ESG investing

Growing demand for environmental, social and governance (ESG) investing has been driven in part by investors seeking to enhance long-term value, and align with environmental resilience. To this end, environmental (E) pillar scores and indices produced by rating providers and investment funds strive to integrate metrics aligned with environmental performance, climate risk mitigation, and strategies towards renewable energy. This chapter assesses the landscape of criteria and measurement within the E pillar of ESG investing, to understand if it is fit for purpose in its current form.

2.1. Introduction

As market participants show greater awareness and concern that climate transition may present material and non-material risks to companies and a wider range of stakeholders; environmental, social and governance (ESG) products are increasingly being used as a tool to assess the alignment of companies with low carbon economies and to identify financially material sustainability issues. To meet growing demand for these products, investment funds and ESG rating providers are working to integrate metrics aligned with environmental impact, climate risk mitigation, and strategies toward renewable energy. These efforts can be broadly considered the environmental (E) pillar of ESG ratings and investing.

At the same time, two important developments are occurring within sustainable finance that relate to the purpose of ESG. First, there is a sharp growth of institutional investors using ESG approaches with the aim to enhance the long-term value of their investments, as measured by superior risk-adjusted financial returns. Incorporating risks from climate change and stranded assets as a result of the climate transition is increasingly recognised as a central element to this assessment. Second, there is a growing commitment by institutional investors – with financial or impact objectives -- to strengthen the climate resilience of economies by disincentivising carbon emissions. While ESG assessment methodologies of major ratings providers and global investors appear to strive to incorporate both perspectives, questions remain as to whether this is being achieved in practice. Chapter 1 of this Outlook assesses the alignment of ESG investing with superior performance of risk-adjusted returns, finding little evidence of outperformance over the past decade. Building on this analysis, this chapter focuses on the environmental pillar of ESG investing and assesses the extent to which E score methodologies in their current form align with the expectations of the investors and stakeholders that use them.

The extent to which E scoring and investing reflect the environmental impact, carbon footprint and resource use of these investments is critical to enable market participants to make informed decisions relating to a low carbon transition. This can include a strategic re-orientation towards renewables, climate-related risk management and adaptation,[1] as well as operational processes to improve water use, waste management and impact on biodiversity. In its current form, the E pillar includes metrics across all of these areas, with limited scope to distinguish between those that require strategic re-orientation in the long-term and those that require easily implementable operational changes in the short-term. In addition, as market participants seek to understand their exposure to potential risks, the E score itself does not prioritise carbon footprint or intensity within the range of metrics that comprise the E score, so may be of limited value in protecting portfolios from climate transition risks such as stranded assets. This means that E scoring may not yet be suitable for use by investors wishing to use it as a proxy for judging the carbon footprint of companies in line with low-carbon economies.[2]

To varying degrees, institutional investors and central banks are using ESG considerations, and in turn E scores, to rebalance their portfolios for long-term value, and in some cases as a proxy for a greening of the financial system. This raises two important points for consideration. First, for those wishing to invest in products with long-term risk adjusted returns, the E scores should have a transparent methodology to help investors recognise the extent to which these scores can be used to contribute to long-term value. Second, for investors wishing to reduce carbon exposure, the environmental pillar should be clearly discernible as to the extent to which it aligns with risk management or carbon exposures. Establishing consistent E scoring metrics and methodologies within ESG ratings will be an important step to contribute to these efforts. This should include clear and publicly available information on metrics with guidance on the underlying methodology. This should go hand in hand with greater clarity on required E pillar reporting by companies; establishing core metrics with associated metadata for measurement would be a valuable first step. While ESG rating providers tend to have similar metric categories for E scoring, there are wide differences in both the number and choice of quantitative metrics and the way in which metrics are calculated and weighed. Within this, methodologies that score companies positively based on superior climate risk management and renewables transition plans, despite poor performance on emissions and other metrics, can be valuable, but may merit further scrutiny. At the very least, disparities in underlying metrics should be made available to market participants to reduce green-washing and any misconception that environmental scoring is consistent with a low carbon framework.

This chapter assesses the extent to which E scores align with carbon emissions and core metrics that negatively affect the environment, to examine whether E scoring and reporting effectively serve markets and investors that are using ESG investing in part as a tool to make portfolios more resilient to physical and climate transition risks. This point of inquiry will have implications for the approaches of rating providers, institutional investors, central banks and asset managers who wish to use it as a proxy to green the financial system. Section 2.1 outlines related efforts by central banks, financial regulators and governments. Section 2.2 includes empirical analysis of how E scores may contribute to efforts to tilt portfolios toward low-carbon investments, and the extent to which these E scores may influence the emission composition of high-ESG portfolios. Given limited publicly available information in this area, the analysis focuses on the three main rating providers for which information has been shared. Given the abundant availability of their data, this assessment is intended to reflect more broadly on industry practices, rather than to scrutinise their practices. Beyond this, alternative investment products tailored to low carbon activities are also discussed, to illustrate that a range of products exists to align investments with low-carbon transitions. Section 2.3 reflects on implications following the outbreak of the COVID-19 pandemic, including potential opportunities to support a sustainable economic recovery. In addition, policy considerations to improve the E of ESG scoring and reporting going forward are provided.

The key findings in this chapter suggest that E scores often do not align with current carbon emissions exposures, and can be difficult to interpret due to the multitude of diverse metrics on environmental factors. Some of the ESG rating providers analysed exhibit a low correlation between the E score and the overall ESG score. While this is not unexpected, given that the E score is distinct and ESG scores include social and governance metrics, it confirms that investing in high-scoring ESG portfolios does not necessarily equate to a positive environmental impact or greening of the financial system. The analysis also shows that for some ESG rating providers, high E scores positively correlate with high carbon emissions.

ESG scoring and reporting has the potential to unlock a significant amount of information on the management and resilience of companies in line with sustainability, including environmental and physical climate risks when pursuing long-term value creation. It could also represent an important market based mechanism to help investors make decisions on long-term carbon prices and climate transition risks implied by climate mitigation policies and the Paris Agreement.[3] Institutional investors, including central banks, use ESG ratings, and possibly E scores, as tools to green their portfolios and in turn the financial system. This means that more effort is needed to ensure that E scoring provides the information that market participants need to design and implement effective strategies to address environmental factors and the transition to low carbon economies.

Looking ahead, greater consistency on the high-level purpose of the E of ESG investing could provide stakeholders and investors with a framework to assess the level of environmental[4] and financial materiality[5] for aspects of the E pillar. This is ever more pressing in the context of COVID-19 as governments channel significant resources into investments that will inevitably impact the path of the climate transition.

2.2. Putting the E pillar in context: greening the financial system

Many investors around the world, including a number of central banks, are paying greater attention to sustainable activities in their investment portfolios and risk assessment practices with the aim of addressing physical and transition risks as a result of climate change. In turn, ESG investing is seen as an important tool to reduce information asymmetries using non-financial reports, which could be utilised to help facilitate greening of portfolios, and in aggregate, the financial system. It represents an important market-based mechanism to help investors make decisions based on environmental aspects of firms, including emissions, resource use and how the company is forward looking in terms of climate innovation. In this regard the E pillar can support investors seeking to also incorporate long-term expectations on carbon prices and transition risks implied by the Paris Agreement (see Box 2.2). As a step to realign the financial system toward low-carbon economies, governments and other public institutions are increasingly seeking ways to incorporate environmental and climate related risks into investments. Initiatives such as the OECD's Centre and Forum on Green Finance and Investment[6] and the Network for Greening the Financial System (NGFS)[7] have been established to support better alignment with low-carbon economies and enhance activities such as investment approaches and risk management, incorporating climate transition and its subsequent physical risks (NGFS, 2019a; OECD, 2017).

Governments have the primary responsibility for developing policy frameworks to address climate risks, yet central banks and financial market participants are playing an important role in supporting this by mainstreaming ESG considerations and identifying potential risks to market actors and the financial system. Separately, market participants and businesses are struggling to accurately estimate and price the financial impact of future climate-related risks. To improve these tools, additional collective leadership and globally coordinated action to improve the E pillar may be warranted to strengthen practices that support transparency and market integrity. This section outlines the steps undertaken by these actors to integrate ESG criteria into their roles and responsibilities.

2.2.1. Steps taken by central banks and financial regulators

The legal mandates of central banks and financial regulators vary throughout the OECD membership, but they typically include responsibility for price stability, financial stability and the safety and soundness of financial institutions. The primary responsibility for ensuring the success of the Paris Agreement rests with governments, yet it is increasingly considered as within the responsibility of central banks and supervisors to deliver on their substantial role in addressing climate-related risks to financial stability within the remit of their mandates. For example, understanding how structural changes affect the financial system and the economy is core to fulfilling these responsibilities. These risks might have persistent impacts on macroeconomic and financial variables (for instance, growth, productivity, food and energy prices, inflation expectations and insurance costs) that are fundamental to achieving central banks' monetary policy mandates.

Also, physical and transition risks that can have system-wide impacts on financial stability and might adversely affect macroeconomic conditions. Physical impacts include the economic cost and financial losses resulting from the increasing severity and frequency of extreme climate change-related weather events (such as heat waves, landslides, floods, wildfires and storms) as well as longer term progressive shifts of the climate (such as changes in precipitation, extreme weather variability, ocean acidification, and rising sea levels and average temperatures). Transition impacts relate to the process of adjustment towards a low-carbon economy (reaching 'net zero'). The process of reducing emissions is likely to have a significant impact on all sectors of the economy affecting financial asset values.

This financial impact of climate related risk is likely to take two forms: i) the physical risks (which are the most immediate and visible) caused by the proliferation of extreme weather events such as floods, storms, wildfires and rising water levels, and the subsequent damages that insurance firms, for instance, will have to cover;[8] and ii) the transition risks associated with public authority measures or private initiatives to support the move towards a low carbon production model. Both of these factors will have an inevitable impact on valuations, demand and output, effecting financial stability, which could in turn feed back into the real economy through market losses or credit tightening (OECD, 2017).

In addition to the activities of central banks (see Box 2.1), a number of financial regulators have established work on reporting for climate-related information as well as integration of environmental risks. These are largely focused on ESG disclosure by companies,[9] with guidance emerging for financials and intermediaries. Looking ahead, two considerations in this area should remain a priority. First, investors and markets need accurate and comparable information on companies' environmental and climate-related performance and activities in order to assess to what extent this fits with investment strategies they have in place today. Second, and perhaps more difficult, investors and markets also need information on how companies are assessing and responding to risks posed to their operations in the medium and long-term as a result of carbon transition. Independent reporting frameworks are being developed, yet these vary significantly and cater to a range of stakeholders. They feed into the range of metrics used by major ESG rating providers, and often include qualitative guidance on environmental and climate related issues (OECD, 2020b). Section 2.2 further addresses these considerations.

Box 2.1. Central bank ESG practices in OECD countries

As numerous central banks have committed to help green the financial system, they have sought to integrate ESG practices into their investment processes. Given limited capabilities with respect to ESG criteria and climate stress scenarios, a number of central banks are making use of third party products, such as ESG indices and asset managers that provide stylised ESG portfolios. Some are using such advice to help align reserve portfolios with high-ESG ratings and, to a lesser extent, investments in green bonds. Therefore, the performance of high-ESG funds, and also the extent to which the E score is aligned with greening the financial system, is relevant for policy makers.

Effective management of government reserves is a key driver for central banks' consideration of ESG factors and responsible investment practices, in addition to market stability. Complying with generally recognised international conventions and national laws, improving the long-term risk-return profile of investments, and promoting sustainable development are key reasons. In this respect, various central banks are now considering ESG factors in their reserve management, with respect to: (i) managing reputational risk; (ii) enhancing broader risk management, including financial risk; and (iii) promoting sustainable and responsible investment, aligned with corporate social responsibility (CSR) within the remit of their mandates.

This includes both explicit and implicit integration of ESG factors. Explicit integration includes specifying sustainability as one of the policy purposes for holding reserves to guide portfolio choice (i.e. by supporting the transition to a low-carbon economy). Implicit ESG integration refers to the introduction of ESG considerations to achieve the traditional economic uses of reserves, by recognising the indirect ways in which the lack of ESG integration may affect central banks' existing policy objectives. Green bonds have also been introduced, and there appears to be a tendency for central banks to use negative screening (i.e. excluding companies with controversies and unethical practices) when considering CSR, and for engaging in positive screening and portfolio tilting toward exposures with higher ESG scores when considering risk-return dynamics.

Despite notable progress in recent years, central banks have identified a number of challenges to further integrate ESG considerations in the near-term. Such challenges include: (i) methodological issues with ESG benchmark providers and credit rating agencies, including transparency and lack of harmonisation; (ii) lack of standardised disclosures on ESG data; (iii) issues with returns and volatility of ESG branded products, including uncertainty, lack of established performance and trade-offs (e.g. higher deviation from performance of traditional indices); (iv) limitations associated with green bonds, including definitions and standardisation. Altogether, the lack of comparability of ESG methodologies and ESG data makes it very challenging for reserve managers to compare available ESG branded product issuers. Compliance and verification costs create additional transaction costs for reserve managers to consider ESG investing factors.

Source: Central Bank websites and publicly available information; BIS (2019); NGFS (2019b); supplemented by a survey of delegates of the OECD Committee on Financial Markets.

2.2.2. Steps taken by governments

In addition to efforts by central banks and financial regulators, there is a growing concern among both governments and businesses regarding the fundamental role of carbon pricing in this transition. While carbon pricing policies remain at an early stage of implementation, a number of OECD countries have increased their average effective carbon tax rates in the real sector, yet these efforts remain limited and in some cases are only targeted to a handful of industries (OECD, 2019c). As a result, financial markets may not be efficiently incorporating future prices of fossil fuels (see Box 2.2).

Box 2.2. Carbon pricing and financial markets

The under-pricing of externalities associated with carbon emissions from fossil fuels is widely acknowledged to be a contributing factor in the continued growth of average temperatures beyond two degrees (OECD, 2018). Notably, the potential damage from these externalities would give rise to growing physical risks, in the form of damage from climate and weather-related events (OECD, 2017). The consequences of physical risks in the coming decades could have material impacts on the real economy and financial systems. As these physical risks become more extreme and widespread across geographies and industries, potential losses would become much harder to diversify, and risks would become more systemic in nature (Bank of England, 2019; BIS, 2020).

While it is difficult to determine how efficiently financial markets are currently incorporating future prices of fossil fuels, an unanticipated increase in policy commitment with respect to the price of carbon could contribute to widespread repricing of financial assets whose valuations would be determined in part by carbon prices. This sudden change, while helping anchor the transition to low-carbon futures, could lead to substantial disruptions as investors would absorb losses on 'stranded' assets. This asset stranding effect could lead to impaired company valuations in the natural resource and extraction sectors, with possible implications for other sectors. In addition, given the very high leverage of the corporate sector of many OECD member countries, sharp disorderly adjustments in asset prices could trigger corporate defaults and potential bouts of financial instability. The Bank of England and NGFS estimate that credit losses from a sudden repricing could range between USD 1 trillion and 4 trillion on fossil fuels (NGFS, 2019a).

This raises a critical question: while the transition is important to reduce physical risks to the financial system over time, can financial markets absorb current estimates of transition risks? Clearly, the size and timing of potential losses will be important. If the transition path extends over multiple business cycles, then there is a much higher likelihood that global markets are able to absorb these losses over time. Indeed, the climate transition is already contributing to defaults associated with stranded assets in the coal industry. To put this in context, investors have been able to absorb trillions of USD losses during brief acute crises, though contributing to financial stability risks, and have been able to absorb losses more efficiently over time. For example, credit losses in banks and other financial institutions exceeded USD 4 trillion in the aftermath of the Global Financial Crisis (IMF, 2009), and European banks have since written off over USD 600 billion of Non-Performing Loans over the past five years (EBA, 2020). Therefore, a well-designed regulatory framework and information on risk and pricing externalities could help drive an orderly repricing in which losses could be spread or absorbed through traditional financial and accounting channels over two or more business cycles. However, should this process begin too late, disorderly losses could impose acute strain on financial markets as the climate transition is accelerated to address escalating physical risks.

Financial markets can facilitate a transition through the managing and transferring of risks and assets, as well as capital mobilisation. While losses on any legacy assets would be expected, financial markets exist in part to facilitate transitions to new technologies and innovations that can create opportunities for economic gains and growth. Therefore, despite significant transition risks, there may also be significant opportunities for organisations focused on climate change mitigation and adaptation solutions. At times, this may even occur within the same industries and companies; for example, as energy conglomerates transition to a planned reduction of fossil fuels, they may also transition to a mix including renewables. This is also taking place more broadly among users of energy, with a number of companies signalling their commitment to become carbon neutral by 2030. At the same time, the growth of green markets, along with renewables and green technologies, are developing to help finance activities to meet existing climate mitigation targets. To the extent that these new activities may displace old systems and disrupt parts of the existing economic system, winners and losers will likely emerge from this process of 'creative destruction' (TCFD, 2017a). At the same time, returns in these high-growth areas could eventually help mitigate the losses from stranded assets to the financial system.

To the extent that financial market participants are already using ESG integration as a tool to facilitate the transition toward a greening of the financial system, climate-related disclosures, metrics and methodologies should be transparent, consistent and effective in order to ensure broader market efficiency can be met, and to help channel capital to areas where financial and environmental materiality are optimised.

Source: OECD (2017), Investment in Climate, Investing in Growth; Giuzio M. et al. (2019), "Climate change and financial stability", Financial Stability Review, ECB, May; European Banking Authority (2020), EBA Report on NPLs: Progress Made and Challenges Ahead; Bank of England (2019), Avoiding the storm: Climate change and the financial system, Speech given by Sarah Breeden; NGFS (2019a) A call for action: Climate change as a source of financial risk; OECD (2018), Effective Carbon Rates 2018: Pricing Carbon Emissions Through Taxes and Emissions Trading; Bank of England, (2019), Climate change: what are the risks to financial stability?; BIS (2020), The green swan: Central banking and financial stability in the age of climate change.

Countries are increasingly planning to implement carbon pricing policies, yet a carbon price gap remains,[10] suggesting that many governments continue to under-price externalities from carbon emissions. In turn, this has an inevitable impact on the ability of markets to price risks associated with carbon-intensive activities and transition to low-carbon alternatives. Ultimately, addressing the mispricing of carbon and effectively taking into consideration the misprice risk associated with carbon-intensive activities will depend on the extent to which governments and financial market actors can accurately estimate the true financial cost of a transition to low-carbon economies.

2.3. In practice: E scoring and performance

Two important developments have occurred in sustainable finance that relate to the purpose of the E pillar. First, there is a sharp growth in institutional investors using ESG approaches with the aim to enhance the long-term value of their investments, as measured by superior risk-adjusted financial returns. In this respect, incorporating risks from physical risks and stranded assets as a result of the climate transition is increasingly recognised as a central element to this assessment.[11] Second, there is a growing commitment by institutional investors – with financial or impact objectives – to strengthen the climate resilience of economies by disincentivising carbon emissions.[12] While ESG assessment methodologies of major rating providers and global investors appear to strive to incorporate both perspectives, questions remain as to whether this is being achieved in practice.

To meet growing demand for sustainably branded finance products to support transitions to low-carbon economies, ESG rating providers and investment funds are striving to integrate metrics aligned with environmental resilience, climate risk mitigation, and strategies toward renewable energy. This section assesses the extent to which E scores within ESG ratings are currently suitable as a tool to guide efforts to shift portfolios to low-carbon investments, and how these E scores may influence the emission composition of high-ESG portfolios. Data from the three main rating providers (Bloomberg, MSCI, and Thomson Reuters) are used to assess the alignment of E scores with environmental metrics such as carbon emissions and waste. In addition, a comparison of portfolios weighed toward issuers with high-ESG scores and non-weighted traditional portfolios is undertaken to assess their emissions content.

Notably, this section finds that for some providers, high E scores positively correlate with high emissions, suggesting that the content of the E score is not always synonymous with low emissions or an alignment with a low-carbon trajectory. These findings raise questions as to the benefit of ESG portfolios for investors that wish to prioritise low-carbon investments or near-term carbon transition objectives. In particular, the E score in its current form is not an effective tool to differentiate between companies' activities related to outputs that affect the environment, climate risk mitigation to improve risk-adjusted returns, and medium-term strategies to align portfolios with lower-carbon activities. Scores tend to incorporate each of these factors, but the inputs and weighting are not transparent. By contrast, other types of investment products, such as those tailored to climate transitions, provide ample opportunities for investors to rebalance portfolios away from companies with carbon-intensive outputs or supply chains. However, highly tailored low-carbon or carbon-transition portfolios may have asset compositions and risk characteristics that stray widely from standard market benchmarks that are most commonly used by institutional investors, so risks need to be balanced against climate and long-term return objectives.

2.3.1. Alignment between ESG ratings, E pillar scoring and environmental metrics

Financial and official sector participants, including central banks, institutional, and retail investors, have shown an increasing interest in ESG investing as a tool to support a greening of the financial system. Yet, there remains some ambiguity about the extent to which such investors are willing and able to invest in low-carbon portfolios that deviate significantly from broad-based market indices. Despite a growing interest by many countries' policymakers in seeing investment utilised to facilitate a climate transition through low-carbon portfolios, the question remains as to whether the criteria in ESG investing[13] are sufficient to isolate and address the obstacles to this transition, or to accelerate the transition to sustainable assets and support financial markets in absorbing potential transition risks. In this respect, if ESG investing does not divert material financial resources away from those companies that currently contribute the highest levels of emissions, it raises questions about the efficacy of ESG investing to achieve green transitions and mitigate portfolio risks. Evidence of this, however, remains to be seen, and analysis in this section suggests that E scores can be difficult to interpret and do not always reflect strong performance on individual, environmental and climate related metrics.

Importantly, individual E scores do not align with overall ESG ratings for all rating providers, suggesting that high ESG scores cannot necessarily be used as a proxy for environmental performance. Depending on the rating provider and methodology, however, there is scope to use ESG ratings to align with a focus on environmental standards, in the event that investors carefully choose ESG rating providers or develop in-house rating methodologies, or in the event that transparency as to the methodology used for performance in line with E, S and G improves. Figure 2.1 illustrates that for two of the three rating providers analysed, the R squared is high, denoting a correlation between the overall ESG ratings and the E score. For a third provider, however, a low R squared signals a low correlation between a high ESG rating and a high E score. Therefore, a better understanding of the methodologies used by ESG rating providers, in particular to generate E scores, is important to understand the methodological aspects that drive these findings.

Figure 2.1. Overall ESG ratings and E scores do not align for all ESG rating providers

E pillar score and ESG ratings' R squared for global companies rated by selected providers

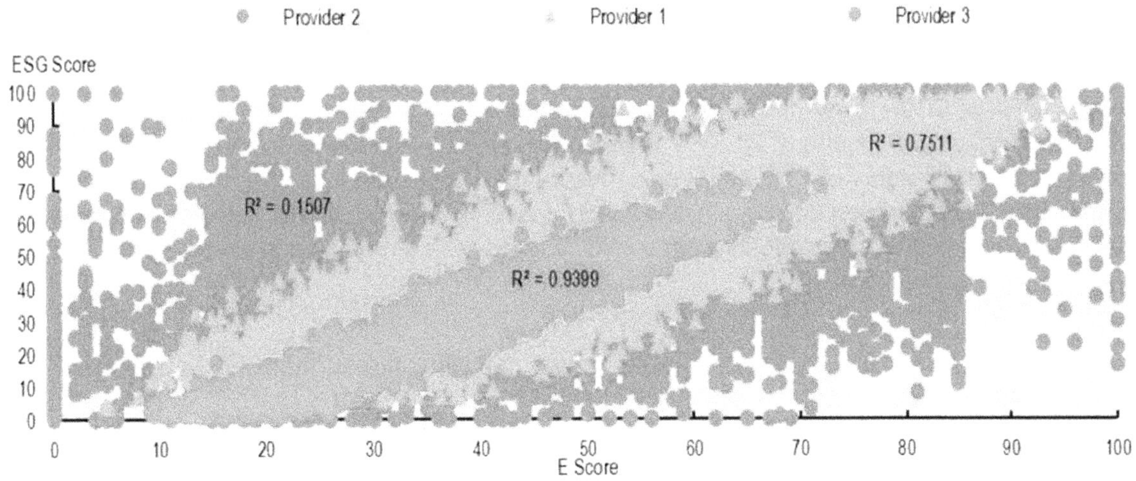

Note: For full methodology, refer to OECD (2020c), ESG Investing: Practices, Progress and Challenges.
Source: Bloomberg, MSCI, Refinitiv, OECD calculations

Environmental and financial factors that are material to a company can differ depending on the industry and place in the global value chain. Financial materiality refers to sustainability topics that potentially have a significant financial impact on a company's performance, while environmental materiality considers the factors that will have a long-term impact on the society and future generations. In some cases, factors that are environmentally material can also be financial material, for example metrics used to measure environmental impact can also be important in measuring transition risks, and may change over time. Nevertheless, there are a number of environmental metrics that could be considered core in assessing any company's impact on the environment that may not be considered financially material today. These are, overall CO2 emissions, total waste production, total energy use and total water withdrawals (see Table 2.1).

Table 2.1. The materiality of environmental factors may differ by industry and company, yet a core set of environmental metrics can be identified as a starting point to analyse E scores

Core output measures that negatively affect the environment

Metric	Description
CO2 Emissions	Total Carbon dioxide (CO2) and CO2 equivalents emission in tonnes. Direct (scope1) + indirect (scope 2). The following gases are relevant: carbon dioxide (CO2), methane (CH4), nitrous oxide (N2O), hydrofluorocarbons (HFCS), perfluorinated compound (PFCS), sulfur hexafluoride (SF6), nitrogen trifluoride (NF3). (GHG) protocol followed for all emission classifications by type.
Total Waste Production	Total amount of waste produced in tonnes. Non-hazardous waste + hazardous waste. Only solid waste is taken into consideration except if liquid waste reported in 'tonne'. For sectors like mining, oil & gas, waste generation like tailings, waste rock, coal and fly ash, etc. are also considered.
Total Energy Use	Total direct and indirect energy consumption in gigajoules that has been purchased and consumed within the boundaries of the company's operations. For utilities, transmission/ grid loss as part of its business activities is considered as total energy consumed and electricity produced by utility companies to sell. Raw materials such as coal, gas or nuclear used in the production of energy are not considered under 'total energy use.
Total Water Withdrawals	Total water withdrawal in cubic meters from any water source that was either withdrawn directly by the reporting organisation or through intermediaries such as water utilities. Different sources of water such as well, town/utility/municipal water, river water, surface water, etc. are considered.

Source: Refinitiv, OECD

The challenges investors face relate to how sub-metrics that go into calculating these metrics may differ, ranging from the information each company reports to how rating providers aggregate this information. The methodological practices that are then used to aggregate sub-metrics and environmental metrics to define the E score are important. This section addresses these concerns by analysing the alignment between E scores and individual core environmental metrics, as well as assessing the underlying methodology used to define the E score.

The overall level of CO2 emissions is higher in companies with high E scores for two of the three rating providers assessed (see Figure 2.2). This means that for two providers, higher scoring companies generate higher gross output of CO2 emissions. This includes those stemming from the direct burning of fossil fuels and indirect carbon dioxide emitted during consumption of solid and liquid gas, gas fuels and gas flaring.[14] The third ESG provider shows the inverse trend, with a reduction in average CO2 emissions observed as the E score increases.

Figure 2.2. For some E score providers, high-E scores correlate with higher CO2 emissions

CO2 Emissions by E pillar score for a global set of companies across the three providers

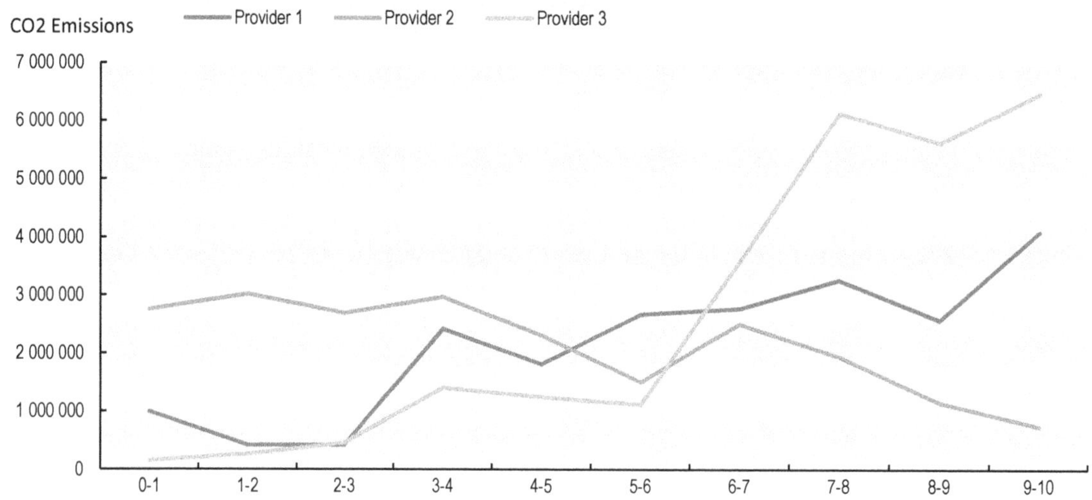

Note: Average tonnes of estimated CO2 emissions (Scope 1 and Scope 2, as reported by Refinitiv's methodology for estimating emissions) by E pillar deciles for different providers.
Source: Bloomberg, MSCI, Refinitiv, OECD calculations

Box 2.3. Tracking carbon emissions and carbon intensity

Scope 1 emissions refer to all direct emissions from the activities of an organisation or under their control. Including fuel combustion on site such as gas boilers, fleet vehicles and air-conditioning leaks.

Scope 2 emissions include all indirect emissions from electricity purchased and used by the organisation. Emissions are created during the production and use of the energy.

Scope 3 emissions refer to all other indirect emissions from activities of the organisation, occurring from sources that they do not own or control. These are usually the greatest share of the carbon footprint, and occur in the value chain of the reporting company, including both upstream and downstream.

In addition to a direct exposure to, and measurement of carbon emissions, investors are increasingly interested in companies' carbon reduction strategies, including carbon emissions targets to reduce their carbon footprint in the future. While an increasing amount of information is available to investors from a growing portion of companies, the measurements are still at an early stage of development and do not appear adequately captured in ESG methodologies.

A suitable metric would be the level of reduction in CO2 emissions divided by revenues over time (i.e. year by year). This way investors could understand if the company is reducing the overall level of CO2 emissions despite a possible growth of the company. While the carbon intensity metric is generally available for a specific year, it is uncommon to find a growth measure over time. Investors could use the available data to retrieve the change in carbon intensity over time, of which currently only one provider includes metrics that measure emissions intensity over time.

It is more difficult to track carbon targets and strategies, and there are currently no formal mechanisms to ensure that the company will be held accountable for timely implementation. Despite this, E score providers conduct both qualitative and quantitative analysis to try to measure this.

This issue raises the need for further consideration of appropriate metrics to track both carbon emissions and intensity in the E scope of ESG.

Source: Greenhouse Gas Protocol (2020); TCFD (2017b)

Similarly, rating providers that show alignment between high CO2 emissions and high E scores, typically exhibit an increase in both the scope 1 and scope 2 CO2 emissions when E scores are high (see Figure 2.3, Panel A and Panel B).[15] This suggests that higher CO2 emissions for high scoring companies is not driven by an irregularity in the measurement of a certain type of emissions. In addition, there is an indication that when direct emissions are high, indirect emissions from production may also be high, without a clear differentiation in the rating segment of companies with these characteristics.

Figure 2.3. Rating providers that exhibit an alignment between high CO2 emissions and high-E scores, see both higher scope 1 and scope 2 CO2 emissions

Breakdown of CO2 emissions by E pillar score, scope 1 and scope 2 measurement for Provider 1 and 3

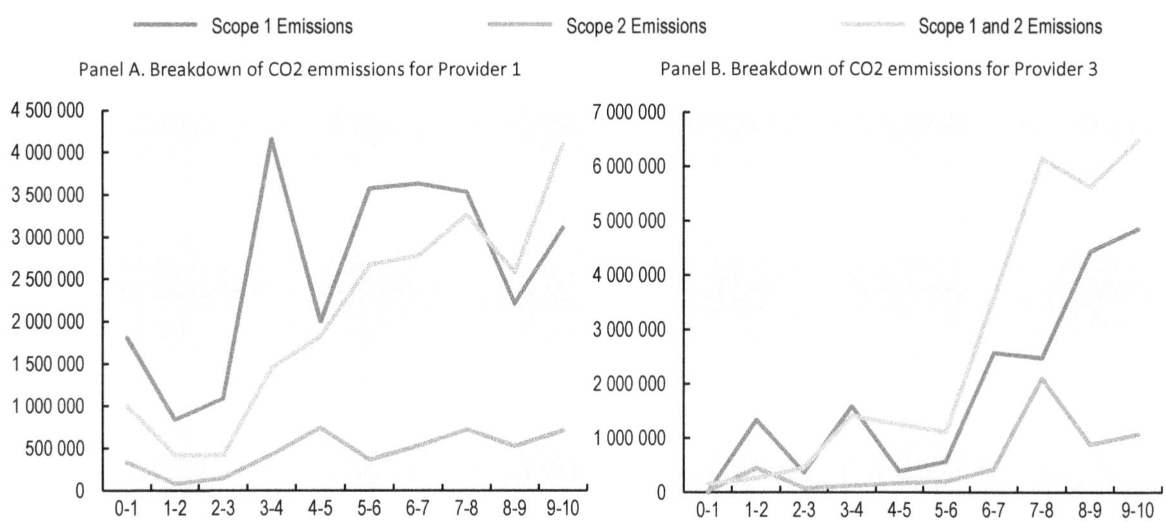

Note: Scope 1 refers to direct emissions and scope 2 refers to indirect emissions from direct production.
Source: Bloomberg, Refinitiv, OECD calculations

Accounting for revenue, it is possible to measure intensity of CO_2 emissions by unit of output (see Figure 2.4). This can reduce the bias associated with higher emissions of larger companies within high ESG ratings, and can be used as a proxy for the extent of greening by issuers, and in turn for portfolios. Using this measure, one provider still exhibits a notably higher level of emissions by higher E-scoring companies. To have a fuller picture, it will be important to measure over time the rate of change of revenue adjusted CO_2 emissions (see Box 2.3), which currently none of the rating providers analysed measure.

Figure 2.4. For one provider, higher E-scoring companies exhibit higher revenue adjusted CO2 emissions

CO2 emissions adjusted for revenue by E pillar score for a global set of companies across the three providers

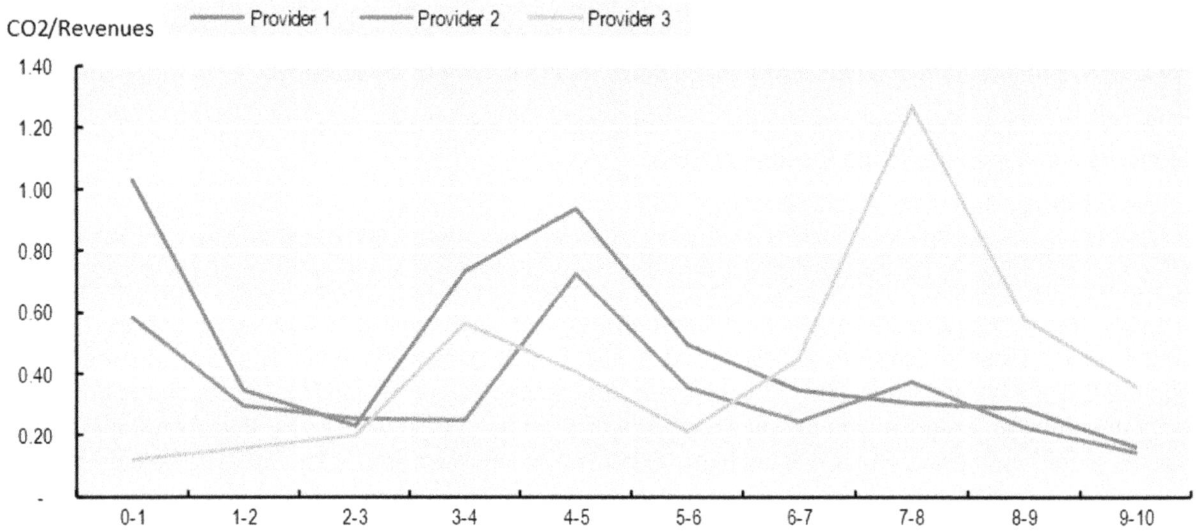

Note: Average tonnes of estimated CO2 emissions divided by Revenues, by E pillar deciles for different providers.
Source: Bloomberg, MSCI, Refinitiv, OECD calculations

Total waste produced and total water withdrawals are also greater in higher E scoring companies across at least two out of three rating providers analysed (see Figure 2.5). Total waste produced refers to both hazardous and non-hazardous waste produced by companies, and can include plastic waste that contaminates waterways and ecosystems. Separately, treatment and disposal of waste can also generate carbon dioxide and equivalent emissions. Higher E scores for two providers appear to correlate with higher waste produced for two of the three rating providers analysed. On the other hand, higher water withdrawals[16] are seen for higher E scores across all rating providers analysed.

Figure 2.5. For some E score providers, high E scores correlate with higher waste produced and water withdrawals

Total waste produced and total water withdrawals in tonnes by E pillar score for three providers

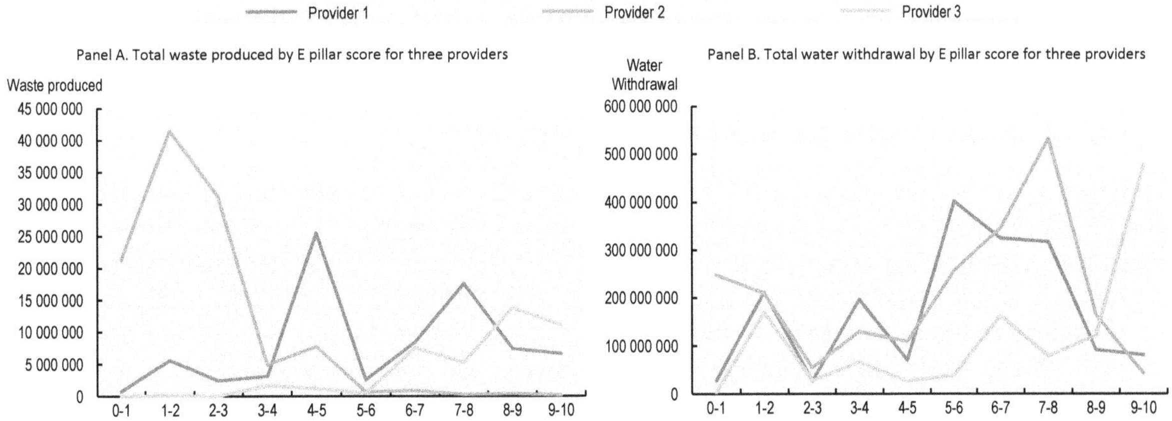

Note: Average tonnes of waste produced (hazardous and non-hazardous) by E pillar deciles for different providers. Average cubic meters of water withdrawal by E pillar deciles for different providers.
Source: Bloomberg, MSCI Refinitiv, OECD calculations.

Interestingly, total energy use for higher E score companies is lower for two out of three providers analysed (see Figure 2.6). This is measured by gigajoules of energy use, accounting for renewable energy. Without additional information, it is difficult to decipher exactly the extent to which renewable energy is adopted, yet a reduction in non-renewable energy use for higher E scoring companies could indicate that high E score companies are also increasingly adopting renewable energy options in their production and operations.

Figure 2.6. For some E score providers, high E scores correlate with lower non-renewable energy use

Total energy use in tonnes by E pillar score for three providers

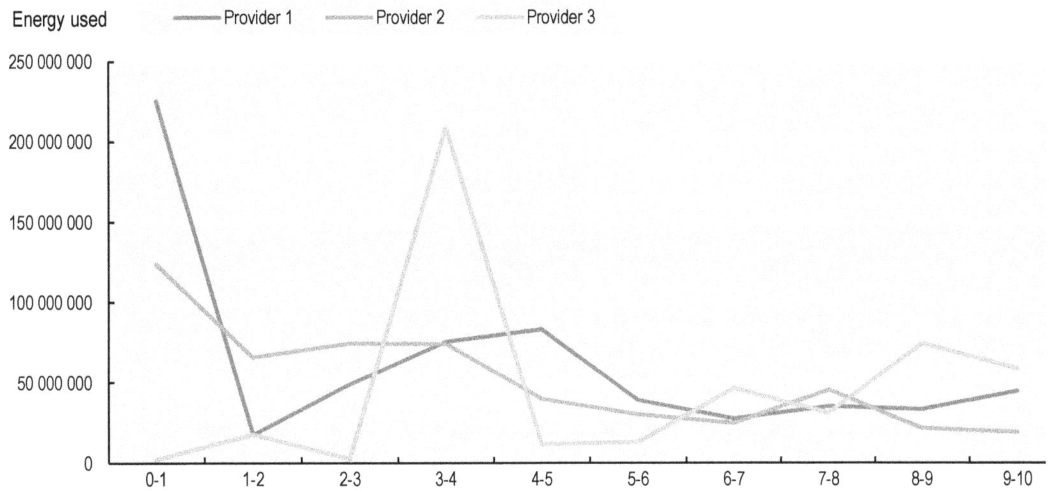

Note: Average Gigajoules of energy used after accounting for renewable energy by E pillar deciles for different providers.
Source: Bloomberg, MSCI, Refinitiv, OECD calculations.

Therefore, if investors aim to use these E scores as a proxy for environmental performance and/or to create a portfolio that aligns with lower-carbon activities, this analysis raises questions as to the usefulness of E scores in achieving this. The findings of this analysis indicate that there is little alignment between ESG ratings, E scores and individual environmental metrics. In order for markets to use E scores effectively, investors will be required to understand and choose a rating provider whose E score components and weightings fits their criteria. This would require further analysis of the extent to which underlying metrics of the E score of the rating provider they use align with their view of environmental materiality.

2.3.2. Understanding E scoring methodologies

Transparent, accurate and comparable ESG data are critical for effective investment analysis and decision-making. In the context of the environmental pillar, it is equally important that investors have reliable information in order to prepare their portfolio for future risks that may arise from the carbon transition, and to facilitate decisions that deliver risk-adjusted returns on investment. The analysis conducted in this section suggests that when looking at the top performing companies by environmental pillar scores across leading ESG rating providers, outcomes at the metric level do not always represent a positive effect on carbon emissions and the environment. Notably, the E score captures a range of information and metrics beyond carbon emissions that may drive this trend. This is valuable in that it provides information on activities that may require environmental risk management. This said however, for investors wanting ESG portfolios to align with low-carbon economies, the E pillar may not be an appropriate proxy.

Figure 2.7. Despite homogeneity in the naming of metric categories, the number of metrics, weighting, and supplementary analysis differ significantly

.Environmental pillar approaches by rating providers

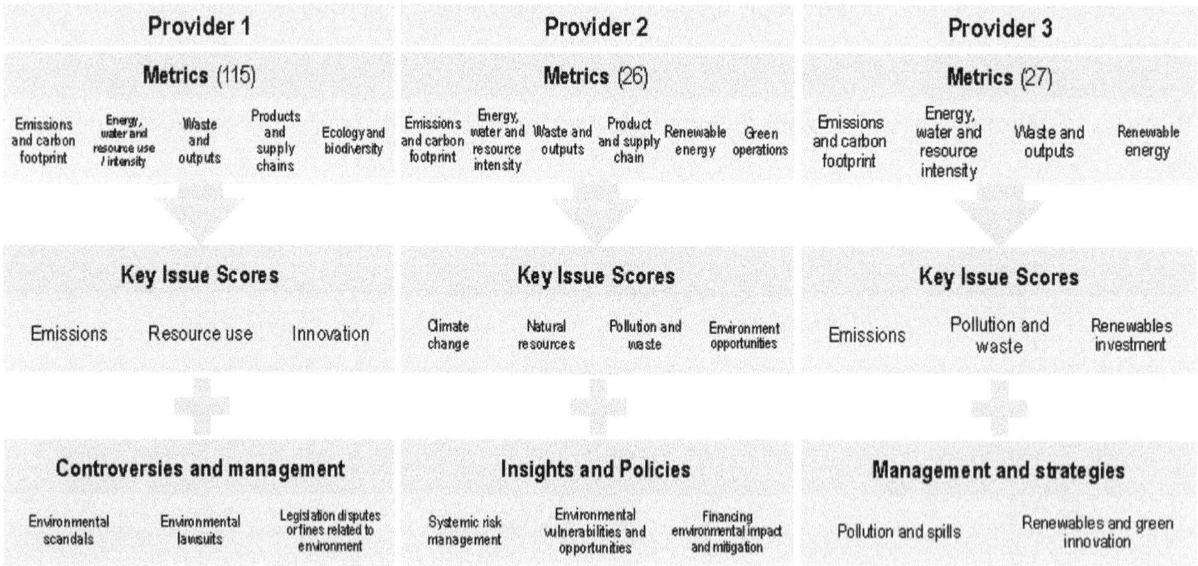

Note: Indicative categorisations based on available information
Source: Bloomberg, MSCI and Thomson Reuters, OECD analysis

Given the result of the analysis performed, the indication is that criteria other than carbon emissions tend to drive E score rating methodologies through the divergence of environmental performance for various tranches of scores across prominent ESG rating providers. This section elaborates on this by outlining the underlying methodologies of E pillar scores and discusses differences in the scope and measurement of metrics across these providers. As such, it explores to what extent differences in environmental pillar scores by rating providers are the result of variations in methodology, or of an underlying difference in the rationale of what constitutes good environmental performance, for example an emphasis on company management versus outright emissions and environmental outcomes. Initial findings suggest that it is a combination of both. Beyond this, wide differences in the number and choice of quantitative metrics, as well as the way in which the metrics are calculated and weighed, can impact the overall E score, making the comparison of ratings between providers difficult, even when referring to the same company (see Figure 2.7). Similarly, supplementary analysis in the form of subjective or qualitative research by rating providers can also impact the overall rating, with the impact of different metric calculations and weights on the overall E score being considerable.

Despite similarities in categories of metrics, the difference in the number of metrics used and measurement criteria contributes to considerable rating inconsistencies. Preliminary research indicates that these differences may be the result of a combination of the following:

- Differences in the scope of metrics, namely those outside of the core;
- Difference in the measurement (i.e. absolute vs. relative) or input indicators to measure metrics;
- Difference in weight.

Practices such as estimation in the case of missing data may also exacerbate differences between providers. The number of input metrics used by rating providers varies significantly, with Provider 1 using a selection of around 115 metrics,[17] Provider 2 uses around 26 and Provider 1 around 27 metrics on environment (see Table 2.2).[18]

Table 2.2. Despite similarities in broad category names, the difference in the number of metrics used and measurement criteria contribute to inconsistencies

Environmental pillar metrics by category across rating providers

Type	Category	Sub-category	Provider 1 (115)	Provider 2 (26)	Provider 3 (27)
Inputs	Product and supply chain	Materials sourcing and efficiency	5	2	-
		Supply chain management	6	1	-
	Renewable energy management	Use of renewables	4	1	1
		Investment in renewable energy	2	-	1
	Green operations	Green buildings	1	1	-
		Green products or operations	11	-	-
	Resource use	Total resource intensity	3	2	1
	Total in percent		*28%*	*27%*	*12%*
Outputs	Emissions and carbon footprint	GHG / carbon emissions	16	2	6
		Air quality	3	-	2
	Energy output and management	Energy output	8	-	3
		Energy management	4	1	2
	Water output and management	Water and wastewater outputs	7	-	3
		Water and wastewater management	4	2	2
	Waste and other outputs	Hazardous waste outputs and management	8	-	2
	Total in percent		*43%*	*19%*	*74%*

Type	Category	Sub-category	Provider 1 (115)	Provider 2 (26)	Provider 3 (27)
Outcomes	Ecology and biodiversity	Ecological impact	2	2	2
		Biodiversity impact	6	-	-
	Total in percent		*7%*	*8%*	*7%*
Processes	Risk management and policy	Climate impact and risk mitigation	1	3	-
		Environmental management systems	4	3	1
		GHG / carbon policy	4	-	-
		Environmental policy	5	3	-
		Environmental reporting	7	1	-
		Systemic risk management	1	2	-
	Sustainable finance	Sustainable finance	3	-	1
	Total in percent		*22%*	*46%*	*7%*

Note: Number of metrics in each sub-category are noted, with the total number of environmental metrics in parentheses. Lack of publicly available information to a comparable level of detail between rating providers may hinder a full comparison, with potential variation from internal studies conducted by rating providers (for example, some only make composite indicators available with several proprietary metrics driving these, while others list outright measurement metrics). The aim of this table to present an indicative example of the scope of metrics within the E pillar. For a full list of metrics, please see OECD (2020b), ESG Investing: E scoring and reporting.
Source: Bloomberg, MSCI and Thomson Reuters, OECD analysis.

Thomson Reuters and Bloomberg adopt an outright metric value measurement approach (for example, direct CO2 equivalent emissions measured in either parts-per-million or units of micromol mol-1), whereas MSCI adopts a binary approach for all metrics (for example, three-year trend of average carbon emissions intensity measured by either -1, 0, or 1), which could include the calculation of several sub-metrics in order to decipher the overall metric score (revert back to Figure 2.7). These metrics are then used to create composite sub-scores across key issues, or rather categories used by rating providers. This quantitative element of the rating is complemented by additional analysis (in some cases qualitative analysis) of company management strategies or insights (in the case of MSCI), which can have a notable impact on the rating. The logic for this is to also assess how well a company may be preparing to deal with environmental and carbon transition risks and opportunities in future, yet the approach and methodology used for this portion of the rating can differ, and often relies on subjective judgement.

The types of environmental metrics included in each of the E rating frameworks appear to vary widely, with a multitude of possible measurement methodologies as well as underlying rationales for the inclusion of metrics. To illustrate this, metrics can be grouped as falling somewhere along the input-output-outcome-process chain (see Figure 2.8). Production-related metrics such as those measuring energy consumption or water withdrawals tend to be inputs. Emissions metrics, including CO2 and GHG emissions by source, regardless of whether they are expressed in unit value or as a share of revenue, tend to represent outputs. Outcome focused metrics can include those that look at impact such as ecological and biodiversity. Process metrics can include binary metrics or descriptions of policies and risk management practices as discussed above, including for example, information on board oversight related for climate related risks.

Figure 2.8. Environmental metrics can be grouped as falling somewhere along the input-output-outcome-process chain

Types of environmental metrics used by E rating providers

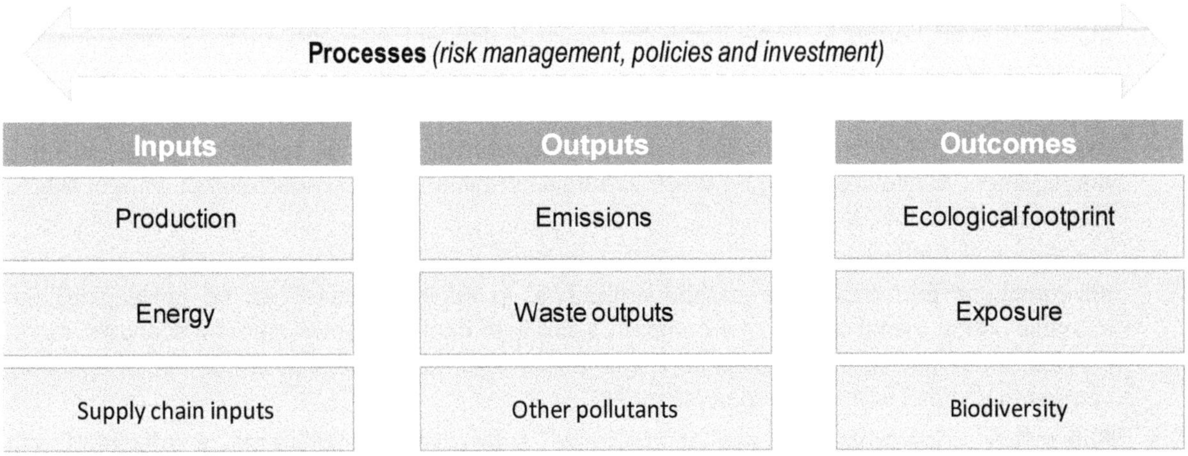

Source: OECD illustration.

The logic used in this chain can also be applied to frameworks such as those set out by the Task Force on Climate-related Financial Disclosures (TCFD) which recognises the importance of: (a) metrics on climate-related risks associated with water, energy, land use, and waste management (inputs and outputs); (b) greenhouse gas emissions using the scope 1 (direct emissions), 2 (indirect emissions from direct production), and 3 (indirect emissions from activities along the value chain) definitions (outputs and outcomes), and; (c) company management processes, anticipated regulatory requirement, market constraints or other goals (TCFD, 2017b).

In addition to the difference in metrics and their associated measurement, the source and type of underlying data used differs among providers. Bloomberg collects public ESG information disclosed by companies through their sustainability reports, annual reports and websites. In some cases, Bloomberg also integrates metrics from third party rating agencies, such as Sustainalytics, the ISS quality score, and the Carbon Disclosure Project (CDP) score. Thomson Reuters also collects reported data from the public domain, including company sustainability reports, annual reports and third party providers. MSCI uses a multitude of sources, including company disclosure, third-party databases, as well as direct co-operation with companies to develop qualitative and binary metrics.

The difference in the scope of metrics, related measurement of input data, and difference in weighting used by Bloomberg, MSCI and Thomson Reuters, can account for differences in E rating scores and similarly the lack of correlation between the scope 1 and 3 emissions metrics (refer back to Figure 2.2 and 2.3) and tranches of E scores. In addition, not all metrics align well with what is financially material today (i.e. already included in company reporting or board committee activities), which may be more commonly found in the process group of metrics, nor with environmental impact and carbon footprint (i.e. output and outcome groups of metrics), nor with the longer-term transition to renewables.

Issues discussed within this section give rise to a number of challenges that may limit the usefulness of E scores, and ESG ratings more broadly, for environmental considerations in investment approaches, and may necessitate greater scrutiny by market participants using these scores. Key issues include:

- *Limited comparability:* While diversity of analytical approaches may be welcome, the current state of approaches has resulted in the limited comparability of E scores across major providers.

- *Lack of transparency:* Disclosure of all relevant elements of the rating methodology is vital for investors. This should include information on the main metrics used, as well as clarity on when supplementary judgements or estimations are used to arrive at the resulting E score. The majority of this information is labelled as proprietary with little made available publicly. In addition it is difficult to find information regarding weighting of various categories or underlying sub-metrics, making it even harder to understand the focus of different elements of E, S, and G within methodologies.
- *Selection bias:* Larger companies have the resources to implement and communicate E pillar related strategies from renewable energy programmes, internal carbon pricing and risk management. Limited reporting on these strategies within smaller companies may impact overall E scores (OECD, 2020c).
- *Limited scope within metrics:* The use of binary indicators can limit the value of metrics to measure environmental performance or carbon emissions. In addition, these can be misleading. For example, in the measurement of a company's ability to deal with environmental scandals, rating providers may assess more favourably a company that has weathered a number of scandals compared to those that have had no scandals.
- *Subjectivity judgements:* The use of qualitative, subjective questionnaires or interviews with companies, as well as research conducted in collaboration with rating providers have a significant impact on E scores and in some cases call into question the consistency of assessments (both within the agency and across key rating providers) that are highly judgement-based to contribute to the E rating process.

2.3.3. Alignment between sustainable indices and carbon emissions

Interest by investors in ESG compliant investments has also spurred demand in more targeted sustainable indices and funds. This section seeks to understand how these funds and indices are built and to what extent their framework, and particularly sustainability integration, may differ from the parent benchmarks that they are derived from. This also includes an assessment of the difference in overall CO2 emissions between standard index and fund constituents compared to those in the targeted ESG index or fund. Alternative investment products tailored to the low-carbon transition are also outlined to see what benefit these may bring to investors who wish to invest in low-carbon activities.

The number of sustainable indices and funds has increased significantly in the past several years, with many large indices having ESG counterparts. The analysis in this section focuses on the S&P 500, STOXX 600 and their ESG counterpart index,[19] as well as MSCI World, MSCI ESG leaders and MSCI ESG screened counterpart funds.[20] Analyses of their methodologies are undertaken to understand the variation of levels of CO2 emissions between the parent index or fund and its related ESG index or fund to understand if high ESG portfolios have a lower carbon footprint than traditional funds with similar constituents. This analysis reveals a stronger presence of exclusionary screening, which removes companies based on predefined criteria,[21] such as the exclusion of specific industries (i.e. tobacco); rather than titling or integration of ESG scores[22] to build the ESG counterpart indices or funds. An assessment of the presence of companies from the most polluting industries is undertaken,[23] to understand if and how these companies are removed or limited in ESG counterpart indices and funds, indicating a portfolio rebalancing towards companies with a lower carbon footprint.

The findings of this section highlight two issues. First, similarly to ESG ratings, ESG indexes do not currently represent low-carbon investment option for investors. Second, inconsistencies across indices in terms of the extent to which ESG indices and funds reflect stronger E performance, highlight the considerable amount of analyses required to determine which ESG investment products align with these objectives.

As such, investors may find it difficult and time consuming to extrapolate information on ESG indices and funds to the extent metrics and ratings vary, and sub-metrics that unlock more specific information may not be readily available. By contrast, other types of investment products, such as those tailored to climate transitions, provide ample opportunities for investors to rebalance portfolios away from companies with carbon-intensive outputs or supply chains. However, highly tailored low-carbon or carbon-transition portfolios may have asset compositions and risk characteristics that stray widely from standard market benchmarks that are most commonly used by institutional investors.

Table 2.3. There is little change in the major constituent companies between the STOXX 600 index and its ESG counterpart

Comparison between STOXX 600 and STOXX ESG-X indices, 2020

	STOXX 600	STOXX ESG-X	STOXX 60	STOXX ESG-X
Number of constituents	600	580	Largest companies by market capitalisation	
Basic Materials	7.2%	7.6%	Linde Air Liquide Rio Tinto	Linde Air Liquide Rio Tinto
Energy	5.1%	5.4%	Total BP Royal Dutch Shell	Total BP Royal Dutch Shell
Industrials	12.8%	11.4%	Airbus Siemens Schneider Electric	Siemens Schneider Electric Vinci
Utilities	5.3%	5.4%	Enel Iberdola National Grid	Enel Iberdola National Grid

Source: Refinitiv, STOXX, OECD calculations

Notably, in some cases, the weight of high polluting industries, such as the energy sector, increased in the ESG index (with little change in the constituent companies). For example, this is the case for the S&P 500 ESG and STOXX 600 ESG indices. Focusing on S&P 500 and its ESG counterpart (S&P 500 ESG) there is little difference in terms of the largest holdings and industry representation. A more detailed comparison of the STOXX 600 index and the STOXX ESG-X index, shows that the ESG focused index does little to improve the sustainability of the parent index (see Table 2.3). The integration methodology appears to remove 20 companies (from the original 600) with little difference in the characteristics of constituents in terms of sector and ESG criteria. For example, in the energy sector, Total, BP and Royal Dutch Shell remain the largest companies for both the STOXX 600 and STOXX ESG-X index. Despite the overall level of emissions and perceived impact on the environment, these companies exhibit high E pillar scores for some rating providers, at or above 90 out of 100 for Refinitiv and between 77 to 92 out of 100 for Bloomberg. This is in part due to transition policies enacted by companies and targets for lowering the carbon footprint, which often make up a large part of the E score. In contrast, MSCI World funds and ESG counterpart indices show clear differences in the constituents included (see Table 2.4),[24] with the MSCI ESG leader fund, for example, including companies based on their MSCI ESG ratings, through a best-in-class approach.

Table 2.4. There is a clear difference in major constituents between the MSCI World fund and ESG counterpart funds

.Comparison between MSCI World and MSCI ESG funds, 2020

	MSCI World	MSCI ESG Screened	MSCI ESG Leaders	MSCI World	MSCI ESG Screened	MSCI ESG Leaders
Number of constituents	1 207	1 540	847	Largest companies by market capitalisation		
Basic Materials	4.3%	3.8%	4.6%	Bhp Group Rio Tinto Linde	Linde Air Liquid Basf	Linde Air Liquid Air Prod&Chem
Energy	4.6%	4.2%	3.8%	Exxon Mobil Royal Dutch S Chevron	Exxon Mobil Chevron Total	Total ConocoPhillips Equinor
Industrials	11.7 %	10.5%	12.0%	Boeing United Tech. Honeywell	Union Pacific 3M Siemens	Union Pacific Siemens United Parcel
Utilities	3.6%	1.8%	3.9%	Nextera En. Duke En. Enel	Nextera En. Iberdrola Exelon	Iberdrola Dominion Southern C.

Source: MSCI, Refinitiv, OECD calculations

Understanding what impact differences in the composition of parent indices and funds and their ESG counterparts have on the environmental performance of these indices and funds is important. Focusing on CO2 emissions, and taking into consideration a weighting for market capitalisation when relevant, this section compares aggregate CO2 emissions between parent and ESG indices and funds, as well as analysing tilting methodology (that takes into consideration market capitalisation weighting before and after ESG integration).

Table 2.5. CO2 emissions in some sectors appear higher in the S&P ESG when tilting is applied

Comparison of estimated CO2 Emissions for S&P 500 indices, 2020

	Aggregate CO2 Emissions (millions of tonnes)		*Average CO2 Emissions (millions of tonnes)*		*Weighted CO2 Emissions (thousands of tonnes*	
	S&P 500	**S&P 500 ESG**	**S&P 500**	**S&P 500 ESG**	**S&P 500**	**S&P 500 ESG**
Basic Materials	195	134	8	10	235	269
Energy	391	314	14	22	1 997	2 608
Industrials	262	166	3	3	388	391
Utilities	880	589	31	31	1 253	1 182

Source: Refinitiv, S&P, OECD calculations

CO2 emissions for the S&P ESG index appear lower than the S&P 500 on face value, yet when tilting is applied by sector, CO2 emissions in some sectors appear higher in the S&P ESG compared to the parent S&P 500. This could be due to exclusion of low polluters (relative to the index average) from some sectors, resulting in an increase in the weighting of the sector in the index (see Table 2.5).

In parallel, a number of alternative investment products tailored to low carbon transition have emerged, and may bring benefits to investors who wish to invest in instruments with a focus on environmental outcomes or low-carbon activities. These include green bonds (see Box 2.4) and specialised climate funds, such as PIMCO Climate Bond fund, the Blackrock iShares Global Green Bond ETF, and the Invesco

WilderHill Clean Energy ETF. These funds focus on investing in green bonds as well as bonds from issuers showing innovative approaches to environmental sustainability. The bonds in which the investments are made are certified to be green by third parties or by institutional investors internally, thereby providing greater assurance that the investment mechanisms are supportive of the transition to low-carbon economies. [25] In line with this, PIMCO and iShares funds invest in bonds of companies and countries specifically issued to back green projects, while the Invesco fund invests in equities that are involved in renewable and clean energy. These may increase with the implementation of the European Commission's climate benchmarks in 2019.

As the portfolio composition would deviate more from the traditional indices, the returns and variance might differ from a standard portfolio, and therefore may not align with existing investment strategies of portfolio managers. However, for those that have flexibility of portfolio composition within their strategies, existing metrics and investment products allow investors to construct portfolios that appear to align with transitions to low-carbon economies. These types of investments might, for example, be benchmarked to specialised climate funds, such as the Bloomberg Barclays MSCI Green Bond Index which tracks the global market for fixed income instruments that are certifiably invested in green projects.

Box 2.4. Sovereign green bonds

A strong momentum in sovereign green bond issuance

The green bond market, which was initiated by multilateral investment institutions more than a decade ago, has deepened and expanded with a diversified issuer profile, including various corporate entities and local governments. Increased investor demand for green bonds, including by large sovereign wealth funds and pension funds committed to responsible investment and integration of Environmental, Social and Governance (ESG) factors, has encouraged potential issuers and supported the growth of this market in general. While corporate bonds have dominated the universe of green financing so far, sovereign issuers who entered the market only five years ago, have been increasing their presence rapidly with large issuance.

Sixteen sovereigns have now issued green bonds to finance green projects in governments' budget, exceeding USD 80 billion (see Figure 2.8). Amid the COVID-19 pandemic, sovereign green bonds issuers has kept the issuance momentum in 2020 with several re-openings and a few inaugural issuances including Germany and Sweden. Looking forward, the governments of Denmark, Italy, Mexico, Spain and Slovenia are considering issuing one.

In terms of maturity structure and volume size, sovereign green bonds vary significantly: Maturity of bonds varies from 5- to 30-year, with 18-year weighted average maturity, and size of bonds ranges from USD 15 million to above USD 3 billion. While France stands as the largest issuer, Euro area issuers account around 75% of the total issuance.

From the perspective of a sovereign issuer, issuing green bonds may contribute to diversification of investor base as well as developing and deepening of the market for sustainable finance instruments. In addition, country experiences suggest that the issuance of green bonds brings about a positive market story with supportive new flows (OECD, 2019b). In terms of borrowing cost, the 2019 survey on primary market developments amongst sovereign debt management offices of OECD countries revealed that issuers of sovereign green bonds have not observed a consistent, material difference (e.g. a premium or discount in terms of spreads at issuance) in the pricing between green and conventional bonds, as the financial risk as well as the credit risk are the same for investors. In terms of secondary market liquidity, however, slightly poorer conditions have been observed for green bonds, except in a few rare cases. This reflects the relatively small size of green bonds and the strong presence of buy-and-hold investors in green bond markets. In order to address this concern, a few sovereign issuers including Denmark and Germany have been looking into a new models of green issuance. Denmark is considering a model where a conventional bond and a green add-on can be traded separately. Germany have recently introduced the so-called twin bond concept which comprises the issuance of green bonds bearing the same characteristics (such as maturity and coupon) as already existing, conventional bonds.

Figure 2.9. Sovereign green bond issuance

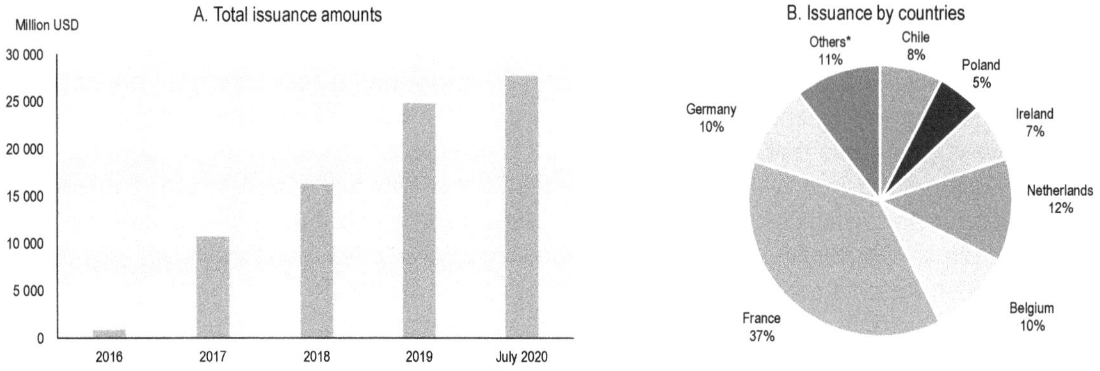

Note: Others include Fiji (2017), Hong Kong (China) (2019), Hungary (2020), Indonesia (2018, 2019 and 2020), Lithuania (2018), Korea (2019), Nigeria (2017), Seychelles (2018) and Sweden (2020).
Source: Refinitiv, national authorities' websites, OECD calculations.

The future size of the sovereign green bond market will be subject to green eligible projects

Despite its rapid growth, the size of the sovereign green bond market is quite small compared to traditional bonds. For example, in the OECD area, sovereign green bonds account for only 0.1% of all government debt securities (OECD, 2020a). Although still nascent, sovereign green bond market can be expected to keep growing over the longer horizon, as increasing number of governments assess green bond issuance as a valuable tool to display moral leadership on climate change and sustainability, increase awareness of the country's climate plan, and fund commitments under the Paris Agreement. In addition, the sovereign issuance of green bonds aims at supporting the development of sustainable financial markets and in particular the green market segment by providing investors with risk-free benchmark green securities. However, green eligible public investment in a government budget which is often quite small relative to overall government borrowing needs, put a natural barrier to green bond issuance.

Across OECD countries, overall government investments amounted to 7.7% of government expenditures (i.e. on average 3.1% of GDP), and investment in environmental protection represented only 4% of total investment in 2017 (OECD, 2019a). In this regard, a few issuers (e.g. Belgium and the Netherlands) have financed green eligible operating expenditures and tax expenditures through the proceeds of sovereign green bonds in addition to green investments. Against this backdrop, the potential size of the sovereign green bond market will to a large extent depend on the size of government expenditures in green projects such as renewable energy, clean transportation and climate change adaptation.

In sum, ESG approaches provide benefits in unlocking a significant amount of information about corporate practices that affect the environment. Nevertheless investors should not draw generalised conclusions that the E pillar is synonymous with corporate behaviours that are better for the environment. In this regard more work is needed to assess the consistency of metrics, their significance and how they are integrated along with other metrics related to environmental risks and opportunities to derive the E pillar score.

2.4. Supporting low-carbon transition and resilience into an economic recovery

This chapter acknowledges that the E pillar has been instrumental in combining a wide range of information that draws new attention to environmental factors. E scores include valuable information on outputs such as emissions and waste; climate change scenarios and risk management; and strategies to transition to renewable energy. This information is of growing importance as a number of public sector authorities, from central banks to financial regulators, contemplate how to incorporate climate risk and environmental resilience into their policymaking and activities. Furthermore, climate-related disclosures are of critical importance to institutional investors trying to meet the demand by asset owners for products that align with sustainability in terms of risk-adjusted returns and/or with the climate transition.

In addition to the health and economic crisis caused by COVID-19, the pandemic has also brought to light the materiality of ESG-related risks and the deep linkages between businesses and their stakeholders across the value chain. For investors, ESG approaches can help unlock a significant amount of information about the management of and preparedness for sustainability risks, including environmental and climate risks, when pursuing long-term value. However, fragmented ESG ratings do not deliver the transparent, accurate and comparable data investors need to manage climate risks. For policymakers, ESG investing and ratings are seen as important tools to green the financial sector. They represent important market based mechanisms to help investors make decisions based on long-term carbon prices and transition risks implied by the Paris Agreement. Clearly governments cannot depend on E scores in their current form to align financial and corporate value with carbon targets in the current market environment.

In an economic recovery context, ESG risk management could play a strong role by ensuring that material sustainability risks are managed and properly priced, so that business do not sacrifice long-term value even as they struggle to meet immediate challenges. This is particularly important for countries committed to a green recovery, which if implemented accurately, could allow private finance to properly price and efficiently allocate capital to green projects. Looking forward, the pandemic has underlined the importance of managing financial and non-financial risks, including ESG risks, throughout company operations and supply chains. Addressing these risks is an important element to long-term resilience against future shocks, both in financial markets and the economy as a whole (see Box 2.5).

Box 2.5. The role of the E pillar in supporting a sustainable economic recovery

As an immediate response to the economic turbulence resulting from measures to tackle the COVID-19 pandemic, governments have implemented monetary and fiscal measures on an unprecedented scale to support financial markets and the real economy. These measures have been necessary to limit acute and permanent economic damage caused by the economic contraction. As policy makers consider recovery measures, it will be important to look beyond the immediate crisis and think about what opportunities and risks lay ahead.

In doing this, policy makers may want to integrate considerations on climate and biodiversity, applying the lessons learnt from past crises to facilitate a fair, low carbon recovery. This could include the systematic integration of environmental considerations into the economic recovery and stimulus process. In a recent Reuters survey of asset managers, asset owners and other stakeholders, 74% of respondents claimed that the current COVID-19 situation has hastened the adoption of ESG considerations into mainstream investment policy. The European Central Bank also released a consultation document on the European Commission's Renewed Sustainable Finance Strategy, stating that the COVID-19 pandemic is an opportunity to step up efforts to achieve the environmental objectives of the European Union by incorporating sustainability considerations when steering the financial response to the crisis.

The use of confinement to address the spread of COVID-19 put a temporary break on CO_2 emissions, along with air pollutants from transportation and industrial activity. As governments work on the economic recovery, there is an opportunity to include policies that support and build on the short environmental gains made. Nearly three quarters of CO_2 emissions are the result of human activities and recent figures suggest that these are beginning to rise again as economic activity restarts. Actions such as the German government's EUR 130 billion stimulus package that includes around EUR 40 billion of climate-related spending can be used as an example. Notably, this includes EUR 7 billion for new hydrogen projects, EUR 2 billion for green auto innovations, and EUR 2.5 billion for the upgrade of the energy efficiency of buildings.

Source: ECB (2020), OECD Website (2020) A green recovery in the age of COVID-19.

As an increasing number of investors look to invest in environment and climate transition products, a more standardised and comparable approach across E rating providers may support more sustainable capital realignment away from carbon intensive economic activities. This chapter highlights where there is a lack of consistency across rating providers and identifies areas that may give rise to constraints. Also, further consideration may be given to the extent to which corporate reporting frameworks consider financial materiality and separately environmental materiality in the environmental pillar and the extent to which it is aligned with the carbon transition. Greater clarity from corporate reporting frameworks on their approach as to what constitutes material information in the context of environment would also be beneficial.

Today, the lack of comparability between E pillar ratings illustrates a fragmentation that may limit the benefits of E scores as a tool to assess environmental impact. Similarly, opacity in the measurement of longer-term management and strategy metrics limit the E pillar's use as a tool to assess companies' conformity to the carbon transition, which in turn, raises concerns as to the extent to which financial market participants can rely on E scores as a key tool to manage environmental and carbon transition risks. Therefore, for the E pillar to be most useful to investors with differing motivations, methodologies to generate E pillar scores will need to contain metrics that measure financial materiality and distinct aspects of environmental materiality in a mutually exclusive and transparent manner, where possible, so that investors have no doubt as to what is driving the E pillar score.

In line with this, the following considerations should be addressed to improve the relevance of the E pillar:

- Greater consistency on the high-level purpose of the E pillar could provide stakeholders and investors with a framework to assess the level of environmental and financial materiality for aspects of the E pillar. This would help untangle the various metrics and information that serve disparate stakeholders, which may undermine the value of underlying metrics and information. This should also include clear boundaries as to which areas of the E pillar are relevant to greening the financial system, and which focus on other objectives, such as long-term financial value.
- Improved transparency on the methodologies used to generate E scores and sustainable indices is vital to make the E pillar fit for purpose. Ultimately, this should include clear and publicly available information on metrics with guidance on the measurement of supplementary analysis. This should go hand in hand with greater clarity on required E pillar reporting by companies; establishing core metrics with associated metadata for measurement would be a valuable first step.
- Stronger coordination is required to define the role that the E pillar should play in helping financial market participants navigate the low carbon transition. Notably, the E pillar may have an important role to play as an informational vector supporting the assessment of companies' exposure to physical and transition risks, as well as support broader government policies to meet climate mitigation targets. The extent to which these two approaches support each other can be instrumental in creating clarity for companies, investors and in turn markets.

ESG approaches have the potential to unlock a significant amount of information on the management and resilience of companies in line with sustainability, including physical climate risks and other environmental risks when pursuing long-term value creation. It could also represent an important market based mechanism to help investors make decisions based on long term carbon prices and climate transition risks implied by climate mitigation policies in response to the Paris Agreement. Looking ahead, more needs to be done to ensure that the E pillar provides investors with the insight needed to help both long-term value and a greening of the financial system. Irrespective of investor needs, steps to improve transparency and market integrity will ensure markets are efficient and resilient to best contribute to a transition and deliver long-term value. This is ever more pressing in the current COVID-19 environment, in which governments are channeling a significant amount of resources to investments that will inevitably impact the economic path of the recovery.

References

BIS (2019), Green bonds: the reserve management perspective, Bank of International Settlements Quarterly Review, https://www.bis.org/publ/qtrpdf/r_qt1909f.htm

Bloomberg (2020), ESG Stock Resilience Is Paving the Way for a Surge in Popularity, https://www.bloomberg.com/news/articles/2020-03-31/esg-stock-resilance-is-paving-the-way-for-a-surge-in-popularity

Climate Bond Initiatives (2019), Greening the financial system Tilting the playing field The role of central banks, https://www.climatebonds.net/files/reports/cbi-greening-the-financial-sytem-20191016.pdf

ECB (2020), Eurosystem reply to the European Commission's public consultations on the Renewed Sustainable Finance Strategy and the revision of the Non-Financial Reporting Directive, https://www.ecb.europa.eu/pub/pdf/other/ecb.eurosystemreplyeuropeancommissionpublicconsultations_20200608~cf01a984aa.en.pdf

Greenhouse Gas Protocol (2020), Technical Guidance on Scope 1, 2 and 3 Emissions, https://ghgprotocol.org/scope_2_guidance

GSIA (2019), Global Sustainable Investment Review 2018, Global Sustainable Investment Alliance, http://www.gsi-alliance.org/wp-content/uploads/2019/03/GSIR_Review2018.3.28.pdf

IMF (2009), Global Financial Stability Report: Responding to the Financial Crisis and Measuring Systemic Risks, https://www.imf.org/en/Publications/GFSR/Issues/2016/12/31/Global-Financial-Stability-Report-April-2009-Responding-to-the-Financial-Crisis-and-22583

IOSCO (2019), Final report, Sustainable finance in emerging markets and the role of securities regulators, www.iosco.org/news/pdf/IOSCONEWS534.pdf

I4CE (2018), Carbon pricing across the world: how to efficiently spend growing revenues?, Climate Brief N°55, https://www.i4ce.org/wp-core/wp-content/uploads/2018/10/20181106_PC55_Carbon-Revenues_vENG.pdf

I4CE (2019), Global Carbon Account 2019, https://www.i4ce.org/wp-core/wp-content/uploads/2019/05/i4ce-PrixCarbon-VA.pdf

NGFS (2019a), A call for action Climate change as a source of financial risk, Network for Greening the Financial System First comprehensive report, https://www.banque-france.fr/sites/default/files/media/2019/04/17/ngfs_first_comprehensive_report_-_17042019_0.pdf

NGFS (2019b), A sustainable and responsible investment guide for central banks' portfolio management, https://www.ngfs.net/sites/default/files/medias/documents/ngfs-a-sustainable-and-responsible-investment-guide.pdf

OECD (2020a), Sovereign Borrowing Outlook for OECD Countries, https://www.oecd.org/finance/Sovereign-Borrowing-Outlook-in-OECD-Countries-2020.pdf

OECD (2020b), ESG Investing: E Scoring and Reporting, www.oecd.org/finance/esg-investing-e-scoring-and-reporting.pdf.

OECD (2020c), ESG Investing: Practices, Progress and Challenges, www.oecd.org/finance/esg-investing-practices-progress-and-challenges.pdf.

OECD (2019a), Government at a Glance 2019, OECD Publishing, Paris, https://doi.org/10.1787/8ccf5c38-en.

OECD (2019b), Sovereign Borrowing Outlook for OECD Countries, http://www.oecd.org/finance/Sovereign-Borrowing-Outlook-in-OECD-Countries-2019.pdf

OECD (2019c), Taxing Energy Use 2019: Using Taxes for Climate Action, OECD Publishing, Paris, https://doi.org/10.1787/058ca239-en.

OECD (2018), Effective Carbon Rates 2018: Pricing Carbon Emissions Through Taxes and Emissions Trading, OECD Publishing, Paris. https://doi.org/10.1787/9789264305304-en

OECD (2017), Investing in Climate, Investing in Growth, OECD Publishing, Paris. http://dx.doi.org/10.1787/9789264273528-en.

OECD (2015), Aligning Policies for a Low-carbon Economy, OECD Publishing, Paris, https://doi.org/10.1787/9789264233294-en.

Refinitiv (2019), ESG Carbon Data & Estimate Models, https://www.refinitiv.com/content/dam/marketing/en_us/documents/fact-sheets/esg-carbon-data-estimate-models-fact-sheet.pdf.

S&P (2020), The ESG Lens on COVID-19, Part 1, https://www.spglobal.com/ratings/en/research/articles/200420-the-esg-lens-on-covid-19-part-1-11444298.

S&P (2019), S&P 500 ESG Index, https://us.spindices.com/indices/equity/sp-500-esg-index-usd.

STOXX (2019), STOXX Europe 600 ESG-X https://www.stoxx.com/index-details?symbol=SXXPESGX.

TCFD (2017a), Recommendations of the Task Force on Climate-related Financial Disclosures, https://www.fsb-tcfd.org/wp-content/uploads/2017/06/FINAL-2017-TCFD-Report-11052018.pdf.

TCFD (2017b), Implementing the Recommendations of the Task Force on Climate-related Financial Disclosures, https://www.fsb-tcfd.org/wp-content/uploads/2017/12/FINAL-TCFD-Annex-Amended-121517.pdf.

World Bank (2019), State and Trends of Carbon Pricing, http://documents.worldbank.org/curated/en/191801559846379845/pdf/State-and-Trends-of-Carbon-Pricing-2019.pdf.

Notes

[1] Climate related risks include either physical risks, which occur from exposures to more frequent and more devastating disasters caused by natural hazards, and; transition risks that arise from uncertainties surrounding the timing and speed of the transition to a low-carbon economy.

[2] A low-carbon economy is an economic output based on low carbon power sources that therefore has a minimal output of greenhouse gas emissions, with specific reference to carbon dioxide. More information on policy alignment needed to achieve the transition to a low carbon economy can be found in OECD (2015).

[3] The Paris Agreement is the first universal climate agreement. It was adopted on 12 December 2015 at the 21st Conference of the Parties (COP21) of the United Nations Framework Convention on Climate Change (UNFCCC). The Agreement lays out the foundation for meaningful long-term action, providing transparency and review mechanisms that should allow countries to assess and adjust the scale of their efforts. In doing this, it aims to strengthen the global response to climate change over the course of the 21st century by: i) "holding the increase in the global average temperature to well below 2°C above pre-industrial levels and pursuing efforts to limit the temperature increase to 1.5°C above pre-industrial levels, recognising that this would significantly reduce the risks and impacts of climate change"; ii) "increasing the ability to adapt to the adverse impacts of climate change and foster climate resilience and low greenhouse gas emissions development, in a manner that does not threaten food production"; and iii) "making finance flows consistent with a pathway towards low greenhouse gas emissions and climate-resilient development" (Article 1, UNFCCC, 2015).

[4] There is no single definition of environmental materiality. For the purpose of this paper, a working definition, adapted from Global Reporting Initiative, is: those topics that have a direct or indirect impact on an organisation's ability to create, preserve or erode environmental value for itself, its stakeholders and society at large. (see GRI G4 Guidelines).

[5] Materiality as a concept defines why and how certain issues are relevant for a company or a business sector, this can refer to issues that are financially material (i.e. the approach taken by SASB) or issues that are material from the perspective of a range of stakeholders (i.e. the approach of GRI), for example by representing a material risk or importance for the business model of a company. Materiality is applied in a wide variety of contexts, including in accounting, reporting, business model, financial, legal, risk and more recently, environmental, social, and governance issues. In this context, there appears to be two major perspectives on materiality. The first is with respect to financial materiality, centering on the impact the environment and climate change – both physical and transition risks – could have on a company. This provides a basis for financial materiality in the context of risk-adjusted returns for a company. The other is a stakeholder-oriented concept of materiality, which emphasises the impact a company has on the wider environment and society.

[6] In addition, OECD recommendations on due diligence for responsible business conduct include guidance to help integrate risks from transitions into operations and business activities.

[7] In 2017, nine central banks and supervisors established the Network of Central Banks and Supervisors for Greening the Financial System (NGFS). Driving this, was a view that "climate-related risks are a source of financial risk, [and are] therefore within the mandates of central banks and supervisors to ensure the financial system is resilient to these risks." (NGFS, 2019). Since 2017, the network has grown to 69 international Members and 15 Observers as of 24 July 2020. The NGFS aims to accelerate the work of central banks and supervisors on climate and environmental risk and on scaling up green finance.

[8] For example, the number of extreme temperature events has more than tripled since the 1980s (Munich Re, 2018).

[9] For example, financial regulators, through the International Organisation of Securities Commissions (IOSCO), have established a sustainable finance network. The objective of this work is to introduce and improve standards for ESG disclosures recommended by regulators (IOSCO, 2019).

[10] The OECD estimates that the carbon pricing gap was 76.5% in 2018, representing EUR 30 per tonne of CO2. By the current rate of gap narrowing, carbon prices will only meet real costs in 2095 (OECD, 2018).

[11] See the Taskforce for Climate-related Financial Disclosure (2017), Final Report: Recommendations on Climate-related Financial Disclosures.

[12] One example is the Climate 100+ initiative, which is an investor initiative launched in 2017. More than 450 investors have joined the initiative, with over USD 40 trillion in assets collectively under management (AUM), with the aim to engage companies to: curb emissions, improve governance and strengthen climate-related financial disclosures.

[13] Environmental, social and governance (ESG) investment refers to a set of standards for a company's operations that investors use to screen potential investments. ESG investing is therefore not a clearly defined investment strategy, but a broad criteria that can be applied to any kind of investment strategy that takes into account issues within the E, S or G. Please refer to Chapters 1 and 4 for more information.

[14] In line with the Task Force on Climate-related Financial Disclosures' (TCFD's) scope 1 (direct emissions), 2 (indirect emissions from direct production).

[15] Due to lack of available data for scope 3 emissions, scope 1 and 2 emissions have been used for the analysis.

[16] Water withdrawals refer to all freshwater usage, excluding evaporation losses from storage basins. This can include water used for agricultural irrigation or industrial use such as through cooling for thermoelectric plants.

[17] Number of metrics estimated using publicly available information provided by ESG rating providers.

[18] Bloomberg (2019), MSCI (2019) and Thomson Reuters (2017) have been used to as the publically available source of the frameworks and categories used by rating providers. Individual metrics as sourced in the annex, and referred to throughout this chapter have been shared with the Secretariat by the rating provider (not for publication), or downloaded from the Bloomberg Terminal and Thomson Reuters Refinitiv platforms.

[19] S&P 500 ESG and STOXX 600 ESG-X.

[20] MSCI World ESG Leaders and MSCI World ESG Screened.

[21] Exclusionary screening in ESG occurs when specific assets are screened out of an index or portfolio for value reasons, for example excluding any company from the coal or oil production industry (regardless of their ESG score), resulting in divestment.

[22] Tilting occurs when an index or portfolio provider uses data from ESG rating agencies to rank the ESG scores of the companies within their parent product, to create an ESG counterpart. For example, by tilting the portfolio towards high ESG firms by excluding those with the ESG scores below a certain threshold.

[23] Industries are grouped by economic sector using Refinitiv data. Economic sectors have been selected according to the most polluting industries using International Energy Organisation CO2 emissions data.

[24] In terms of number of companies included, the MSCI World fund includes 1 207 companies, with the MSCI ESG screened includes 1 540 companies, and the MSCI ESG leaders includes 847.

[25] In this regard, the certification of the projects does not necessarily mean that benefits like CO2 emission reductions have been quantified.

3. Corporate governance and the management of ESG risks

At the very heart of a sustainable and resilient economy is a dynamic business sector that is willing and able to assume risk. To finance and manage risk taking is therefore as old as the corporate form itself. As new types of risks emerge or become more salient, the company, its shareholders and society at large all have an interest that these risks are properly managed and disclosed so that scarce resources can be allocated in the most efficient manner. In recent years, this has brought increased attention to environmental, social and governance risks that may influence corporate and economy wide resilience. This chapter address the outlook with respect to evolving tools and corporate practices for managing ESG risks and the challenges that remain with respect to establishing a commonly accepted high quality framework for disclosure of comparable, consistent and verifiable data.

3.1. The corporation, risk management and resilience

The corporation is a key engine for sustainable economic prosperity and societal progress. Corporations do not only provide income opportunities, goods and services. Through a dynamic process of technological and organisational innovation, they also contribute to economy-wide transformations of patterns of production and consumption. In well-functioning markets, this process results in an ever more effective use of scarce financial, human and natural resources.

In order to serve this dynamic function, the corporate sector requires access to equity capital with its unique ability to assume the financial risks that are associated with forward-looking investments that have uncertain outcomes. This includes investments in critical economic activities such as research, development, innovation and skills development that will upgrade human resources, generate new products, develop more efficient processes and increase productivity. Hence, it is not only the absolute amount of capital that matters for dynamic sustainable economic growth. At least as important is the kind of capital that is made available. Work by the OECD, for example, shows that at a given level, relatively more credit financing can actually slow down growth, while an expansion of stock market equity funding in general boosts economic growth (Cournède and Denk, 2015).

Equity capital also has the unique characteristic, that once it is provided to the company, it generally remains committed for the company's entire lifespan. And since the providers of equity are residual claimants without any fixed return, equity provides the financial resilience that helps the corporation overcome temporary downturns and still meet its obligations to fixed claimants, such as employees, creditors, bondholders and suppliers. In the wake of the 2008 financial crisis for example, publicly listed non-financial companies raised a historical record of USD 496 billion of new equity capital through the stock market during a time when access to bank credit became scarce or vanished (Isaksson and Çelik, 2013). More recently, while initial public equity offerings in other industries practically halted in March 2020 as a result of the Covid-19 pandemic, the healthcare industry still managed to raise new equity capital at a level comparable to its 2015-2019 average.[1] Because of its long-term nature, the willingness to assume risk and the adaptability to new circumstances, the equity-financed corporation provides an important contribution to the process of creative destruction, which in itself is one of the most important prerequisites for economy-wide sustainability and resilience.

A working paper published by the European Central Bank (ECB) illustrates that also from an environmental perspective, not all forms of finance are equal with respect their potential. Analysing a large panel of countries - and with data from 1990 to 2013 - the ECB working paper concludes that for given levels of economic development, financial development and environmental regulation, CO_2 emissions per capita are lower in economies that rely more on market based equity funding (De Haas and Popov, 2019). The working paper identifies two main reasons for the relationship between the use of equity capital and lower carbon emissions: first, stock markets reallocate investment towards less polluting sectors more effectively than other types of financial markets; second, equity markets also push remaining carbon intensive sectors to develop and implement greener technologies. The working paper concludes that carbon-intensive industries produce more green patents when national stock markets deepen. In general, broad and deep public equity markets that present investors with the ability to diversify the firm-specific risks associated with technological innovation lower the overall societal cost of capital for research and development that result in new patents, products and processes that have a smaller carbon footprint.

Considering the society wide importance of the corporation and the unique characteristics of equity capital, it is not surprising that systems for managing and communicating corporate risks are as old as the legal form of the corporation itself. The history of the corporation is one where checks and balances continuously have been adapted to new circumstances and successively become embedded in legal and regulatory norms, such as company law, corporate statutes, securities regulation, auditing and accounting standards. As secondary markets for equity developed high-quality standards for public disclosure of comparable, consistent and verifiable information has also developed in order to facilitate for market participants to "measure what they manage" and make rational decisions and choices with respect to different investment alternatives.

The purpose of these checks, balances and disclosure practices that are at the heart of the corporate governance framework is to ensure that equity providers and other investors at any given time have the necessary information to assess, and as necessary the means to address, the resilience and future sustainability of the corporation. A critical component of this is information about risk. Failure to furnish capital providers with a credible assessment of the risks that face the corporation not only increases uncertainty about expected performance and the long-term viability of the individual company; it also leads to an increase in the cost of capital and ultimately, a misallocation of society's resources.

When new risks appear, or existing risks become more salient, it is inevitable that the company, regulators, shareholders, creditors and other stakeholders with an interest in the long-term value of the company, will insist that these risks are properly identified, measured, mitigated and disclosed. As described in Chapters 1 and 2, this inherent necessity to adapt risk management and disclosure to new circumstances has in recent years brought increased attention to information about environmental, social and governance (ESG) risks that may influence the corporation's sustainability and resilience.

3.2. The nature and occurrence of corporate ESG risks

From the corporate perspective, the value proposition for managing individual ESG risks is not fundamentally different from managing any other risks that the company may face. However, and to the extent that they have not yet been considered, the company is likely to need new types of expertise, additional information channels, better analytical tools and novel internal policies and practices that are specifically tailored to assessing the company's ESG risks.

Like other risks, the occurrence and significance of ESG risks will vary between individual companies and across industries. Such differences may arise with respect to products, processes, organisational structure, business relationships and geographical location. A company engaged in the extractive industries, for instance, is likely to face a different set of ESG risks than a health care provider. Hence, to generically discuss how companies should go about identifying, assessing and mitigating ESG risks can be a rather complex task. For practical purposes it is therefore useful for policy-makers, standard setters, markets and companies to unbundle them and understand their individual characteristics. Such an analysis can also serve as a starting point for identifying priorities for disclosure of comparable, consistent and verifiable information to the market.

Environmental risks may have different origins and can be both exogenous and endogenous with respect to the corporation itself. An increase in environmental hazards in the form of more frequent and forceful hurricanes in populated areas, for example, may be entirely exogenous to the operations of an insurance company but still have a substantial impact on its risk profile. Likewise rising sea levels may adversely affect the value of assets in low lying areas held by a resort company and changes in local climate may alter the risks for the agriculture business in that area. But there may also be important endogenous environmental risks that are generated by the very character of the company's own products, processes or organisational structure. Examples include potential liabilities as well as reputational costs that may follow from neglectful oil spills and emissions of toxic substances. When identifying and addressing environmental risks, the company needs to pay attention to risks that stem from exogenous factors as well as endogenous risks that are generated by their own operations, by those of companies in their supply chains and by the use of the company's products and services by consumers.

Social risks are not only associated with specific stakeholders, such as the company's own employees. They can also stem from violation of human rights in global supply chains and from conditions in local communities affected by the company and its suppliers. Social risks can also be related to how social attitudes, norms and regulations with the respect to the company's activities may differ between markets and evolve over time. They may also be influenced by changes in the corporation's organisational structure and its contractual arrangements. Increased outsourcing, for example, is likely to require increased attention to local conditions throughout the supply chain and additional resources to simultaneously monitor multiple layers of sub-contractors and joint-venture partners. Social risks may also emerge from new communication technologies and the use of social media that can trigger and amplify changes in consumer sentiments possibly resulting in reputational risks.

Governance risks are associated with the robustness and resourcefulness of the company's procedures for compliance with the framework of relevant laws and regulations within which the corporation operates. This includes a wide spectrum of legal domains such as environmental standards, labour law, tax law, corporate law, securities regulation, anti-bribery, money laundering and disclosure requirements that establishes the legal and regulatory boundaries for the corporation's operations. It may also include any self-declared corporate commitments, for example with respect to business strategy or standards for responsible business conduct (RBC) even when these are not embedded in laws and regulations.

Key quality indicators for governance are the quality of reporting lines, the design of incentive structures and a functional allocation of responsibility and accountability throughout the organisation and among the different company organs, such as the shareholders meeting, the board of directors and management. It should be noted, however, that investor assessments of governance risks often goes beyond evaluating just the formal routines for compliance to also include an appraisal of the internal corporate culture as well as RBC standards.

One factor that can impact the risk assessment across the entire spectrum of environmental, social and governance risks is the occurrence, or the probability, of legislative and regulatory intervention. The introduction of new environmental laws for example may alter the valuation of corporate assets or influence the demand for certain products. Assessing the effects or likelihood of regulatory intervention is therefore a natural part of a company's risk management. One way to mitigate risks related to regulatory intervention is to commit to voluntary company and industry ESG standards. While it is difficult to estimate the costs and benefits of such voluntary undertakings, it is plausible to assume that they would only be justified from the company's perspective when the costs to the company (or industry) from introducing voluntary commitments will be lower than the costs of complying with the alternative mandatory standards. The reason why the compliance costs may be lower may not necessarily be that voluntary undertakings are less ambitious or efficient. Cost savings could for example occur if the voluntary undertakings are adaptable in a way that makes their implementation more effective than the alternative black letter law would allow. However, while the absence of mandatory environmental regulation or improved labour safety standards for example, may be beneficial for the company and its shareholders, it may not necessarily be optimal from a wider economic perspective when market failures, such as differences in bargaining power or the lack of an appropriate market price for clean air exist and would suggest regulatory solutions.

To be sure, ESG risk management, due diligence processes and their related disclosure practices do not evolve in a vacuum. Even when a company's board and auditors in good faith and in compliance with their fiduciary duties consider a specific risk immaterial, certain investors and stakeholders may disagree and request that it is addressed or disclosed. There may be multiple reasons for such disagreements. A particular investor may have holdings in other companies impacted by the first company's activities, which from the investor's portfolio perspective amplifies a certain risk in the first company. The question then arises whether the costs associated with addressing the portfolio risk of one investor should be borne by the company rather than by the investor itself. This illustrates the fact that the investor community is a heterogeneous group that differs with respect to investment strategies, risk appetite and qualifications. And what one investor considers a risk may even be seen as an opportunity by another investor. Such pluralism with respect to judgement, attitudes and competencies is the cornerstone of a well-functioning market economy and a good corporate governance framework provides efficient rules-based mechanisms to arbitrate any differences in preferences between investors, including exit opportunities for dissenting shareholders.

As mentioned above, and to serve the wide variety of interests of market participants, extensive work has been undertaken over decades to establish disclosure requirements for relevant information in order to be comparable, consistent and verifiable. This is indeed an on-going process where the relevance, quality and cost of disclosure items are assessed. When not being of material importance to the company or its stakeholders, it not obvious whether it is the company or the specific investor that requires the information that should foot the bill for the costs associated with producing and processing the information.

Conflicting assessments of risks may not only occur between company officials and its shareholders or among different shareholders themselves. They may also exist among different stakeholders, for example when the risk and associated costs of unemployment at a certain plant are weighted against the risks of its continued negative impact on the environment.

There are also cases when certain investors may militate for ESG actions or practices, indifferent to the costs it will impose on the company. Such actions may have little to do with risks to the sustainability of the company's operations or its long-term resilience but rather with specific preferences of the particular investors. In this case, it is less about the company's risk level and more about the intrinsic nature of the company's business or its operations. Individual shareholders are obviously entitled to have views on matters also with no material consequences for risk or return, keeping in mind that from the managers' and the board's perspective, accommodating such demands against the interest of the company could imply a breach of their fiduciary duties.

However, if the demand for attention to certain ESG risks that are deemed immaterial by the company is backed by capital providers that are indispensable to the company's capital supply, neglecting them may in itself become a material risk, affecting the company's cost of capital. Under such circumstances the remaining shareholders may still be well served if the board and management cater to the demands of indispensable capital providers, assuming that it complies with equal treatment of shareholders.

Since the sustainability and resilience of the company typically coincide with the interests of the shareholders, the existence of differences with respect to their risk assessments should not be exaggerated. Also, shareholders who make substantial investments in independent information gathering may themselves, with the help of modern information systems and qualified advisors, be able to complement the quality of risk analysis that is generated through the company's own internal processes. When this is the case, it may indeed be beneficial to the company to establish a dialogue that will provide additional information and help the company to identify hitherto neglected or unknown risks. In such a dialogue it remains important however that any material corporate information is equally shared with the market.

3.3. The G20/OECD Principles of Corporate Governance, risk management and ESG considerations

The need for robust structures and procedures for risk management and high-quality disclosure is firmly articulated in the G20/OECD Principles of Corporate Governance (the G20/OECD Principles; OECD, 2015). Their scope and recommendations extend beyond traditional financial and operational risks and point to the need to also address company policies and performance with respect to environmental and social issues.

Importantly, the quality of risk management with respect to environmental and social factors cannot be seen in isolation from the totality of the recommendations for good corporate governance provided by the G20/OECD Principles. This includes the rights of shareholders, the functioning of capital markets, the role of stakeholders, the quality of disclosure and the role of the board of directors. Effective risk management requires that all aspects of the governance framework, individually and in concert, work well in a functional and purposeful fashion. This is indeed why investors and regulators have identified weak overall governance arrangements as a potential risk along with environmental and social factors. As a consequence, the G20/OECD Principles recommend that explanation of the company's corporate governance practices should be mandated as part of corporate reporting.

While the G20/OECD Principles identify some key areas to address and the main elements of ESG related risks management, the responsibility for the detailed design and implementation remains with the individual company, which must take its own firm- and industry-specific circumstances into account. Analogous to the internal organisation of financial and operational risk management and disclosure, there is today a growing range of tools in the form of mandates, standards, frameworks and guidance that boards and managers can use as tools when they develop the company's system for managing and disclosing ESG risks. Some examples of the more common tools are discussed in sections 3.4 and 3.5.

3.3.1. Board responsibilities over strategy and risk

The G20/OECD Principles recommend that the corporate board of directors is vested with the responsibility to oversee the company's risk management and the related systems that are designed to ensure that the corporation operates in conformity with the extensive legal framework that set the boundaries for their operations, including tax, competition, labour, environmental, equal opportunity, health and safety laws, company law and securities regulations.[2]

Importantly, this duty encompasses the distribution of accountability and responsibility for managing risks; specification of the types and degree of risk that a company is willing to accept in pursuit of its goals; and how it will manage the risks that it creates through its operations and relationships. As mentioned above, this responsibility should be linked to the responsibility to monitor the company's governance practices and a continuous review of the internal structures that the company has established. Such on-going assessment and adjustments may be particularly important as new ESG risks emerge or existing ones become more salient.

The G20/OECD Principles also point to the usefulness of establishing compliance programmes that will support risk management. Such compliance programmes may cover different areas of risk exposure depending on the nature of the company's operations and include issues related to safety conditions, human rights and the environment. It is worth noting that in large complex organisations, the parent company may be exposed to ESG risks beyond its own legal person. The G20/OECD Principles therefore recommends that compliance programmes should extend also to subsidiaries and where possible to third parties, such as agents and other intermediaries, consultants, representatives, distributors, contractors and suppliers, consortia, and joint venture partners.

Because of the increased importance of risk management, the G20/OECD Principles also recommend that companies consider setting up a specialised risk committee that can support the full board in performing its function. However, in order to avoid board fragmentation and to ensure that all board members assume collective responsibility for all aspects of its work, the setting up of specialised committees should be based on an assessment of the company's size and risk profile. Again, in order to ensure objective independent judgment, it is important that the full board retain the final responsibility for oversight of company risks and it may for that purpose consider special reporting procedures around risk management, including direct reporting by staff members to the board.

In fulfilling its responsibilities, it is important for the board to encourage also other means of reporting of unethical/unlawful behavior without fear of retribution. Unethical and illegal practices by corporate officers may not only violate the rights of stakeholders but also be to the detriment of the company and its shareholders in terms of reputational damage and an increasing risk of future financial liabilities that may jeopardize financial sustainability and resilience.

As a consequence, the G20/OECD Principles recommend that stakeholders, including individual employees and their representative bodies, should be able to freely communicate their concerns about illegal or unethical practices to the board and that their rights should not be compromised for doing this. The G20/OECD Principles therefore point to the possibility in many countries to bring cases of non-observance of the *OECD Guidelines for Multinational Enterprises* to a National Contact Point (OECD, 2018). Moreover, the G20/OECD Principles recognise that the application of high ethical standards by the board and management is in the long-term interest of the company as a means to making its long-term commitments credible. In this context, aggressive tax planning is referenced as an example of practices that can give rise to both legal and reputational risks.

3.3.2. Disclosure and transparency

While the management of relatively minor risks may be handled internally in the company under the supervision of the board, certain risks may for the sake of materiality or other reasons also be disclosed to the market. Investors are particularly interested in information that may shed light on the future performance of the companies to which they have committed their capital, which may indeed be affected by growing ESG risks.

Based on this premise, many jurisdictions apply the concept of materiality, which can be defined as information whose omission or misstatement could influence decisions taken by the users of the information. However, the G20/OECD Principles recognise that material information can also be defined as information that a reasonable investor would consider important in making an investment or voting decision. They also point to the usefulness or obligation to provide information on issues that may have a significant impact on employees and other stakeholders. Considering their potential adverse impact and costs to the company, these concepts may indeed call for the disclosure of ESG-related risks in the financial statements or the management's discussion and the analysis of operations, which typically are also included in the annual report. The G20/OECD Principles also encourage disclosure relating to business ethics, the environment, social issues and human rights. It is increasingly considered good practice to also provide disclosure about the company's system for identifying, assessing and mitigating such risks.

The G20/OECD Principles advocate that both financial and non-financial information should be based on high quality disclosure standards, since this improves the ability to monitor the relevance, reliability, consistency and comparability of corporate reporting - something that in society's interest should be equally important for the disclosure of financial risks as for the disclosure of ESG-related risks. In the area of financial and operational results, it is at least in principle relatively straightforward to meet this requirement by relying on the two leading, time tested and internationally recognised accounting and reporting standards. As will be discussed in section 3.5, the picture is more scattered for the comparability, consistency and verifiability of ESG risks and ESG information more generally. And as concluded in Chapter 2, greater clarity from corporate reporting frameworks on their approach to what constitutes material information in the context of environment would be beneficial for investors to make informed decisions regardless of their ESG investment strategy.

3.4. Evolving practices and challenges in managing ESG risks

As fiduciaries of the company and its shareholders, the board and its senior management are responsible for ensuring that the company has in place a comprehensive and robust approach to risk. The main elements of this responsibility, outlined in the G20/OECD Principles, are today established law or regulation in virtually every jurisdiction. According to the OECD Corporate Governance Factbook 2019, at least 90% of the 49 OECD and non-OECD jurisdictions surveyed now require or recommend the establishment of an enterprise-wide internal control and risk management system that goes beyond ensuring high quality financial reporting (OECD, 2019: 123).

This implies that in order for board members to meet their fiduciary duties, they must ensure that the company's internal policies, structures and procedures for risk management are up to the task of identifying, measuring and monitoring risks that could have a material impact on the company's performance. The board should also ensure that the company's approach and the system for managing ESG risks is fully aligned with the company's business model and its value proposition. The board must also ensure that company's approach to ESG risk is consistent with its overall approach to risk.

3.4.1. Challenges and the need for adaption

Whichever way a particular risk is classified – as a traditional financial, operational or reputational risk and/or under a separate rubric of "sustainability", "resilience" or "ESG" risk – the duties of the board and senior management to ensure the adequacy of the company's response are the same. While the management of ESG risks is no exception in this regard, appropriate management of ESG risks is likely to pose some special challenges that companies should address upfront:

- Some ESG issues may be novel and outside the experience of existing board members, senior management and even the company's risk professionals.
- ESG issues are often complex and multidisciplinary in nature, with responsibility for various components resting with sets of personnel that have heretofore had limited interaction and coordinated oversight.
- Even when the company relies on both internal and external sources of ESG information and analytics that they regard as accurate, timely and reliable, investors and stakeholders that use other sources may reach different conclusions.
- Years of routine reporting to the authorities on certain ESG issues, for example, health and safety standards, may have nurtured a compliance/check-list mentality rather than a truly pro-active approach to identify potential ESG risks.
- Those with responsibility for identifying, measuring and monitoring particular risks that come under the rubric of ESG may not consider investors and other stakeholders (or even the board and senior management) as important parts of the audience for information about how such risks are managed by the company (Lubrano, 2017).

Considering the great variety of potential risks and the great diversity between companies and industries, there is no one-size-fits-all solution to the challenges of establishing a robust company level ESG risk management system. While the general framework and duties around responsibility for risk management are common to the corporate community, the operations, business model, value proposition and risk appetite do differ. Accordingly, the board and management must work together to tailor the company's implementation of the basic principles of risk management to its particular circumstances, including the specific set of ESG risks that are salient to the company's operations and performance.

Considering the need to tailor risk management systems to company specific circumstances, it is not surprising that governments, regulators and stock exchanges have largely refrained from providing detailed mandatory requirements around how companies should organise and resource their internal risk management systems. As a matter of fact, a certain degree of heterodoxy among companies in their approaches to risk may in principle contribute to the resilience of an industry and the economy as a whole by reducing the likelihood that a single event or confluence of unpredicted events will have identical negative impacts on all actors. Particularly with respect to forward looking assessments of ESG risks that often require a more pro-active approach, overly rigid and detailed regulatory requirements around internal risk management practices could also result in counterproductive boilerplate and box ticking responses that replace the more pro-active approach that every company must exercise in order to identify and assess its particular and often complex ESG risks. Within certain boundaries and subject to existing regulations in areas such as labour law and environmental law, companies are therefore left with the responsibility to determine their own risk appetites, set risk tolerances, and establish a matching risk management system that is fit for purpose.[3]

3.4.2. Tools for designing the ESG risk management system

The absence of mandatory, detailed and off-the-shelf templates for ESG risk management implementation at company level doesn't mean that boards and management are flying blind. A growing body of resources exists today to help boards and management to develop and adapt policies and practices to address the challenges that are related to establishing a high quality internal ESG risk management system.

An increasingly global reference tool for integrating ESG risks into corporate risk management systems is the OECD's Due Diligence Guidance for Responsible Business Conduct (OECD, 2018). This set of recommendations developed in 2018 by the OECD in consultation with business, investors and stakeholders provides an overarching framework on supply chain due diligence to help companies implement the recommendations on responsible business conduct in the OECD Guidelines for Multinational Enterprises (OECD, 2011). This risk based framework enables companies along any part of the value chain to identify, avoid and address adverse impacts related to workers, human rights, the environment, bribery, consumers and corporate governance that may be associated with their operations, supply chains and other relationships. Guidance is also provided to companies on how they can provide remedy for their actions, when relevant. The OECD due diligence recommendations also provide coherence to the ESG approach by aligning its key tenents to the UN Guiding Principles on Business and Human Rights and the ILO conventions on labour. The OECD Due Diligence Guidance for Responsible Business Conduct is also used as a tool for non-financial disclosure, notably by companies that are reporting under the EU Non-Financial Reporting Directive and is described in more detail in section 3.5. It is increasingly used as a basis for laws, such as the EU Regulation on Conflict Minerals and the French Duty of Care Act and referenced in EU discussions on mandatory due diligence.

A frequently referenced source of guidance on the design and implementation of corporate risk assessment and internal controls is the Committee of Sponsoring Organizations of the Treadway Commission - COSO.[4] COSO's Enterprise Risk Management – Integrated Framework, first issued in 2004 and most recently revised in 2017, provides guidance for integrating risk management into strategic planning, operational reviews, internal reporting and compliance, with risk considered at the enterprise, division and business unit levels. In October 2018, COSO also released specific guidance on how to integrate internal processes for identifying, assessing and managing ESG risks in its overall enterprise risk management framework (COSO and World Business Council for Sustainable Development, 2018). In its essence, COSO's ESG risk management guidance applies fundamental risk management principles to the ESG space. Consistent with its guidance on integrating internal processes for ESG risks referred to above, the following eight steps in COSO's framework for implementing effective risk management is applied to ESG risks:

1. Internal environment (risk culture);
2. Objective setting (strategy; risk appetite and tolerance);
3. Event identification (analysis of risks of potential business activities);
4. Risk assessment (likelihood and severity);
5. Risk response (actions to prevent or mitigate impact);
6. Control activities (policies and procedures to ensure planned responses);
7. Information and communication (capturing and reporting on risk-related processes and activities); and
8. Monitoring (analysis of data and revision of policies, procedures and practices).

While their ESG guidance was designed with COSCO's own Enterprise Risk Management – Integrated Framework in mind, the guidance can also be applied to other risk management frameworks a company may choose to follow, such as ISO 31000 and company-specific approaches. Consistent with its intended purpose, COSO's ESG guidance relies on or references such existing ESG frameworks, guidance, practices and tools, rather than providing its own taxonomy of risks, standards and metrics in the manner that, for example, the Sustainability Accounting Standards Board (SASB) does with respect to disclosure.

Box 3.1. Integrating ESG into a company's risk management systems

In a September 2017 "thought paper", sustainability and accounting experts Herz, Monterio and Thompson emphasise the importance at this point in time of improving enterprise risk and performance monitoring systems to ensure the quality of the company's metrics around ESG risk for both internal (board and management) and external (investors and stakeholders) decision-making. Among the examples they give for how companies can adapt their internal systems to include the management of ESG risks are Denmark's Novo Nordisk and Italy's Pirelli.

Novo Nordisk is a major healthcare and pharmaceutical company whose charter has since 2004 reflected the company's commitment "to conduct its activities in a financially, environmentally and socially responsible way". In 2008 it undertook a process applying the COSO Framework to bring ESG within the company's existing control framework. Recognising that resources are limited and that not all risks deserve equal attention, Novo Nordisk decided on "a top-down, risk-based approach and materiality assessment to identify the most crucial areas" to be brought within the scope of its systems. Novo Nordisk's management put together a team of both finance and ESG specialists to work together across units to design and implement "entity- and transaction-level controls, manual and automated controls, and preventative and detective controls" in all sustainability areas deemed material.

Pirelli is one of the world's leading tyre producers, with manufacturing operations in 13 countries and sales in virtually all markets. To encourage fuller integration of ESG risks within the company's overall risk management approach, Pirelli includes its enterprise risk management (ERM) and sustainability (ESG) units in the same department. The company has also developed a proprietary information technology system for collecting and consolidating environmental and social performance data across units and including suppliers. While both of these innovations of course contribute to streamlining the company's integrated reporting, just as importantly, they greatly increase the likelihood that the board and management will have the high-quality information they need regarding Pirelli's ESG risks and its systems to monitor risk management targets, including those around water usage, carbon emissions, energy consumption and workforce training.

Source: (Herz et al., 2017).

A number of national institutes of directors and their associations also recognise ESG risk management as an important issue for boards and have issued guidance for directors on how to approach particular ESG issues in board oversight of risk management. One example is the Global Network of Director Institutes (GNDI), which has issued guidance papers on integrated reporting, cybersecurity and governance of data.[5] And in its response to the European Commission's 2018 public consultation on institutional investors and asset managers' duties regarding sustainability, the European Confederation of Directors Associations (ecoDa) affirmed its members' view "that ESG factors do play an important role (for investors), not only in societal terms but for the business firms directly. They may not only pose important potential risks if neglected, while also offering strategic opportunities when optimally exploited. So sufficient attention for ESG factors is a component to secure long term business success."[6]

Responding to increased demand, a growing number of commercial advisory services have also become available to companies, including all the major auditing and consulting firms, as well as consultants that are specialised in particular industries and categories of risk. The growing amount of ESG data and analysis generated by specialised providers, such as Bloomberg, MSCI and Sustainalytics, are additional sources of information and metrics that can assist companies with respect to information gathering, benchmarking, peer group analysis both at company level and with respect to individual ESG risks.

3.4.3. The allocation of responsibility and accountability

While guidance, advisory services and standards can help companies craft their more detailed and firm-specific ESG risk management systems, its ultimate effectiveness will always rely on a functional division of responsibility and accountability among the different company organs, which is consistent with their incentives, statutory roles and fiduciary duties.

3.4.4. The board and board committees

According to the G20/OECD Principles, it is the board of directors that should set the company's risk appetite, specifying the types and the degree of risk that a company is willing to accept. It should also articulate how the company will manage the risks that arise through its operations and relationships in order to provide the necessary guidance to the managers that must ensure that risks are managed in a way that meets the company's desired risk profile.

In order to act in a manner consistent with their fiduciary duties in their role to formulate and oversee the company's approach to ESG risks, board members must first and foremost inform themselves. ESG encompasses a very broad range of sometimes new or emerging risks that often are interdisciplinary, complex and technical in nature, such as climate change estimates and effects. To continuously and systematically follow what possible ESG risks the company is exposed to from its operations is therefore essential, just as the board on an on-going basis keeps itself informed about technological developments, market sentiments and competitors. Also, the constant evolution of stakeholder expectations, regulations, mandates, standards, frameworks and guides with respect to ESG topics can be hard to keep up with even for specialists. But much the same as every board member should have at least a basic understanding of financial accounting and operations in order to serve effectively as a director, a similar minimum level of familiarity with the nature of ESG risks and the associated societal expectations, standards, metrics and frameworks for ESG risk management is today essential.

In addition to the various external sources for integrating ESG risk into risk management systems mentioned above, boards may also make use of different established ESG reporting tools to orient directors about what ESG risks are generally considered material to the sectors and industries in which the company operates. A basic grounding in such reporting tools empowers directors to make more effective use of the information that management provides them and to ask the right questions as the company's approach to ESG risk evolves. For example, it behoves every director to know which categories of ESG risk are indicated as relevant to the company's operations on SASB's materiality map.[7] Likewise, familiarity with the recommendations of FSB's Task Force on Climate-related Financial Disclosures (TCFD) allows directors to make better sense of, and contribute to, the company's approach to dealing with climate-related issues even when the company may not explicitly use that particular reporting tool for its disclosure.

Staying informed on ESG risks requires above all regular board interaction with management and the subject matter experts inside and outside the company that support the company's ESG risk management work. In order for this dialogue to truly contribute to the effectiveness of the company's approach to ESG risk, it must go beyond the mere exchange of compliance-related information and respond to the current era dynamics with respect to ESG risk management, including the use of information technology tools. In appropriate cases, board members may also engage directly with investors and other stakeholders to understand their views and expectations. For communications between the board, management, experts and stakeholders to take place in an efficient and effective way, policies and procedures need to be in place to ensure that the board receives relevant, high quality information on ESG issues in a timely fashion. Accordingly, the board and management must work out policies and practices for keeping the board updated and adequately informed on emergent ESG issues and ensuring that the board has the information it needs to assess the continuing adequacy of the company's ESG risk management practices and planning.

Importantly, directors must ensure that their own board structure, composition and procedures accommodate the consideration of ESG risk within the firm's overall risk appetite and approach to risk management. In line with the recommendations in the G20/OECD Principles, some boards today rely on special risk committees to take the lead in this area. Companies may also rely on an audit committee for the same purpose or a combined audit and risk committee. However, an audit and/or risk committee composed entirely of board members with a traditional finance or operational background may not be well suited to adequately consider non-traditional risk factors, or to decide whether the board has access to the right internal and external resources. In most cases, direct involvement by the Chair and the governance committee is also essential to ensure that the board's needs in this area are taken into account in the overall programme for board evaluation and succession planning.

Regardless of how the board structures itself to oversee ESG risk, it will need to fashion policies and procedures for its interaction with ESG assurance providers in a manner analogous to that between audit committees, internal auditors and external auditors. As discussed further below, ESG assurance is a nascent but developing field. Just as in the case of financial and other operational risks, those with responsibility for oversight of ESG risk need to understand the nature of ESG audit and assurance practices, their value and their limits. This requires development of a programme of interaction between the board, relevant company staff and assurance providers.

Engagement with stakeholders and others is for the most part management's role. However, it is for the board to assure itself that the company's management, including its investor relations functions and other channels of communication with outsiders, foster productive feedback and expectations management around the company's ESG policies, procedures and practices. It is therefore seen as a useful practice that the board goes through the exercise with management of mapping the company's different stakeholders to the ESG issues that affect them, the operations of the company that impact those issues, the company's responses in each area, its engagement with affected stakeholders, its objectives and recent outcomes. Especially for companies with elevated environmental or social risks, it can be considered good practice for management to monitor the ESG information flows that investors and other stakeholders rely on by gathering the same information and tracking how the company is being portrayed.

In assuming its responsibility, the board should also ensure that the company's approach to ESG risk remains at all times coherent and consistent with existing legislation, the company's strategy and value proposition. Not all risks are of equal importance to the company. Each company needs to articulate internally and externally how its ESG risk policies, procedures and practices, are focused on those risks that are likely to have the greatest material impact on the company's sustainability and resilience. This includes both upside and downside risks and can be reflected in the company's integrated reporting as will be discussed in the next section of this chapter. It is inevitably a complex task to ensure that ESG risk oversight and management does not take place in a vacuum. Integrating and adapting a company's approach to ESG risk into the value proposition, business model and overall risk appetite demands careful coordination between all the committees and individuals at the board and senior management level responsible for strategy, business development, compliance, risk management, investor relations and public communications.

Box 3.2. Board committees and ESG risk

Boards can choose from at least four options in organising how to structure oversight of ESG risk: full board, audit committee, risk committee; or specialised ESG/sustainability committee. Deciding which approach is best requires consideration of a variety of industry and company-specific factors, as well as legal/regulatory considerations in the jurisdiction in which the company is organised or listed. The listing rules for the New York Stock Exchange, for example, require audit committee review of risk policies.

Leaving the full board to exercise oversight of risk without the support of a board committee is increasingly disfavoured. The OECD Corporate Governance Factbook reported a marked increase from 62% to 87% in the number of jurisdictions requiring (50%) or recommending (37%) assigning responsibility for risk to a board committee between 2015 and 2019. (OECD, 2019: 123) A pattern of the audit committee taking on responsibility for supporting risk oversight has emerged in a number of jurisdictions since the beginning of the century. Reasons why the audit committee might be selected to help the board oversee risk include the independent composition of most audit committees, a desire to ensure that oversight of financial and non-financial risk are well-coordinated and the historical pattern of risk management functions reporting to the Chief Financial Officer, who in turn reports to the audit committee.

A board typically establishes a stand-alone risk committee when operational risks (as opposed to the financial risks that are the focus of the audit committee) are particularly salient and/or the company's systems are rapidly evolving in response to such risks. A separate risk committee of the board allows directors more versed in operations than finance and accounting to take primary responsibility for supporting the board's work in overseeing the company's non-financial risk management system. In some jurisdictions and industries (notably banking and finance) the financial statement and accounting compliance burdens imposed on audit committees may leave its members with little capacity to play an effective role in oversight of non-financial risk. The technical nature of a company's business may also militate for establishment of a stand-alone risk committee whose members have the requisite professional expertise and experience to understand and evaluate risks inherent in its operations. Mining, energy and financial companies often establish stand-alone risk committees. In 2019, approximately one-third of jurisdictions require or recommend stand-alone risk committees, double the number in 2015. (OECD, 2019: 124).

A small but growing minority of companies have established dedicated ESG/sustainability committees of the board. Stand-alone committees to support the board's oversight of ESG risk and disclosures may be desirable where such risks are especially salient and/or where establishment and monitoring of key performance indicators (KPIs) around ESG require a high degree of technical expertise.

Last but not least, it follows from its responsibility that the board needs to pay attention to how the company's limited resources are allocated to address actual and potential risks to the company in the most cost effective way. Selectivity is a fundamental element of effective risk management. The company's resources, including the "bandwidth" of board members and senior managers, are not unlimited. While boards should be accorded at least legal deference to make their own business judgments about the allocation of resources, the basis for such judgment must always be rooted in their fiduciary duty to act in the best interests of the company.

Management

On a day-to-day basis, it is management that has to make the ESG risk management system work within the context of the company's overall risk management system. As noted above, important guidance for incorporating ESG risks into a company's overall policies, practices and management structures already exists and can be expected to continue evolving. One particular management challenge when integrating ESG risk management within the existing organisational structure is that ESG risks are often interdisciplinary and cross-departmental in nature.

Often, the "traditional" risk management functions in a company report to the Chief Financial Officer (CFO), who in turn reports to the senior management and the audit committee of the board. Internal risk reporting and control functions more often than not are carried out on an operating unit basis, with those responsible for understanding and implementing the risk processes working with easily identifiable and frequently consulted operational counterparts. For ESG risk management to be effective, it often involves monitoring activities that cut across operational units and therefore require people to work together that have heretofore rarely done so. It may therefore be natural for operational staff to resist new ESG risk management practices and procedures if they do not fully understand how they relate to their immediate responsibilities.

As a consequence, senior management bears particular responsibility for ensuring consistency of the company's messaging around ESG risk. And more importantly, consistency between its messaging and its actual practices. Clear articulation of a company's ESG efforts allows management, staff and other internal audiences to understand why a particular set of policies, procedures and practices have been implemented and what they are intended to accomplish. Clarity also promotes the establishment of effective metrics, targets, performance indicators and incentives. Well-crafted internal communications around the approach to ESG risk also facilitate the setting of proper priorities within the overall risk management framework throughout the organisation and the development of assurance and audit.

In addition to the need to adapt the organisational structure to better capture ESG risks, effective ESG risk management within a firm may also require different reporting lines than those that have been established for financial and more traditional operational risk management functions. As noted above, the CFO, as the chief responsible executive for financial reporting, often plays the central C-suite role in risk management. To mimic this, some companies have created a Chief Risk Officer (CRO) position to coordinate the approach to identifying, measuring and monitoring operational risks. ESG risks however are typically likely to go beyond the scope of the CRO's operational expertise, requiring the CRO to be supported by specialists. It may therefore be necessary for the management team to establish channels of communication and lines of reporting and accountability at the top that ensure that ESG risks are properly considered and managed in a manner consistent with the company's overall approach to risk management.

Shareholders

As noted in section 3.3 above, the G20/OECD Principles recognise that shareholders (and other capital providers) have a high level of interest in the accuracy and completeness of the company's disclosures around material risks, as well as the effectiveness of the company's systems for identifying, measuring and monitoring risks. This information is to be given to shareholders so that they can act on it – not simply as an input into buying and selling decisions, but also in the exercise of their shareholder rights, including the rights to vote, question management and, when part of the legal framework, introduce proposals for resolutions at the shareholders meeting.

Shareholders have a role to play in encouraging better disclosure of ESG risks that are material to their interests and how the company manages such risks. While often considered a mere formality, in many jurisdictions the annual report of the company (not just its financial statements) is subject to the approval by shareholders at the annual general meeting (AGM). Shareholders who feel a company's approach to risk management and/or its disclosure is inadequate can express their dissatisfaction by questioning management at the AGM and by objecting to annual reports they believe inadequately present material ESG risks. Short of such actions, shareholders, including institutional investors in the exercise of their fiduciary duties to beneficiaries, can proactively engage with portfolio companies to encourage them to adopt reporting frameworks and standards that allow for greater comparability across companies. Shareholders also have the opportunity to let companies know their views on the quality of assurance provided on ESG disclosures.

In several markets, it has become commonplace that ESG related resolutions are submitted without any direct relation to material information or risk factors but openly motivated by particular social, environmental or political agendas. When the board and other shareholders in the interest of the company are not able to meet such requests, it may still be in their interest to understand their rationale and possible impact on the company's operations, reputation and long-term performance.

3.5. Challenges and evolving practices with respect to recognition and disclosure of ESG risks

In order to serve the economy and individual users, it is essential that corporate reporting be high quality, consistent, comparable and verifiable. With respect to the recognition and reporting of financial and operational results, this is typically accomplished through the application of two internationally recognised, time-tested and largely mutually recognised sets of accounting standards. These are the International Financial Reporting Standards (IFRS), which are developed by the International Accounting Standards Board (IASB), and US Generally Accepted Accounting Principles (US GAAP), which are developed by the Financial Accounting Standards Board (FASB), designated by the US Securities and Exchange Commission (US SEC) as the standard setter for publicly listed companies. Both bodies have developed their standards over a long period of time with the involvement of innumerable experts and practitioners.

As of today, neither the IASB nor FASB have embarked on setting their own specific reporting standards with respect to ESG factors. The Chair of IASB stated in 2019 that the IASB does not intend to move into standard setting for climate change related financial reporting (Accounting Today, 2019). The Chair also stated that the IASB is not equipped to enter the field of sustainability reporting, adding that setting standards in this area "requires expertise that we simply do not have". This, however, does not mean that the IFRS Foundation and its stakeholders could not play a pro-active and constructive role in lending their expertise to advancing reporting with respect to ESG factors. In a recent remark, the IFRS Foundation Trustee Teresa Ko outlined possible future roles that the IFRS Foundation could play in supporting progress towards the development of high-quality and internationally recognised standards for sustainability reporting.[8] FASB, the scope of whose SEC-delegated authority is basically limited to audited financial statements, has so far declined ambitions in ESG standard setting.

In principle, the recognition and disclosure of material ESG risks would be covered already under existing recognised reporting rules. But as already noted, in order to be effective, the identification and assessment of ESG risks may require different tools and standards than those developed for reporting of more traditional financial and operational risks. It may also be in the interest of the company to issue, and for markets and stakeholders to receive information that may not necessarily be recognised as material.

3.5.1. The evolving universe of ESG reporting

In the absence of the two dominant bodies vested with developing financial reporting standards from the arena of ESG reporting, and considering the challenges involved, it is not surprising that efforts with respect to internationally recognised, consistent, comparable and verifiable ESG disclosure are still at an early stage. No single universally agreed standard that companies can use for recognising and reporting ESG related information has yet emerged. This poses challenges both from the company and the investor perspectives. Just as differences in scope and methodology with respect to ESG ratings, investment strategies and products present a disjointed and inconsistent view of ESG (See Chapters 1 and 2), inconsistencies and lack of comparability between frameworks for ESG reporting may also mislead investors in their investment decisions. Catering to a growing demand, a number of different supporting tools intended for ESG related disclosure have been developed and while these supporting tools may indeed be useful in specific contexts, their multitude and diversity may in itself cause a certain degree of confusion among both issuers and users. Reconciling different approaches and identifying central indicators for comparable, consistent ESG disclosure has therefore emerged as one of the key challenges together with the additional complexities associated with assurance and audit to verify the content.

While there is no established taxonomy to describe the many different kinds of supporting tools for ESG reporting that exist, it may still be useful to point at some broad similarities and distinctions between them according to their character and intended use. In the brief overview that follows, the examples of different supporting tools and the experiences with their use are therefore structured by broadly classifying them as reporting mandates, reporting standards, reporting frameworks and disclosure practice guides.

Reporting mandates

Reporting mandates refer to legal and regulatory provisions imposed by governments that require disclosure of general or specific ESG information. The most prominent example is probably the European Union's principles-based Non-Financial Reporting Directive (NFRD), which came into effect in 2018 and is currently under review, including the related national legislation issued to implement it.[9] As a complement to the review, the European Commission in 2020 also launched an initiative on sustainable corporate governance with the aim to ensure that sustainability is further embedded into the corporate governance framework with a view to align better the long term interests of management, shareholders, stakeholders and society (EC, 2020).

The NFRD is designed with a broad set of stakeholder interests in mind, and so applies a correspondingly broad understanding of ESG risk materiality. The directive instructs member states to require each listed company and significant enterprise ("public-interest entities") to publicly disclose its policies, the outcomes of such policies (including key performance indicators), and the risks associated with the company's operations in the areas of: environmental matters; social and employee aspects; respect for human rights; anti-corruption and bribery issues; and diversity on boards of directors. Approximately 6 000 European companies are subject to the NFRD.

The NFRD does not prescribe integrated reporting. Approximately 60% of the 1 000 companies whose NFRD disclosures were analysed by the Alliance for Corporate Transparency (ACT) in 2019 integrated key ESG information in their annual reports, with the remainder publishing separate ESG or sustainability reports (COSO and World Business Council for Sustainable Development, 2018). Nor does NFRD require companies to follow a particular reporting framework, which obviously gives rise to challenges with respect to comparability. What companies need to do is to specify which domestic or international framework(s) they follow. The Global Reporting Initiative, United Nations Global Compact, Sustainable Development Goals, OECD Due Diligence Guidance for Responsible Business Conduct and its industry specific due diligence guidances, the Carbon Disclosure Project and ILO standards, were the most frequently used according to the disclosures that were reviewed by the ACT.

The ACT's 2019 analysis of NFRD implementation paints a mixed picture of its completeness thus far. While over 80% of the companies surveyed disclosed their policies in the five categories, only 35% included targets and only 28% reported on outcomes. While about half of the companies surveyed by ACT provided disclosure on at least one strategic sustainability-related risk, only 7% described how these risks are reflected in their core business strategies. Not surprisingly, companies whose disclosures were reviewed by the ACT reported best on "traditional" risks that today have come to be classified under the ESG rubric. For example, 99% of companies provided disclosure with respect to employees.

It should be noted that the ACT analysed corporate reporting in the areas covered by the NFRD, not the workings of the internal ESG risk management systems of the corporations. It is therefore difficult to extrapolate from corporate disclosures the intrinsic quality of companies' ESG risk management systems. Their ESG risk management practices and results may in fact be substantially better in reality than they appear from the public reporting. The results of the ACT survey at least point to the possibility that European companies are better at identifying potential ESG risks than at internalising consideration of them into strategic direction, setting key performance indicators and measuring outcomes. Interestingly, the ACT found a positive correlation between companies that reported ESG targets and those that secured some sort of assurance of the information included in their ESG disclosures. This would be consistent with boards and management seeking to have greater confidence around information that they judge may have a direct impact on corporate strategy and performance.

Reporting mandates may also be more rules-based, and narrower in their scope and intended beneficiaries. For example, some securities law regimes require listed companies engaged in mining to report accidents, violations of health and safety laws, fines and settlements for deaths and injuries.[10] Others may require disclosure of employment law claims against the company.

Reporting standards

Reporting standards lay out what metrics should be disclosed for specific ESG topics that are deemed material and can be adapted to particular sectors and industries. For example, SASB requires that oil & gas companies estimate and disclose the amount of CO_2 emissions that would be released by commercialising their proven reserves. Standards, like SASB and the Global Reporting Initiative (GRI), which likewise organises the application of standards by industry, aim to allow for quantitative and like-for-like comparisons between companies, and potentially third-party assurance through an audit (Global Sustainability Standards, 2018). To be credible, standard setters consult widely and seek consensus around the topics deemed material and the key performance metrics to be reported.

The GRI was established in 1997 to develop standards for all organisations (including listed and unlisted firms, not-for-profits and other entities) to report environmental, social and governance information for the benefit of a broad range of stakeholders. It has taken a modular approach, incrementally releasing standards over time as particular ESG issues gained salience. Companies employing GRI standards in their reporting are encouraged to upload them to the GRI website, which now catalogues disclosures from over 14 000 organisations.

The GRI standards are set by the independently operated Global Sustainability Standards Board (GSSB) consisting of 15 members "representing a range of expertise and multi-stakeholder perspectives on sustainability reporting" (GSSB, 2020). GRI standard setting involves regular stakeholder consultation, public notice and comment procedures. The GSSB's meetings are open to the public and made available online. GRI recently modified its universal reporting standards to integrate and align with recommendations of the OECD Due Diligence Guidance for Responsible Business Conduct.[11]

The SASB started as an initiative largely focused on US companies but has over the past two years seen significant uptake also from non-US companies and investors. According to data provided by SASB, as of 31 July 2020, 169 US companies and 110 non-US firms report their ESG disclosure in accordance with SASB standards. 163 of these firms are included in the S&P Global 1200 index.[12] Of the 41 global institutional investors surveyed for Morrow Sodali's 2020 Institutional Investor Survey, 81% recommend SASB as the best standards for companies to communicate their ESG information (Morrow Sodali, 2020). Currently, more than 130 institutional investors from 18 countries incorporate SASB's standards in their investment processes as licensees and/or have joined SASB as Alliance Members or as members of its Investor Advisory Group.

SASB's governance structure and standard-setting process are similar to those of the internationally recognised bodies that set disclosure standards for the benefit of investors, such as the Financial Accounting Standards Board (FASB) and the International Accounting Standards Board (IASB) (SASB, 2017). SASB's standards are developed and revised under the guidance of its Standards Board and a Standards Advisory Group for each of the 11 SASB sectors. Members of the Advisory Groups include industry representatives, investors, technical experts, legal and accounting professionals, academics and others who engage with the Standards Board with the goal of settling on standards and metrics that are practical and fit-for-purpose. Standard-setting takes place in accordance with a fully transparent six stage process, progressing from project screening through research, standard-setting agenda, comment period, update and post-implementation review phases. The standard-setting agenda and comment period phases of the process in particular are designed to ensure that new standards and revisions "are developed based on extensive feedback from companies, investors, and other market participants as part of a transparent, publicly-documented process" (SASB, 2020). SASB has also established an Investor Advisory Group of leading asset owners and asset managers "to encourage companies to participate in SASB's on-going standards development process, so that outcomes reflect both issuer and investor viewpoints". GSSB similarly commits itself to "due process" and multi-shareholder engagement and input in setting GRI standards, the main differences arising from the GRI standards' broader set of intended beneficiaries (Global Sustainability Standards, 2018).

While usually cited as the most comprehensive ESG disclosure standards, SASB and GRI differ importantly with respect to their audiences, and thus their definitions of materiality. SASB is first and foremost a set of accounting standards for investors to consider in allocating capital while GRI's definition of materiality takes into account the broader interests of non-financial stakeholders and societal impacts.

Reporting frameworks

Reporting frameworks such as the International Integrated Reporting Council's (IIRC) framework and the framework issued by the Task Force on Climate-Related Financial Disclosures (TCFD) for climate-related disclosures are examples of principles-based frameworks that provide guidance on how reporting companies should organise and present ESG related information (IIRC, 2013; FSB, 2020). For example, TCFD recommends that every company include in its non-financial reporting an explanation of how its strategic planning process takes into account greenhouse gas emissions. 77% of the respondents to Morrow Sodali's 2020 Institutional Investor Survey recommended TCFD as the preferred framework for climate-related disclosures (Morrow Sodali, 2002). The latest artificial intelligence review of the reporting of 1 126 companies from 142 countries and eight industries conducted by TCFD found that the percentage of companies disclosing information aligned with each of its recommendations increased between 2016 and 2018. The average number of the 11 recommended disclosures addressed by companies grew from 2.8 recommendations in 2016, to 3.1 in 2017, and to 3.6 in 2018. Seventy-eight percent of the companies in the review disclosed information aligned with at least one of the Task Force's recommendations in 2018, up from 70% in 2016. However, climate-related disclosure remains patchy and "only around 25% of companies disclosed information aligned with more than five of the 11 recommended disclosures and only 4% of companies disclosed information aligned with at least 10 of the recommended disclosures" (FSB, 2019).

Some companies choose to organise the presentation of all or part of their ESG reporting along the lines of more aspirational objectives, such as the Sustainable Development Goals, or recommendations for operational best practices, like the OECD Due Diligence Guidance for Responsible Business Conduct and its complementary sector-specific guidance (OECD, 2018). The OECD Due Diligence Guidance supports the implementation of the OECD Guidelines for Multinational Enterprises and "help[s] enterprises avoid and address adverse impacts related to workers, human rights, the environment, bribery, consumers and corporate governance that may be associated with their operations, supply chains and other business relationships". Together with its complementary sector-specific due diligence guidance for the minerals, agriculture and garment and footwear supply chains, and good practice reports for the extractives and financial sectors, the OECD Due Diligence Guidance provides companies with guidance for identifying and assessing potential adverse impacts of its operations, supply chains and business relationships and examples of practical actions for managing the risks that these present for both the company and others. Seventeen percent of respondents to a recent survey carried out by the Alliance for Corporate Transparency (ACT) of compliance with the EU Non-Financial Reporting Directive cited the OECD Due Diligence Guidance and its complementary sector specific guidance among the frameworks employed for reporting the ESG-related information required by the directive and national implementing legislation (Alliance for Corporate Transparency, 2019: 34).

Practice guides

Disclosure practice guides typically lay out certain disclosure principles in the expectation of voluntary compliance, often recommending the application of more detailed tools that usefully can be applied. Stock exchange initiatives intended to encourage public company disclosure of ESG information generally fall into the category of practice guidelines.

NASDAQ's ESG Reporting Guide is one such effort to help companies listed on its exchanges to identify suitable reporting methodologies appropriate for their activities as well as to "help both private and public companies navigate the evolving standards on ESG data disclosure" (NASDAQ, 2019). In parallel, NASDAQ has established an ESG Reporting Platform to facilitate the distribution of listed companies' ESG information to users, including data services, ESG rating services and index providers. NASDAQ also maintains a team of ESG experts available to work with client companies to "analyse, assess and action ESG programs with the goals of attracting long-term capital and enhancing value creation" (NASDAQ, 2019).

In early 2020, the Japan Exchange Group and the Tokyo Stock Exchange released their "Practical Handbook for ESG Disclosure" (Japan Exchange Group, 2020). The Handbook is intended to help Japanese listed companies respond in a meaningful way to demands for quality ESG information from investors. It advocates a step-by-step approach, encouraging boards and management to begin by gaining an understanding of market expectations around ESG disclosure and identifying the ESG issues relevant to the company's operations. Companies should then articulate how these issues figure into the formulation of the company's strategy. Once the links between ESG issues and strategic direction are clear, the company can "[p]ut in place an internal structure for oversight and implementation of ESG issues and set metrics/targets, to enable steady progress on ESG activities." Finally, in dialogue with investors and other stakeholders, the company should be in a position to determine what existing disclosure frameworks and standards best communicate the company's approach to ESG risk and how it fits into the company's business model, value proposition and overall risk management system.

3.5.2. Selecting and communicating the tools for recognition and disclosure of ESG risks

At this point in the development of ESG reporting, a threshold question for the board and management of each reporting company is which set of ESG reporting tools would serve as the best foundation for presenting its exposure to ESG risks and the company's approach to identifying, measuring and monitoring them. Reporting that uses high quality, comparable, consistent and verifiable tools that are well suited for the company's activities would help to build consensus among investors and stakeholders on what are reasonable expectations for ESG risk disclosures.

However, and considering that some of the available supporting tools are still at an early stage of development, companies, investors and other stakeholders sometimes express near exasperation with the proliferation of tools for ESG reporting. The World Business Council for Sustainable Development's Reporting Exchange catalogues more than 2 000 mandatory and voluntary ESG reporting requirements and resources from more than 70 jurisdictions (World Business Council for Sustainable Development Reporting Exchange, 2020). As a consequence, directors and managers, may be unclear about their purposes and audiences and whether and how investors and other stakeholders expect them to be applied in combination. As many companies are themselves at a fairly early stage of integrating financial and non-financial reporting, many boards and managers are themselves also new to the challenge of deciding what ESG information on the company's operations their companies should report and how to present it.

As a basic rule and overall guidance when identifying reporting tools and formats, the reporting of ESG risk and performance should: 1) convey all materials information accurately and in a timely manner; 2) be as responsive as possible to expectations of investors, the market and relevant stakeholders impacted by the company's actions; 3) be pro-active; 4) facilitate to the extent possible the users' ability to meaningfully evaluate the information conveyed; and 5) be consistent with the company's messaging to other stakeholders and special interests.

3.5.3. The selection process

The first step for the board and management in the selection of the supporting ESG reporting tools is to consistently tie the discussion of each element of ESG risk to its potential impact on the company's business model, strategy and value proposition. The board must ensure the accuracy and completeness of communications with shareholders and investors around those ESG risks that are relevant to them - that is, primarily those that are material to the company's financial condition and long-term performance.

However, there is also likely to be considerable diversity within the universe of a company's investors, other market participants and the company's stakeholders when it comes to their expectations about information on the company's approach to ESG risk and its assessment of such risks. The challenge for the board and managers is to decide which issues are relevant to which stakeholder, and which among all the available standards, frameworks and guidance policies can justifiably be applied. This may not be straightforward, because the interests even among different types of capital providers may not be identical with respect to their risk appetite and exposure. As a consequence, companies can be tempted to be ambiguous, exaggerate or even, misallocate resources in the hopes of satisfying all stakeholders. This may not only create uncertainty for the prime users of the information, it can also be financially costly and distract attention from focusing resources on the most pertinent risks. Inevitable failures in these respects will compromise credibility with all constituencies.

A company's non-financial public disclosures may, obviously, extend beyond items of material relevance to the company. Indeed, as noted above, the OECD Due Diligence Guidance and its complementary sector-specific guidance, the TCFD framework and the GRI standards are crafted to elicit disclosure of information that can be of material relevance to a broad set of stakeholders and potentially non-stakeholder interests. Transparency around environmental and social impacts of the company's operations (both positive and negative) that do not present material risks to the company's long-term financial performance may indeed be justifiable on a cost-benefit basis, taking into account the potential for adverse publicity and reputational damage to the company.

3.5.4. Consistency of messaging to stakeholders

Beyond the selection of supporting tools for reporting and the choice of metrics, it is also important that the company communicate the rationale for how this selection is consistent with the company's approach to ESG risks. Such disclosure is an essential part of transparency and a sound relationship with markets, investors and other stakeholders.

The communication can form part of the company's integrated reporting. According to the International Integrated Reporting Council (IIRC), integrated reporting means providing "a concise communication about how an organisation's strategy, governance, performance and prospects, in the context of its external environment, lead to the creation of value in the short, medium and long term" (IIRC, 2013). In the context of ESG disclosure, integrated reporting ideally gives the users the opportunity to understand how the board and management have tied together the company's approach to ESG risk with its value proposition, business model and strategy.

A public company's initial forays into ESG disclosure rarely begin with the full integration in its annual report of ESG information provided along the lines of generally accepted reporting frameworks and standards. As discussed in Section 3.4, putting in place systems for the identification, measurement and monitoring of what are sometimes novel risks is a complex and painstaking process. Connecting these systems to a process for generating quality reporting on the same timeline as the company's annual financial statements is equally challenging. The CFO may therefore argue that the company's internal ESG reporting need to be a "well-oiled machine" before they feel comfortable to take the leap to fully integrated ESG reporting (SASB, 2020). When this is the case, it is probably more common for a company to begin by preparing a stand-alone ESG report on a separate timetable. Sometimes even on a biannual rather than annual basis.

Legal, regulatory and assurance considerations may also come into play in deciding whether to fully integrate ESG disclosure with financial performance reporting. The highest degree of legal responsibility is ordinarily attached to information provided in annual reports. Boards and management may therefore seek to gain more experience and confidence in the quality of ESG risk management and reporting before potentially exposing themselves to any legal liability. For this reason, they may also be well served if they can rely on a core set of high quality, comparable, consistent and verifiable ESG disclosure items.

3.5.5. Assurance and audit

Assurance and audit of ESG-related information collected and reported by the company has evident benefits for the board, management and investors. Independent assurance provides investors and other stakeholders with a greater degree of confidence in the accuracy and completeness of the ESG-risk information provided by a company in its disclosures. As is the case of financial statements, quality auditing ensures greater clarity, consistency and comparability of reporting over time and between companies. The process of obtaining independent assurance on emerging issues, including ESG risks, can also assist boards and management teams to more thoroughly understand the risks that they present and the options that are available for measuring and monitoring such risks. The very process itself of determining the scope of the audit, planning its execution and negotiating the level of assurance provides an important framework for keeping the board, its responsible committee(s), management and staff focused and committed.

By all accounts, the existing framework for consistent, comparable and verifiable ESG information provided by companies to investors, markets and stakeholders, and the current capacity of potential providers of assurance in these areas, are incipient. And as concluded in this and other chapters of this Outlook, the current state of affairs may not only lead to confusion but also misguide investors that explicitly aim to allocate their investments in accordance with a company's ESG profile and performance. By its nature, the audit process requires a clear set of consistently applicable principles and rules against which to evaluate the veracity and comparability of company statements. And until such a unified standard exists, auditors can probably be expected to push back against providing assurance of ESG information that is presented in a sui generis fashion. Efforts like SASB and GRI have contributed importantly to the process of reaching market consensus on what issues can be considered material and how they should be discussed in relation to the company's strategy and value proposition. But there is still some way to go before companies, investors, auditors and regulators can conclude on how relevant information should best be verified and presented. That said, growing demand for assurance may ultimately prove to be the driver of rationalisation and convergence of ESG disclosure practices.

Box 3.3. Assurance and audit in practice: Vornado Realty Trust

Vornado Realty Trust's 2019 Environmental, Social and Governance Report may provide some clues to the direction in which ESG assurance is heading, and perhaps some general insights into the current trajectory of ESG reporting by public companies. Vornado is a real estate investment trust (REIT) organised under the laws of the US state of Maryland. Its principal offices are located in New York City and the company's shares trade on the New York Stock Exchange under the ticker VNO. The company invests in retail and office buildings, with the bulk of its assets located on in New York's borough of Manhattan. The company professes a strong commitment to sustainability. It is a TCFD signatory, a SASB sector advisory group member, a corporate member of the US Green Building Council and an Energy Star Partner of the Year award winner.

Vornado does not fully integrate its financial and non-financial reporting, choosing instead to publish a yearly ESG Report separately from its annual report and financial statements to shareholders. It has adopted the TCFD framework for presenting its climate-related disclosures and reports sustainability metrics against both GRI – Core Option and SASB standards for real estate. The same firm that audits Vornado's financial statements (Deloitte) is contracted by the company's management to provide assurance on the accuracy and completeness of the GRI- and SASB-compliant reporting in the company's ESG Report. Using the same firm for auditing both financial and non-financial reporting makes sense from a practical point of view – the firm's financial auditors should have a firm grasp of the company's operations and value proposition and be in a better position to understand the potential impact of ESG factors on the company's financial and operational performance than stand-along auditors of its ESG risk management systems.

Interestingly, Vornado's auditors produced two reports to the company's trustees in connection with, and included in the ESG Report. The first is a "Review Report" of the company's disclosures against GRI standards and provides only limited level of assurance ("we are not aware of any modifications that should be made to [Vornado management's assertion that the disclosures conform to GRI standards]"). However, Deloitte delivered an "Independent Accountants' Report" reflecting a full examination of the company's SASB disclosures and including a statement of its opinion that such information "presented in accordance with SASB Real Estate Sustainability Accounting Standard is fairly stated, in all material respects". The higher level of assurance provided by Deloitte with respect to the SASB disclosure (comparable to the level of "reasonable assurance" provided with respect to the financial statements) is traceable in large part to SASB's narrower definition of materiality. Audit firms can have considerably greater confidence in their ability to gauge what information is likely to be material to the traditional audience of investors ("material to financial performance") and, accordingly, to estimate what risk they take on in providing assurance with respect to such information. But they and their clients are surely on shakier ground when it comes to what might be material to the more remote (and maybe even amorphous) set of stakeholders for whose benefit GRI disclosures are directed.

References

Accounting Today (2019), "Sustainability standards seen as too fragmented", 17 October, https://www.accountingtoday.com/news/sustainability-standards-seen-as-too-fragmented.

Alliance for Corporate Transparency (2019), 2019 Research Report: An analysis of the sustainability reports of 1000 companies pursuant to the EU Non-Financial Reporting Directive, https://allianceforcorporatetransparency.org/assets/2019_Research_Report%20_Alliance_for_Corporate_Transparency-7d9802a0c18c9f13017d686481bd2d6c6886fea6d9e9c7a5c3cfafea8a48b1c7.pdf

Cournède, B. and O. Denk (2015), "Finance and economic growth in OECD and G20 countries", OECD Economics Department Working Papers, No. 1223, OECD Publishing, Paris, https://doi.org/10.1787/5js04v8z0m38-en.

COSO and World Business Council for Sustainable Development (2018), "Applying Enterprise Risk Management to Environmental, Social and Governance-related Risks", October 22, 2018, https://gndi.weebly.com/papers.html.

Dee Haas, R. and A. Popov (2019), Finance and carbon emissions, ECB Working Paper Series No. 2318/September 2019.

ECODA (2019), https://ecoda.org/wp-content/uploads/2019/08/20180123_Investors_Duties_and_Sustainability-ecoDa_final_response.pdf.

EC (2020), Ares(2020)4034032 on Sustainable Corporate Governance, Proposal for legislation fostering more sustainable corporate governance in companies, European Commission https://eur-lex.europa.eu/legal-content/EN/PIN/?uri=PI_COM:Ares(2020)4034032.

FSB (2020), Task Force on Climate-related Financial Disclosures, Overview, https://www.fsb-tcfd.org/wp-content/uploads/2020/03/TCFD_Booklet_FNL_Digital_March-2020.pdf

FSB (2019), Task Force on Climate-related Financial Disclosures: Status Report 2019, p. 7. https://www.fsb-tcfd.org/wp-content/uploads/2019/06/2019-TCFD-Status-Report-FINAL-053119.pdf.

Global Sustainability Standards (2018), Board Due Process Protocol October 2018, https://www.globalreporting.org/standards/media/2099/gssb-due-process-protocol-2018.pdf.

GSSB (2020), Global Sustainability Standards Board Overview, https://www.globalreporting.org/standards/gssb-and-standard-setting/

Herz, R.H., B.J. Monterio and J.C. Thomson (2017), Leveraging the COSO Internal Control – Integrated Framework to Improve Confidence in Sustainability Performance Data.

International Integrated Reporting Council (2013), The International <IR> Framework, https://integratedreporting.org/resource/international-ir-framework/.

Isaksson, M. and S. Çelik (2013), "Who Cares? Corporate: Governance in Today's Equity Markets", OECD Corporate, Governance Working Papers, No. 8, OECD Publishing, http://dx.doi.org/10.1787/5k47zw5kdnmp-en.

Japan Exchange Group (2020), Practical Handbook for ESG Disclosure, https://www.jpx.co.jp/english/corporate/sustainability/esg-investment/handbook/b5b4pj000003dkeo-att/handbook.pdf.

Lubrano, M. (2017), "EM companies must recognize investors are front-row in the audience for ESG information", Pensions & Investment, November 21, 2017.

Morrow Sodali (2020), 2020 Institutional Investor Survey, https://morrowsodali.com/insights/institutional-investor-survey-2020.

NASDAQ (2019), ESG Reporting Guide 2.0: A Support Resource for Companies (May 2019), https://www.nasdaq.com/ESG-Guide.

OECD (2019), OECD Corporate Governance Factbook 2019, www.oecd.org/corporate/corporate-governance-factbook.htm.

OECD (2018), OECD Due Diligence Guidance for Responsible Business Conduct, https://www.oecd.org/investment/due-diligence-guidance-for-responsible-business-conduct.htm.

OECD (2015), G20/OECD Principles of Corporate Governance, OECD Publishing, Paris, https://doi.org/10.1787/9789264236882-en.

OECD (2011), OECD Guidelines for Multinational Enterprises, OECD Publishing, Paris, http://dx.doi.org/10.1787/9789264115415-en.

Sustainability Accounting Standards Board (2020), SASB, American Institute of Certified Public

Accountants, Webinar: ESG Data Quality & Assurance, Wednesday, May 27.

Sustainability Accounting Standards Board (2017), SASB Conceptual Framework, February 2017, https://www.sasb.org/standard-setting-process/conceptual-framework/.

World Business Council for Sustainable Development Reporting Exchange (2020), https://www.reportingexchange.com/.

Notes

[1] OECD calculations based on data from Thomson Reuters Eikon.

[2] The term "board" as used in the G20/OECD Principles is meant to embrace the different national models of board structures. In the typical two-tier system, found in some countries, "board" as used in the G20/OECD Principles refers to the "supervisory board" while "key executives" refers to the "management board". In systems where the unitary board is overseen by an internal auditor's body, the principles applicable to the board are also, *mutatis mutandis*, applicable.

[3] Governments and regulators may take a different approach to risk management practices in industries, such as banking and finance, where greater similarities and interdependence exist and where business failures can have important systemic or macroeconomic impact.

[4] COSO is a committee composed of representatives from five organizations: the American Accounting Association; the American Institute of Certified Public Accountants; Financial Executives International; the Institute of Management Accountants; and the Institute of Internal Auditors.

[5] Global Network of Director Institutes, https://gndi.weebly.com/papers.html.

[6] European Confederation of Directors Associations. Response to the European Commission's 2018 public consultation on institutional investors and asset managers' duties regarding sustainability, https://ecoda.org/wp-content/uploads/2019/08/20180123_Investors_Duties_and_Sustainability_-_ecoDa_final_response.pdf.

[7] The Sustainability Accounting Standards Board (SASB), an independent non-profit, published the world's first comprehensive set of industry-specific sustainability accounting standards in 2017. SASB's classification system organises companies into 11 sectors and 77 industries in order to identify ESG risks that are expected to be material to particular economic activities. The SASB framework relies on 77 evidence-based, market-informed and industry-specific standards developed by other institutions against which to assess risk exposure and performance.

[8] "Sustainability reporting and its relevance to the IFRS Foundation", https://www.ifrs.org/news-and-events/2020/05/sustainability-reporting-and-its-relevance-to-the-ifrs-foundation/

[9] The EU has recently initiated the process for reviewing and revising the NFRD and developing a uniform European Non-Financial Reporting Standard.

[10] See the US SEC Standard instructions for filing forms under the Securities Act of 1933, the Securities Exchange Age of 1934 and the Energy Policy and Conservation Act of 1975 – Regulation S-K Subpart 229.104 (Mine safety disclosure), https://www.ecfr.gov/cgi-bin/text-idx?SID=fd3f92d14b821275a59c8aeecaabb6e9&mc=true&node=se17.3.229_1104&rgn=div8.

[11] See Review of GRI's Universal Standards (GRI 101, 102 and 103), https://www.globalreporting.org/standards/work-program-and-standards-review/review-of-gris-universal-standards/.

[12] Data provided by SASB on August 24, 2020. A list of companies reporting utilizing SASB standards can be accessed at https://www.sasb.org/company-use/sasb-reporters/.

4. Integrating ESG factors in the investment decision-making process of institutional investors

This chapter reviews the different approaches institutional investors have taken towards environmental, social and governance (ESG) investments, and describes the main methods and tools institutional investors use when integrating ESG factors into their investment decisions. It focuses on the challenges and opportunities specific to pension funds and insurance companies, in light of their fiduciary duty and the long-term prospect of their investments. It also discusses the impact institutional investors' reliance on external ESG data and service providers has on how they approach their ESG investments, outlining issues pension funds and insurance companies need to address if this is the case. Finally, the chapter lists the main information and data points that institutional investors indicate as lacking or missing in order to conduct or rely on a robust ESG analysis. These insights can be of practical assistance to institutional investors looking to develop appropriate ESG governance structures and methods.

4.1. Introduction

Environmental, social and governance (ESG) investment, sustainable investment, socially responsible investment, impact investment, moral investment and other terms are being used more or less synonymously to define the practice of incorporating ESG factors in investment decisions. These factors are of increasing interest for many institutional investors and other market players. However, institutional investors vary in their approach to considering ESG factors for investment decisions, with different types of strategies, datasets and methods they use to integrate ESG factors in their decision-making.

This chapter describes the different approaches, practices and tools institutional investors use to integrate ESG factors into investment policies, and identifies possible trends. It also outlines the main challenges and opportunities they face when considering the integration of ESG factors in their investment decisions. These insights can be of practical assistance to institutional investors looking to develop appropriate ESG governance structures and methods. The COVID-19 crisis also points to the need to build more resilient portfolios that take varied factors into account.

Previous OECD work on the regulatory frameworks that apply to institutional investors in different jurisdictions concluded that integrating ESG factors in investment decisions is generally permitted if consistent with the financial obligations of insurance companies and pension funds towards their beneficiaries and members (OECD, 2017[1]).

The analysis in this chapter is based on several sources of data, including data from the United Nations Principles for Responsible Investment (UN PRI) and from an OECD survey on ESG integration circulated to insurance companies and pension funds in November 2019 (OECD ESG survey). The UN PRI data used includes information only from UN PRI signatories that are insurance companies and pension funds.[1] The OECD ESG survey collected information from institutional investors to better understand if and how ESG factors are considered and applied in their investment process.[2]

To understand these issues, section two examines whether and how insurance companies and pension funds consider ESG factors in their investment decision-making. Section three looks at the investment strategies used to integrate ESG considerations. Section four focuses on the different methods and tools used to analyse ESG criteria, either internally or by relying on external providers. Section five covers the main data points and practical tools that institutional investors report they are still missing to adequately integrate ESG factors in their decision-making processes. Section six concludes and highlights some of the main findings of this chapter.

4.2. Integrating ESG factors in the investment decision-making process

Institutional investors vary in their approaches to integrating ESG factors into their investment decisions. This section looks at whether or not ESG considerations are taken into account and, if so, which part of the organisation is responsible for setting and implementing their ESG strategy. It then describes some of the considerations institutional investors make for integrating ESG factors in their investment decision-making process.

4.2.1. Level of ESG integration

The integration of ESG considerations in investment decisions is becoming a more common practice among institutional investors. According to a survey conducted in 2018 by Natixis Investment Managers, nearly two-thirds of institutional investors believe that the integration of ESG factors will become standard in the industry within the next five years (Natixis Investment Managers, 2019[2]).[3]

However, not all institutional investors integrate ESG factors in their investment decision-making process at the moment. The OECD ESG survey results confirm that:

- Although many insurance companies and pension funds do make ESG considerations when selecting investment opportunities, a significant number do not.
- A majority of respondents declared that they integrate some ESG considerations into their investment decision process: 20 pension funds (out of 25 respondents) and 30 insurance companies (out of 51) considered at least some environmental, social or governance factors on new investments.
- Eighteen insurance companies and four pension funds responded that they do not take any ESG factors into account in their investment decision-making process.
- A small number of institutional investors – three insurance companies and one pension fund – which have not yet started integrating ESG factors -- responded that they were planning to do so in the future. These respondents indicated that the main reasons for not yet integrating ESG factors were a lack of resources, internal knowledge and guidance from policy makers on how to take ESG considerations into account.

According to both the OECD ESG survey and UN PRI data, most institutional investors that choose to integrate ESG factors in their investment decisions implement this through their general investment procedure. A small percentage of the insurance companies and pension funds that are UN PRI signatories offer sustainability themed funds focusing on one or more of the E, S and G pillars. Some themed funds are structured in a way that the investments would be (entirely or mostly) in firms whose products or services aim to meet an environmental or social needs, or firms that focus on long-term and strategic trends. Others may focus on efforts or targets that institutional investors set for themselves, for instance to invest only in firms that take significant steps to cut their carbon footprint.

Among institutional investors that integrate ESG factors, some may only consider one or two of the three dimensions, rather than all three of them. For example, an Asian insurance company responding to the OECD ESG survey stated that governance factors are integrated in all of its investment decisions, but not environmental or social factors. Regulation and the level of market development may be possible reasons for considering only some of the dimensions.

4.2.2. ESG considerations made by institutional investors

Institutional investors integrating ESG factors in their investment decisions face both challenges and potential opportunities and, in addition, estimating the potential risks and returns generated by E, S and G factors is complex. This complexity may be particularly relevant for insurance companies and pension funds that invest on behalf of their beneficiaries and policyholders, and have long-term investment objectives.[4]

ESG integration may be perceived as leading to a trade-off between promoting ESG objectives and risk-adjusted financial returns. As Chapter 1 also shows, empirical and academic studies find mixed evidence on the effect of ESG integration on financial returns:

- ESG integration may **reduce the diversification of portfolios and consequently increase risk**. ESG integration techniques such as exclusionary screening or divestment limit the range of available investments. According to modern portfolio theory, this could have a negative impact on returns over the long-term. Barnett and Salomon (2006[3]) find that applying a low number of ESG filters to build a stock portfolio may reduce the financial performance of the portfolio. However, they also conclude that financial returns can be augmented if a high number of ESG filters are used to select stocks.

- ESG factors in investment decisions may have a **non-negative or even a positive effect on financial returns and risk measures**. Studying equities over five regions between 2009 and 2018, Renshaw (2018[4]) concludes that integrating ESG factors in investment decisions may not always increase portfolio performance, but is also unlikely to be a significant drag on returns. Focusing on worldwide corporate bonds over a period of five years, Ferrarese and Hanmer (2018[5]) analyse that integrating ESG factors may lead to an increase in investment returns and a reduction in their variability.[5] Combining over 2 000 empirical studies since the 1970s, Friede, Busch and Bassen (2015[6]) find a correlation that is at least non negative between ESG investing and corporate financial performance in about 90% of cases, with a positive relation in the majority of cases, while Clark, Feiner and Viehs (2015[7]) show that 80% of 200 academic studies conclude that stock price performance is positively influenced by good sustainability practices.
- E, S and G factors may have **different impacts on financial performance, both in terms of scope and the relevant time horizon**. A correlation study of companies listed in the German Prime Standard between 2010 and 2014 shows that governance performance has the strongest impact on financial performance in comparison to environmental and social performance, where E, S and G performance are assessed through the change in Datastream scores for E, S and G (Velte, 2017[8]).[6] This could be due to the impact of changes to governance being visible more quickly than those from environmental and social changes.
- Any superior performance of portfolios integrating ESG factors may be due to the relatively recent integration of these factors by investors. If better risk-adjusted returns can be obtained by investors integrating ESG factors in their portfolios, then efficient markets should adjust to this reality and lead to a correction in the pricing of ESG factors. In this case, as ESG integration by investors becomes more widespread, **risk-adjusted performances should converge towards those of traditional portfolios**. E, S and G factors may already be reflected in asset prices, partially or fully. Core, Guay and Rusticus (2006[9]) show that firms with weak governance exhibit significant operational underperformance but that market prices already take this into account, which therefore does not translate into poor stock market returns.[7]
- It might take time for the effect of ESG integration to fully materialise. The implementation of E, S and G policies began only in the past decades, while these policies are long-term by nature. Companies that started considering these aspects recently might not immediately observe a positive impact on their share price or on the cost of their debt. E, S and G policies may also bear fruit over several years. Assessing the full impact of ESG integration on **investment returns may therefore only be possible over the long-term**, and it is still too early to know with certainty.

Due to the long-term nature of their investments, institutional investors may be better placed to shape and benefit from ESG policies. Insurance companies and pension funds are so called universal owners that invest long-term and have large and diversified portfolios. This gives them access to long-term opportunities, and the need to assess long-term risks when making their portfolio choices. Investors that do not require short-term liquidity may be in a better position to influence the management of companies they invest in or finance, so that corporate directors focus on long-term firm value (Busch, Bauer and Orlitzky, 2016[10]).

Institutional investors are expected to act according to transparency and financial consumer protection principles and other relevant regulations, and thus disclose whether ESG factors and risks are taken into account in their investment decision-making process. This is important because:

- Disclosure of ESG integration enables individuals to make informed choices concerning both a provider and an investment strategy, when that option is available. For life insurance and voluntary pension products, individuals should choose a provider and an investment strategy appropriate for them by understanding the potential risks and rewards of these investments, including the criteria used to assess their performance. The investment strategy should be in line with their personal circumstances and preferences. Those willing to invest or save with companies that defend certain values may be willing to take E, S or G considerations into account, whereas other individuals might choose to focus on more conventional considerations. In New Zealand, for instance, individuals joining the KiwiSaver voluntary pension scheme who do not actively select an investment strategy are allocated to a default fund. From 2021, the default funds will be banned from investing in companies producing fossil fuel or illegal weapons, and will be required to disclose a responsible investment policy on their website.[8]

- Mandatory pension schemes or occupational pension plans, for which members may not have the option of choosing a provider or an investment strategy, should at least disclose whether ESG factors are taken into account as this may affect the performance of people's retirement savings. Norway's sovereign wealth pension fund, for instance, publishes a responsible investment annual report detailing the principles applied and expected of investee companies, how shareholder rights are used to encourage responsible business conduct, and how sustainability and ethical factors may affect its investment or divestment decisions.[9]

While some institutional investors view ESG as part of their fiduciary duty, others believe ESG integration may breach their fiduciary duty by taking into account interests other than those of the beneficiary (Schanzenbach et al., 2018[11]).[10] Institutional investors may argue that they are required to act according to the best interests of the people whose assets they manage and, given that E, S and G factors may be perceived as being outside of the financial spectrum, they should therefore not be included in their investment considerations. Most OECD countries do not have regulations that prevent institutional investors from investing in ESG opportunities, as long as they comply with their obligations towards their beneficiaries and notably with respect to fiduciary duty (OECD, 2017[1]). The United States requires fiduciaries to consider only the pecuniary benefits to beneficiaries when selecting investments, not collateral goals or other non-financial objectives.[11]

In most OECD countries, there is no obligation for institutional investors to consider ESG factors in the investment process. In the United Kingdom, however, pension funds have been required to integrate ESG issues into their investment approach since October 2019.[12] This includes issuing a statement of investment principles detailing how financially material considerations, including ESG, are taken into account in the investment-making process. The approach to shareholder engagement and stewardship must also be explained. In 2019, the International Organisation of Pension Supervisors (IOPS) published non-binding guidelines for supervisory authorities on the requirements needed for the integration of ESG considerations into investment and risk management processes.[13] In the European Union, the European Insurance and Occupational Pensions Authority (EIOPA) is currently working on an action plan to encourage insurance companies and pension funds to take sustainability considerations into account when making investment decisions.[14]

Differences in regulations related to disclosure requirements may partially explain some of the discrepancies in ESG integration between different jurisdictions. Several jurisdictions, including the European Union and Israel, require disclosure on whether and how any ESG considerations are taken into account by institutional investors.[15] Pension funds and insurance companies in countries with mandatory ESG disclosure requirements tend to exhibit improved ESG risk management practices. It is unclear whether this correlation is due to governments in these countries having a stronger regulatory approach in general, or to more comprehensive disclosure allowing investors to better analyse ESG-related risks and opportunities. It is also possible that regulation follows the market trends and adjusts to more advanced ESG practices that are already in place (UN PRI, 2016[12]).

Many institutional investors choose to comply with guidelines defined by international agreements and initiatives, such as the UN PRI or the Paris Agreement on Climate Action (Paris Agreement).[16] There may be several reasons for investors joining such initiatives:

- Regulations on ESG disclosure may be a catalyst for institutional investors to take part in ESG-related investor initiatives. Almost three quarters of European occupational pension providers surveyed by EIOPA as part of the 2019 stress test report declared subscribing to international principles for responsible investments such as the UN PRI.[17] Whilst regulations in the European Union do not require pension providers to subscribe to international principles for responsible investment, national competent authorities of the EU require institutional investors to report on ESG factors, which may indirectly influence providers to adhere to such principles.
- Institutional investors may do so in response to a demand from their clients, members or other stakeholders such as shareholders or employees. In 2018, 47% of the British pension provider NEST's members stated that it matters a lot to them to know that their pension provider considers how companies and markets they invest in are run, and how they treat people and the planet (NEST, 2018[13]).[18]
- Institutional investors may also wish to take part in the setting of guidelines and common rules applicable to investors.
- Membership of international initiatives such as the UN PRI allows institutional investors to access additional information and aggregated data on ESG factors, which enables them to make better informed investment decisions.
- Institutional investors that choose to join such initiatives publicly demonstrate their commitment to the principles set in the initiative's guidelines. This may have a positive influence on their image and reputation. A worldwide 2018 survey from State Street Global Advisors shows that 35% of pension funds declare adopting ESG principles primarily to avoid reputational risk (State Street Global Advisors, 2019[14]). Civil society input may also influence the behaviour of institutional investors.

4.2.3. Where ESG responsibilities lie

Whether institutional investors have an overall policy regarding ESG issues, or whether they manage ESG-related topics on a case-by-case basis, will affect how embedded ESG considerations will be. Most companies review their ESG policy objectives regularly. Out of the 255 institutional investors in the UN PRI sample reviewed, 147 have reported that they review their ESG policy objectives annually, 72 more frequently (quarterly or more often), and 23 less than once a year. Only 13 institutional investors reported that they review their ESG policy objectives on an ad hoc basis.

In different companies, ESG matters are examined at different levels of the organisational hierarchy. The implementation of ESG considerations in investment decisions does not necessarily mean that the company has a person or a unit in charge of oversight of responsible investments. Whether ESG or responsible investments are overseen and, if so, the seniority of the person or unit responsible – board, CEO, CIO, investment committee, or lower levels – will have an impact on the ultimate decision-making process.

When designing the governance structure for the setting, implementing and overseeing of ESG policy, it is important to consider the implications of the different approaches. On the one hand, involvement from senior management would demonstrate stronger commitment towards the issue. The distance between the person holding ultimate responsibility for ESG matters and the board may be one of the factors considered when estimating the ESG rating of a corporation.[19] On the other hand, ESG principles set at too high a level may be difficult to practically implement in actual investment decisions.

ESG matters are often dealt with at the board level, at least to some extent. Board involvement may demonstrate commitment and the relevance of ESG matters within the company. The board of directors may be involved in different stages of ESG implementation:

- ESG policy and principles: Company boards usually set out a policy that addresses the main ESG principles. The board may also set more concrete ESG targets and goals. Often, the investment committee is held responsible for implementing the set policy in the investment decisions.
- ESG governance structure: Some companies choose to establish a governing body that is designated for ESG topics and holds responsibility for all sustainability-related issues, such as an ESG board or a socially responsible investment (SRI) board committee. ESG governing bodies could consist of several board directors, to which all functional departments are required to report directly on any ESG-related issue.
- ESG oversight: Some boards are not actively engaged and ask to receive periodic reports and to be informed on ESG sustainability-related issues, on a regular basis.

The board of directors may also choose to delegate the responsibility for ESG investment decisions to different levels of management. Segregation of ESG responsibilities may occur, for example, when meeting the set ESG targets is the responsibility of the chief financial officer, while reporting ESG investment decisions to the board is the responsibility of the chief investment officer.

Some insurance companies and pension funds have a designated officer, committee or task force for ESG or responsible investment issues. This is more common in bigger companies or groups with necessary resources to allocate specific functions to ESG topics. In companies with smaller investment teams, ESG-related functions are more likely to be carried out jointly with other responsibilities.

Companies can choose to have a multilevel governance structure dedicated to ESG issues. For example, a large insurance group, which integrates ESG factors in its insurance and investment activities, has structured the governance accordingly. The highest governing body for sustainability-related issues is the group's ESG board, which includes some of the group's board members. The group's corporate responsibility management team acts as the executive office for the ESG board, and is responsible for managing the strategic framework for all group-wide sustainability activities and supporting the different operational functions in the integration of the strategic sustainability approach and policies into the business processes.[20]

4.2.4. The level of ESG integration varies among companies

Given that ESG integration is an ongoing process, investors may approach it in a phased manner. The first phase of integration would be to see ESG through the risk lens, and assess each ESG factor by their potential impact on financial returns. The second phase would be to consider the impact of different investments on ESG-related objectives when choosing between two comparable assets. The third phase for institutional investors more "advanced" in their ESG journey would be to set themselves goals or objectives in terms of ESG effects. These objectives are often linked to the UN Sustainable Development Goals (UN SDGs), the Paris Agreement or other initiatives.[21]

Institutional investors may view ESG factors, mostly, as an additional risk factor. Here, the aim would be to widen the scope of risk management to include ESG factors to complement traditional financial analysis and portfolio construction, and ultimately improve the risk-adjusted financial returns. Some institutional investors may include ESG factors in their overall risk assessment and management, while others will consider ESG factors as an integral part of the traditional analysis performed when examining the risks for specific investments. For example, when investing in real-estate assets, ESG risks would be considered in connection with the property location.

Investors often report that they perceive the incorporation of broader ESG criteria as the next phase in their development. Some insurance companies that have already integrated a number of ESG criteria in their general investment process reported that they plan to further expand their ESG investments into ESG-themed funds, bonds, and other impact investments.

Several institutional investors already approach ESG factors as part of their overall decision-making process and investment decisions not only as financial criteria but also as factors external to financial considerations. This policy usually follows a strategic decision made by the investor or the group. For example, one large insurer, which operates according to the policy of its group, has an ESG strategy and a climate strategy that is applied in the investment process. Here investments are perceived as an effective means to achieve change.[22]

ESG considerations may also play a role when asset management is delegated to an external manager. Some institutional investors require that all external asset managers they contract with must be UN PRI signatories. Others assess the ESG-related policies and practices of their selected asset manager, both during the initial selection process and on an ongoing basis.

Impact investments are often portrayed as a more "advanced" ESG strategy. Investors that focus on ESG objectives, such as climate change mitigation, may put more weight on the ESG factors that are relevant to these objectives, which they may apply either to specific funds they manage or to the whole of their managed assets. For instance, in 2020, a large Danish pension fund that has been integrating responsibility and sustainability principles in its investment decisions for several years introduced a pension product that focuses its investments in selected climate-focused assets. This product targets similar long-term returns as "traditional" pension products offered by the provider. However, since fewer potential investments are available due to the special focus and characteristics of the investment policy, the provider clarifies that it is plausible that the returns of this fund would be more prone to volatility and fluctuation in the shorter term.[23] This is an example of advanced ESG integration, where ESG-related objectives are the main focus of investments, and ESG criteria may overcome traditional ones such as the expected risk-return profile.

4.3. Strategies used for the integration of ESG criteria

Several types of strategies are being used to integrate ESG factors in investment portfolios. Chapter 1 lists the different types of ESG integration investment strategies used by investors. This section discusses the merits of some strategies depending on different objectives and asset classes.

4.3.1. Main strategies to integrate ESG criteria

Exclusion or avoidance is often the first step in ESG integration that nearly all OECD ESG survey respondents use. **Divestment** is also widely used among institutional investors. Controversial sectors such as weapons, coal and tobacco are most-frequently cited for exclusion and divestment. Investors also often exclude investment in fossil fuel exploration and production, alcohol, gambling, gender imbalanced boards and pornography.

Norms-based or inclusionary screening, including best-in-class investing, is frequently used after performing the initial step of exclusion. Among the assets suitable for the portfolio, the choice of the specific assets to invest in may be made according to various E, S and G factors. Investors therefore use a rating system or scale, which has been developed internally or externally, to assess the relative performance and ESG rating of the different assets. The final selection of assets may be done by selecting all companies that are higher than the average, or those that achieve a score higher than a set threshold or achieve the top ratings in each one of the asset classes.

The best-in-class approach may also apply to different sectors and specific ESG objectives. For carbon-intensive sectors, for instance, some investors mention that the best-in-class choice would be based on the carbon footprint and that they invest only in companies with a low carbon footprint or those taking serious steps to improve their current carbon footprint.

Active ownership and engagement are also widely used ESG-integration strategies, although not all institutional investors apply this strategy. The G20/OECD Principles of Corporate Governance (G20/OECD Principles) emphasise the importance of active engagement for fiduciaries but also recognise that not all institutional investors may be willing to engage as active shareholders and that making engagement mandatory may be ineffective. For investors that choose to engage as active shareholders, via voting at shareholder meetings as well as via other channels, the G20/OECD Principles set forth guidelines regarding the disclosure of voting policy and decision-making processes, and the proper management of potential conflicts of interest, (OECD, 2011[15]) (OECD, 2015[16]). It should be noted that regulations may prevent institutional investors from carrying out certain practices related to active ownership. For example, in Colombia and Costa Rica, pension funds are prohibited from voting at shareholder meetings.

When applying an active ownership and engagement strategy, institutional investors may choose to vote in person. However, the most common practice is to use proxy voting, due to the scope of manpower and resources needed for the operation of such a strategy. Some institutional investors as well as some external service providers establish collaboration and joint mechanisms for voting and engagement.

Sometimes, in cases when engagement efforts are not successful and a company is irresponsive to such measures, divestment may be the next step taken by institutional investors. Divestment may also be applied as a response to an ESG-related event that is expected to have an effect on the performance of the company. For example, after pursuing multiple attempts to communicate and engage with a Mexican mining firm concerning the risks posed by the firm's new tailings dam, a large Danish pension fund announced in 2020 that, in the absence of a response to their efforts, the mining firm is now blacklisted and their investments sold off.[24]

Thematic ESG focus is another commonly-used strategy by institutional investors. Some investors direct their thematic investments towards assets that promise secure investment returns as well as positive sustainability impact, such as green, sustainable and social bonds and microfinance funds.

4.3.2. Relevance of different strategies

Responses to the OECD ESG survey show that different strategies may be used to achieve similar goals, or act as a substitution for one another:

- Companies not using exclusion or divestment still declared using active ownership for equity investments and ESG risk management across all asset classes, possibly through external managers that may apply exclusionary screening or divestment.
- The only two insurance companies that declared that they were not using any exclusionary screening process for their investments reported using thematic investment for at least some of their asset classes. This may imply that thematic investment may be used as a substitution to exclusionary screening. Thematic investment could also be seen as a means to apply positive - rather than negative – screening to an investment portfolio.

Not all strategies are relevant to all portfolios, and some of the strategies commonly used for the integration of ESG factors may not be suitable for certain institutional investors. For instance, engagement is sometimes perceived as irrelevant by certain investors. According to UN PRI 2019 data, institutional investors mention two prominent reasons for not engaging: when managing a passive investment portfolio and when amounts invested in companies are small. For investments with such characteristics, the ability of the institutional investor to make an impact by engaging may be limited.[25] Some investors also mention the labour intensive nature of engagement and active ownership as reasons for choosing not to engage.

Strategies may vary according to the relevant asset class:

- In general, the incorporation of ESG factors in the investment decision is more common for some asset classes than others. According to UN PRI 2019 data, most institutional investors incorporate ESG factors when investing in listed equities, fixed income investment instruments, private equity and infrastructure. For other asset classes, especially complex ones such as hedge funds, ESG incorporation is still relevant but less common.

- Some of the ESG integration strategies are relevant only to certain asset classes, while others apply to a broader set of assets. For example, active ownership applies only to holdings where the investors are directly involved in management or have voting rights, such as real-estate or equities. In infrastructure, private equity or hedge funds, the limited partnership format of investments may restrict the ability of institutional investors to apply active ownership strategies. As for engagement, this is applicable to many asset classes, and institutional investors can use it to influence corporate decisions through their equity holdings, as well as investments in debt instruments such as bonds and loans.
- ESG impact investments may be difficult to apply to passive investments, as these investments are based on the tracking of an external index and leave less room for the discretion of the asset manager. Therefore, it is more likely that investors will apply this strategy to active asset classes.
- Thematic investment is frequently applied via investing in designated funds. Many institutional investors mention applying the strategy of thematic investment by investing in funds that invest in companies that are involved in specific activities linked to an environmental or social theme.

Some ESG strategies may be more common for certain asset classes than for others. For example, currently, for impact investments, investors often choose green bonds and ESG-themed funds that focus on targets that relate to E, S or G.

4.3.3. Investment characteristics considered when evaluating ESG criteria

Institutional investors integrate ESG considerations in the investment decision-making process to generate investment ideas and themes, to select individual assets for their portfolio, but also to decide on the weights of different assets in the investment portfolio. This would involve examining ESG factors at the country level, company level and asset level.

Insurance companies and pension funds use various methods to examine the country of an issuer in their ESG assessment. Institutional investors may exclude investment in countries based on their own criteria relative to E, S and G, such as countries subject to international sanctions for instance, or those with an oppressive regime or limited civil rights, based on an internal assessment. Insurance companies and pension funds may also rely on external country ESG ratings to authorise investment in foreign countries. For instance, institutional investors may apply sovereign exclusions based on thresholds for the E, S or G criteria, or the overall ESG rating of a country provided by an ESG rating company. Institutional investors may also use ESG strategies such as active ownership to improve the awareness to ESG criteria in foreign companies, rather than using sovereign exclusions.

When looking at the country level, the ability of the institutional investor to identify and assess any material sustainability risk may be more important than the regulatory approach of the country. Most institutional investors responding to the OECD ESG survey reported that they were mainly concerned with understanding the potential long-term risks threatening a company, rather than the rules and regulations in its country of establishment. As long as institutional investors can access the data required for their ESG assessment, insufficient or lacking local regulatory standards on ESG matters and disclosure will not be obstacles to investing in most cases. Investors may even expect certain ESG standards to be met by potential investee companies, regardless of the local applicable regulation.

By applying a financial approach to ESG, institutional investors may examine the impact of the regulatory framework on future returns as one of the aspects that could affect the value of companies or assets, rather than examining the regulatory framework itself. However, some institutional investors also rely on a country's regulatory approach to ESG to influence their investment decisions. Several pension funds answering the OECD ESG survey indicate that ESG regulations and disclosure of ESG standards in foreign countries are part of the drivers of investment decisions.

The company or issuer level is the main level of assessment of ESG factors when contemplating an investment. Table 4.1 details some of the categories analysed by institutional investors when evaluating the ESG classification of an issuer, together with concrete examples of the criteria examined.

Table 4.1. ESG criteria assessed by institutional investors at the issuer level

Type	Category	Example
E	Climate change	Carbon emissions, climate change mitigation, climate change adaptation, environmental strategy
E	Pollution	Air polluting emissions, spills, waste prevention and management
E	Water	Use of water resources, water management and conservation
E	Energy	Energy consumption
E	Biodiversity	Land, flora and fauna diversity
E	Animal welfare	Animal testing
S	Privacy	Data security
S	Community involvement	Social impact of business operation, products and services
S	Human capital	Diversity and inclusion, training and development
G	Corporate governance	Board skills, balance of power and authority within the board, quality of accounting and audit, management turnover, shareholders' rights, disclosure of remuneration
G	Market behaviour and business ethics	Blocking competition, short-selling, transparency for investors
S and G	Involvement in controversial situations	Corruption, violation of human rights
S and G	Human rights in the workplace	Work conditions, health and safety, non-discrimination

Source: OECD 2019 ESG survey.

Finally, institutional investors may also look at the asset type itself to integrate ESG factors in their investment decision. Some asset types may be directly designed according to ESG criteria, such as green bonds. Other assets may be earmarked for specific projects, purposes or activities in connection with ESG opportunities, such as renewable infrastructure financing for instance.

4.3.4. Are specific ESG strategies more suitable when targeting specific goals?

Some strategies are more common, and perhaps better suited, for specific ESG considerations. Institutional investors may choose to opt out of certain common market practices if they feel that these practices may contradict their general principles or philosophy of investing. For example, a large pension fund recently decided to suspend stock lending on its portfolio, due to the short-term nature of this practice, the potential effect of short selling on capital markets, and the lack of transparency stock lending entails. Such institutional investors promoting a long-term perspective of investments may find that practices such as stock lending are inconsistent with their investment policy.[26]

Environmental factor integration is widely done via impact and thematic investing. Insurers and pension funds may, for instance, have a specific team managing investment in renewables and greenfield within their infrastructure investment allocation, define targets for investments in green bonds, social infrastructure or renewable energy projects, or have specific investment options that invest in green bonds and companies addressing environmental issues.[27]

Engagement is another strategy used for the promotion of environmental objectives. Institutional investors may, for instance, develop engagement activities in countries where the economy highly depends on the coal sector by implementing a dialogue with stakeholders such as companies and customers with the aim of lowering carbon emissions in these countries.[28]

Exclusionary screening may be used to integrate all three aspects of E, S and G factors in investments. A large Australian pension fund offers its members a "socially aware" investment option, which applies exclusions based on E, S and G factors.[29] This investment strategy does not invest in fossil fuels or uranium reserves, companies flagged as having human rights, labour, environmental or governance controversies, companies that produce tobacco, cluster munitions or landmines, and large Australian companies with exclusive male or female boards. Similarly, a large international insurance group excludes sectors and companies that are problematic in terms of social, human rights, ethical or environmental aspects, such as controversial weapons, coal mining and coal-based power generation, palm oil, food commodity derivatives and tobacco.[30]

The integration of social factors in investment decisions can also be achieved through engagement. Institutional investors, for instance, promote social responsibility and sustainable business practices by implementing ESG integration in their investment policy. Criteria such as gender equality, freedom of union and exclusion of child labour can be targeted, and engagement through dialogue with companies and issuers used to promote these objectives.[31] Another example for engagement strategy can be found in the increasing pressure that comes from institutional investors to improve gender diversity in corporate boards and senior levels of management. Some institutional investors set thresholds regarding the share of women on company boards, and engage with the management of companies that fail to meet such thresholds (Goodman and O'Kelley, 2017[17]).

4.4. Methods and tools to evaluate ESG criteria

Institutional investors that integrate ESG in their investments use different methods for the evaluation of ESG factors, whether they conduct the analysis in-house or outsource it.[32] Even investors that perform their ESG analysis internally often rely on external data and other service providers for the evaluation of ESG factors. This section describes the methodologies and tools being used by investors for ESG analysis, and reviews the reasons for using external providers and some of the implications of the broad use and reliance on such providers.

4.4.1. Methodology for in-house ESG analysis

Exclusionary screening is usually the initial step of ESG analysis. The exclusion can apply to specific sectors, or be based on a minimal threshold score for different issues deemed controversial. The minimum ESG rating consists of metrics that are in connection with the different pillars of ESG. For insurance companies and pension funds that are part of a financial group, exclusion policies may apply across the group, or be company specific.

Different factors that are taken into account when evaluating the ESG performance of the company under consideration may then be included in the analysis.

a) ESG issues can be part of the financial analysis performed by investors when analysing the fair value of a company and its micro-economic attributes, rather than a market as a whole. It requires examining the specific ESG factors that can influence a company's valuation or cost of debt.
b) Other investors develop specific methodologies for ESG analysis, which are added as an extra ESG layer to the general investment analysis. Some institutional investors have set up a complete ESG methodology, which is used to assess environmental risks and opportunities based on detailed analysis and indicators.[33]

A best-in-class approach may be applied after analysing and classifying different assets. It is usually applied separately for each asset class and for each sector. The weight of the different criteria may vary according to the sector. For instance, the energy consumption of an issuer from the financial sector is not the same as the consumption of an issuer from the transportation sector, and therefore will be evaluated differently for each of these sectors.

4.4.2. ESG data and analysis tools

Institutional investors use a variety of tools to make ESG-related investment decisions, whether they conduct their ESG analysis in-house or externally.

Insurance companies and pension funds using their in-house model to analyse ESG factors often rely on global frameworks and initiatives as inputs. Several respondents to the OECD ESG survey use a variety of international norms and standards as tools for their proprietary ESG model, including the following:

- **OECD Guidelines for Multinational Enterprises**: these government-backed recommendations set standards for responsible business conduct across a range of issues such as human rights, labour rights, and the environment.[34] Compliance of potential investee companies with these guidelines is a requirement for several pension funds and insurance companies surveyed by the OECD. In 2017, the OECD articulated key considerations for institutional investors in carrying out due diligence to identify and respond to environmental and social risks, within their portfolios (OECD, 2017[18]).
- **International Labour Organization** (ILO) conventions and recommendations: the legal instruments developed by ILO constituents (governments, employers and workers) set out basic principles and rights for workers. ILO conventions are binding, whereas ILO recommendations serve as non-binding guidelines. Including criteria on the application of ILO conventions in their checklist is a common approach for institutional investors.
- **United Nations Global Compact**: this voluntary initiative is based on a commitment by the management of companies to implement strategies and operations according to principles related to human rights, labour, environment and anti-corruption.[35] The ten principles of the Global Compact are derived from the Universal Declaration of Human Rights, the ILO's Declaration on Fundamental Principles and Rights at Work, the Rio Declaration on Environment and Development and the UN Convention Against Corruption.
- **International Organisation for Standardisation** (ISO) standards: these standards apply to products and processes and represent best practices as defined and agreed by experts in different fields of work.[36] ISO standards which institutional investors may require investee companies to fulfil range from health and safety standards, quality standards, to information technology security standards and food safety standards, and environmental management and energy management standards.
- **United Nations Principles for Responsible Investment** (UN PRI): Insurance companies and pension funds may be signatories of the UN PRI. They may also require that any investment-related firm they invest in, or with, also sign the principles and commit to the reporting and accountability framework established by the UN PRI.
- **Sustainability Accounting Standard Board** (SASB): SASB develops standards on the reporting of financially material sustainability information for investors. The 77 standards set out by SASB are industry-specific and come with metrics to assess and compare the materiality of E, S and G factors across companies in a sector. Pension funds and insurance companies use the SASB standards and agreed metrics as inputs to their ESG internal models.

Insurance companies and pension funds may also rely on external data providers for ESG-related data to make related investment decisions: private providers of ESG data through ratings, rankings or indices; and providers of engagement and stewardship advice.

ESG rating and index providers are a common source of data on ESG risks and opportunities. Some providers offer ESG data as a subset of their traditional financial data analysis, while others specialise in ESG data only. ESG data providers may cover all asset classes or focus on an area or category only. Table 4.2 illustrates some of the providers used by pension funds and insurance companies that responded to the OECD ESG survey.

Table 4.2. ESG index and rating providers

	Global data provider	ESG data only	Asset classes covered	ESG ratings/rankings	ESG indices
Bloomberg	X		All	X	X
CDP		X	All	X	
Factset	X		All	X	
GRESB		X	Infrastructure and real estate	X	
ISS Financial		X	All	X	
Morningstar	X		All	X	
MSCI	X		All	X	X
Refinitiv / Thomson Reuters	X		All	X	X
S&P's Trucost		X	All	X	
Sustainalytics		X	All	X	X
TruValueLabs		X	All	X	X

Note: The providers listed were cited by respondents to the OECD ESG survey.

Sources: https://www.bloomberg.com/professional/solution/esg/; https://www.cdp.net/en/data; https://www.factset.com/products-data/esg-solutions ; https://gresb.com/; https://www.issgovernance.com/ ; https://www.morningstar.com/company/esg-investing ; https://www.msci.com/ ;https://www.refinitiv.com/en; https://www.trucost.com/; https://www.sustainalytics.com/esg-data/; https://www.truvaluelabs.com/.

Private data providers may publish rankings of companies according to ESG criteria, or may design indices according to ESG investment strategies. They may also provide ESG-related data based on some internal calculations for institutional investors to use as inputs in their own models. For instance, TruValueLabs provides ESG scores based on the processing of data through artificial intelligence, using custom and standardised criteria such as the SASB standards.

Proxy voting and stewardship advice is also often outsourced by insurers and pension funds to external advisors and pooled among institutional investors. The joint action allows investors to increase their relative share and influence on companies. Two main types of engagement and stewardship advice providers exist:

- Private specialised engagement consultants such as Hermes EOS or CGI Glass Lewis specialise in dialogues with company directors on behalf of shareholders and bondholders to influence management decisions on E, S and G issues. Engagement and voting policies offered by such consultants are based on research and analysis of the underlying companies, and can be accompanied by technical support solutions to manage proxy voting and class action claims.
- Associations or public groups of interest work collectively with other long-term investors to influence corporate behaviour through voting. For instance, the Australia Council of SuperAnnuation Investors (ACSI) provides recommendations to pension funds and other institutional investors holding direct shares of equity on how to vote at annual general meetings

of Australian listed companies.[37] ACSI focuses mainly on board diversity, corporate governance, climate change, workforce issues and corporate culture. Another example is the Red Line Voting campaign developed by the Association of Member Nominated Trustees in the United Kingdom, which defines several key ESG areas on which fund managers in charge of managing the assets of UK pension funds should actively vote against management decisions in annual general meetings.[38] Key areas include topics related to climate change and environmental damage, corporate social responsibility, equal opportunities and labour ethics, and board election and remuneration.

The use of external providers for stewardship advice may facilitate transparency and disclosure requirements for institutional investors. Several OECD jurisdictions have imposed obligations to disclose voting and engagement policies when representing individuals. For example, institutional investors based in the European Union must apply the Shareholder Rights Directives (I and II) which require them to publish (free of charge) online information regarding the development and implementation of their shareholder engagement policy. In the United Kingdom, the statement of investment policy published by pension funds must also include a stewardship policy. External providers may facilitate this process for insurers and pension funds, which may not have the internal skills and manpower to justify the voting and engagement policies, as well as ensuring their consistency and application.

4.4.3. Reasons for the use of external ESG data and service providers

The data necessary for evaluating ESG criteria are not always available publicly as private companies are not always required to disclose information related to ESG issues, such as carbon emissions (E), diversity and inclusion (S), and board decisions (G). Even for publicly listed companies, information that may be required to assess how they function with respect to some E, S or G factors may not be available to the public.

Institutional investors often rely on public sources to obtain relevant ESG data for their internal models. Sources such as government publications, reports from international organisations (including Eurostat, International Energy Agency, OECD, United Nations, World Bank), and non-governmental organisations are commonly used by insurance companies and pension funds when they are analysing ESG risks and opportunities. However, investors are not always able to aggregate and analyse the available data by themselves. This is particularly the case for smaller organisations, which tend to work with external asset managers.

Models and metrics are not yet broadly accepted or agreed upon, and developing models based on existing data requires both funding and manpower, which institutional investors may not have or be willing to use.

In addition to the need for data and metrics in order to assess and evaluate ESG criteria, the ongoing operation of some of the ESG strategies themselves may also require vast manpower and funds that investors may be reluctant to spend. It is common for institutional investors to outsource activities related to strategies such as active ownership and engagement. It is however worth mentioning that using external ESG data providers also has a cost, which not all institutional investors may be willing or able to pay.

4.4.4. Implications of using external providers for ESG analysis services

The models and metrics used by external providers are not transparent and not always robust across different providers. ESG ratings and indices may lack consistency and investments made according to the criteria set by one provider may not fare well according to the E, S or G criteria selected by another provider (Chapter 1).

Many investors rely on the same data for ESG integration, which may have implications on financial markets. Whether relying on indices, on the recommendations of a data provider, or using their own internal models to decide on investment and allocation, institutional investors often rely on similar data providers or sources for their analysis of ESG investments. Using the same data may lead to some form of standardisation of ESG data, thereby improving comparability between sources. However, financial markets may also be relying heavily on data that is not adequate or fit for purpose.

The use of external providers for stewardship advice, especially when pooled and joint with other investors, may increase the effectiveness of voting and engagement policies through the coordination of decisions among shareholders. Yet, using pooled service providers for stewardship advice may also lead to herding behaviour and paradoxically favour disengagement if many institutional investors apply the same rules with little internal analysis of E, S and G factors and impacts.

Outsourcing the analysis of ESG considerations to external service providers may paradoxically result in a decrease in the involvement by institutional investors. Insurance companies and pension funds may rely too heavily on external consultants, and engagement, voting policies and ESG integration in general may become a box ticking exercise rather than rise higher up in the management agenda of asset owners.

The cost of using external providers for ESG analysis and data provision may prevent some institutional investors from integrating ESG factors and risks in their investment decision-making. Many providers of ESG data and indices are private companies and charge for their services, which not all pension funds and insurance companies may be able or willing to purchase.

4.5. Additional data and information that is currently missing

Even institutional investors that rely on several sources of data and modelling to assess ESG criteria may find that there are some gaps in the data and missing information for them to perform their analysis robustly. This section reviews the main data points and analytical tools that institutional investors responding to the OECD ESG survey mention as lacking, and some suggestions brought up by institutional investors as possible solutions.

In general, investors express concerns regarding the lack of transparency and global standards for data disclosure and analysis. Currently, the datasets are inconsistent and incomplete (OECD, 2017[1]). Not all companies disclose information on their ESG polices and performance, and when information is disclosed, companies often tend to give a qualitative and verbal disclosure. The need for a reliable, coherent and comparable information is particularly important for institutional investors, due to their fiduciary duty when managing other people's money.

Thus, many institutional investors voice the need for universal standards for the disclosure of ESG-related data. This will require standardised datasets to ensure their coherence and comparability. Reliable and comparable data is critical in order to improve the quality of ESG analysis. Shifting to a standardised and quantitative disclosure would allow better measurements and evaluation of companies' efforts, leading to a better understanding of the risks and opportunities of investments and compare different companies and assets. It is worth mentioning that several initiatives to establish consistent and comparable disclosure frameworks are currently underway.[39]

There is also a demand for alternative data that does not depend on companies' disclosure. Independent data is considered important in order to increase the ability of investors to understand companies' exposure to ESG-related risks and to have a more comprehensive view of companies' performance.

Specific points of data and information that institutional investors consider important to perform a thorough ESG analysis, and which is missing or inaccessible, include the following items:

- Investee companies' environmental policies:
    - Companies' climate targets.
    - Improved data quality on companies' carbon emissions.

- Social policies:
  - Inequality indicators.
  - Community impact.
  - Evaluation and measurement of impact investment.
- Investee companies' governance:
  - Companies' corporate governance and tax issues.
  - Additional granularity on revenues to better identify positive and negative business units.
  - Companies' ESG policies and strategies.
  - Companies' future capital expenditures and strategic plans.
- Fund portfolio:
  - Breakdown of fund portfolios to the level of individual companies or assets.
  - Analysis of ESG factors for investments in private equity.
  - Climate change scenario analysis at the portfolio level.

As most institutional investors base their investment decisions on different models, rating scales and indices, there is a high demand for transparency of the structure, metrics and relative weights of the models, and for a more detailed explanation of the different ESG rating construction methodologies. Access to granular data upon which analysis is based would enable institutional investors to evaluate external ratings.

In addition to the standardisation of datasets, developing standardised processes and globally accepted indicators that are comparable and financially valid is very important for institutional investors that need to rely on these indicators when making investment decisions.

Establishing publicly available datasets for companies and countries could allow comparing different ESG rating agencies' scores. Some institutional investors call for solutions guaranteeing that the analysis performed by ESG rating agencies and external service providers is done according to set quality measures, which would increase institutional investors' trust when incorporating ESG criteria in their investments. Such datasets could also alleviate the reporting burden on corporates, by reducing the number of different measures and indicators they are required to provide to be assessed by ESG rating agencies. In March 2020, the European Commission published the EU Taxonomy which sets performance thresholds on several E, S and G factors to assist investors and companies that choose to consider such factors.[40]

4.6. Conclusion

Pension funds and insurance companies are increasingly choosing to integrate ESG factors in their investment decisions. Some examine ESG factors mainly via the risk management lens as an opportunity for higher financial returns, while other institutional investors perceive ESG as non-financial objectives such as carbon emissions or other sustainability-performance targets that they aim to promote.

Despite the growing interest in ESG factors, ESG integration is still challenging for many investors. The effect of ESG factors on the financial performance of investments is unclear, and the resources necessary to make informed decisions remain high. Reliable ESG data is not yet widely accessible, which may prevent institutional investors from being able to assess and analyse ESG factors and opportunities.

There are different strategies to integrate ESG factors into investments, and institutional investors select those which are best suited to their portfolio and approach to ESG integration. Insurance companies and pension funds may combine several ESG strategies to achieve objectives, which can be set in their ESG policy or in their general investment policy.

Active ownership and engagement, when available, are ESG incorporation strategies which could be particularly relevant for pension funds and insurance companies due to their portfolio size and long-term focus, with the potential to influence corporate and market behaviours. However, engagement may also be costly and thus less relevant for some institutional investors, in particular those with smaller volumes of assets under management.

External data providers are a significant element in the ESG integration process for institutional investors. There are a broad range of ESG considerations which require specialised data analysis, and may lead institutional investors to rely, at least to some extent, on external data providers and ESG rating indices and agencies. The use of external ESG service providers may contribute to reducing the cost of ESG analysis and to strengthening the influence of institutional investors on corporate and market behaviours. However, using external private providers may also lead to ESG becoming a box-ticking exercise for institutional investors or to them relying heavily on data and models that are not transparent.

Cost implications of integrating ESG factors should also be considered. Whether outsourced or implemented in-house, ESG integration entails some costs for institutional investors, which are likely to be ultimately borne by members, beneficiaries and customers.

Improving the availability, consistency and quality of ESG information could help institutional investors better understand how they might approach the integration of ESG factors and risks, and would allow pension funds and insurance companies to further integrate ESG in their investment decisions, if they choose to do so.

References

Barnett, M. and R. Salomon (2006), "Beyond dichotomy: The curvilinear relationship between social responsibility and financial performance", *Strategic Management Journal*, Vol. 27/11, pp. 1101-1122, http://dx.doi.org/10.1002/smj.557. [3]

Busch, T., R. Bauer and M. Orlitzky (2016), "Sustainable Development and Financial Markets: Old Paths and New Avenues", *Business and Society*, Vol. 55/3, pp. 303-329, http://dx.doi.org/10.1177/0007650315570701. [10]

Clark, G., A. Feiner and M. Viehs (2015), *From the stockholder to the stakeholder: how sustainability can drive financial performance*, University of Oxford, https://arabesque.com/research/From_the_stockholder_to_the_stakeholder_web.pdf. [7]

Core, J., W. Guay and T. Rusticus (2006), "Does weak governance cause weak stock returns? An examination of firm operating performance and investors' expectations", *Journal of Finance*, Vol. 61/2, pp. 655-687, http://dx.doi.org/10.1111/j.1540-6261.2006.00851.x. [9]

Ferrarese, C. and J. Hanmer (2018), *The impact of ESG investing in corporate bonds*, Fidelity International, https://page.ws.fidelityinternational.com/rs/829-LMV-001/images/ESG%20White%20Paper%20FINAL.pdf. [5]

Friede, G., T. Busch and A. Bassen (2015), "ESG and financial performance: aggregated evidence from more than 2000 empirical studies", *Journal of Sustainable Finance and Investment*, Vol. 5/4, pp. 210-233, http://dx.doi.org/10.1080/20430795.2015.1118917. [6]

Goodman, A. and R. O'Kelley (2017), *Institutional Investors Lead Push for Gender-Diverse Boards*, Harvard Law School Forum on Corporate Governance, https://corpgov.law.harvard.edu/2017/04/26/institutional-investors-lead-push-for-gender-diverse-boards/. [17]

Natixis Investment Managers (2019), *Looking for the best of both worlds*, https://www.im.natixis.com/us/resources/esg-investing-survey-2019. [2]

NEST (2018), *Building new norms*, https://www.nestpensions.org.uk/schemeweb/dam/nestlibrary/nest_building_new_norms_2018.pdf. [13]

OECD (2017), *Investment governance and the integration of environmental, social and governance factors*. [1]

OECD (2017), *Responsible Business Conduct for Institutional Investors: Key expectations for due diligence under the OECD Guidelines for Multinational Enterprises*, https://mneguidelines.oecd.org/RBC-for-Institutional-Investors.pdf. [18]

OECD (2015), *G20/OECD Principles of Corporate Governance*, OECD Publishing, Paris, https://dx.doi.org/10.1787/9789264236882-en. [16]

OECD (2011), *OECD guidelines on insurer governance.*. [15]

Renshaw, A. (2018), *ESG's Evolving Performance: First, Do No Harm*, https://www.msci.com/www/research-paper/foundations-of-esg-investing/0795306949. [4]

Schanzenbach, M. et al. (2018), "The law and economics of environmental, social, and governance investing by a fiduciary", No. 971, Harvard Law School, http://www.law.harvard.edu/programs/olin_center/https://ssrn.com/abstract=3244665. [11]

State Street Global Advisors (2019), *Into the Mainstream ESG at the Tipping Point*. [14]

UN PRI (2016), *Corporate disclosure regulations*, https://www.unpri.org/sustainable-markets/how-effective-are-corporate-disclosure-regulations/211.article (accessed on 26 May 2020). [12]

Velte, P. (2017), "Does ESG performance have an impact on financial performance? Evidence from Germany", *Journal of Global Responsibility*, Vol. 8/2, pp. 169-178, http://dx.doi.org/10.1108/jgr-11-2016-0029. [8]

Notes

[1] The UN PRI has an international network of over 3 000 investor signatories which are required to report annually on their responsible investment activities according to a set framework. https://www.unpri.org/about-the-pri. As of 2019, 255 of the UN PRI signatories provide services in connection with pension or insurance: 69 are corporate pension, superannuation, retirement or provident funds or plans; 132 are non-corporate pension, superannuation, retirement or provident funds or plans; and 54 are insurance companies. The geographical split of the UN PRI signatories under consideration demonstrates that a majority (150 out of 255) of pension funds and insurance companies that are UN PRI signatories are based in Europe, whereas 37 are based in North America, 32 in Australia and New Zealand, 16 in Asia, 11 in Central and Latin America and 9 in Africa.

[2] The OECD ESG survey received responses from 51 insurance companies that run life, non-life and reinsurance business lines, with total assets of over USD 2,445 trillion at the end of 2018, and 25 pension funds managing over USD 2.4 trillion in assets at the end of 2018, across 21 countries overall. Insurance companies from 11 countries (Canada, Finland, France, Italy, Japan, Korea, the Netherlands, Portugal, Slovenia, Sweden and Switzerland), and pension funds from 14 countries (Australia, Austria, Brazil, Canada, Croatia, Denmark, Finland, Iceland, the Netherlands, New Zealand, Norway, Russia, Spain and Sweden) responded to the survey. Assets managed were provided by companies responding to the OECD ESG survey and converted to US Dollars using the International Monetary Fund published exchange rate for 31/12/2018.

Given the ESG focus of the survey, it should be noted that the institutional investors who responded may not constitute a representative sample as it is possible that they already have an interest in ESG considerations. This potential self-selection bias does not preclude conclusions being drawn on some of the needs and processes used to integrate ESG factors in investment decision-making processes.

[3] Institutional investors covered by this survey include asset managers, as well as insurance companies and pension funds.

[4] It is worth noting that insurance companies and pension funds might delegate part of the management of their assets to external asset managers, and request them to use similar ESG integration strategies.

[5] The study breaks down the corporate bond universe of the ICE BofAML indices into quintiles, based on ESG scores from Sustainalytics. Over 12 months, the credit spread of portfolio with the best ESG-rated companies tightened by about 20%, compared to a tightening of around 12% for the portfolio with the worst ESG ratings.

[6] The German Prime Standard is a market segment of the Frankfurt Stock Exchange that includes companies which comply with transparency standards higher than those of the General Standard, which is regulated by law. The German Prime Standard is made of the DAX30, TecDAX and MDAX. The DAX30 is a blue chip stock market index consisting of the 30 major German companies (by market capitalisation) trading on the Frankfurt Stock Exchange. The TecDAX stock index tracks the performance of the 30 largest German companies from the technology sector. The MDAX includes the 60 Prime Standard shares from

sectors excluding technology that rank immediately below (by market capitalisation) the 30 companies included in the DAX index.

[7] Shareholder rights are used to represent governance through data from the Investor Responsibility Research Center surveys of investor rights and takeover protection on a sample of American companies between 1990 and 1999.

[8] https://www.beehive.govt.nz/release/default-kiwisaver-changes-support-more-responsible-investment.

[9] https://www.nbim.no/contentassets/aaa1c4c4557e4619bd8345db022e981e/spu_responsible-investments-2019_web.pdf.

[10] The results of a survey by State Street Global Advisors show that 41% of pension funds declared that viewing ESG as a fiduciary duty was the main reason for adopting ESG principles in investments (State Street Global Advisors, 2019[14]).

[11] https://www.federalregister.gov/documents/2015/10/26/2015-27146/interpretive-bulletin-relating-to-the-fiduciary-standard-under-erisa-in-considering-economically.

[12] The 201888 amendment and modification of UK pension fund regulations can be found at http://www.legislation.gov.uk/uksi/2018/988/made/data.pdf.

[13] http://www.iopsweb.org/iops-supervisory-guidelines-esg-factors.htm.

[14] https://www.eiopa.europa.eu/browse/sustainable-finance_en?source=search#EIOPA%E2%80%99sprojectsinsustainablefinance.

[15] The EU regulation on disclosure for financial market participants can be found at https://eur-lex.europa.eu/eli/reg/2019/2088/oj ; the Israeli regulation can be found at Section 9(a)12 of https://www.mof.gov.il/hon/Documents/%D7%94%D7%A1%D7%93%D7%A8%D7%94-%D7%95%D7%97%D7%A7%D7%99%D7%A7%D7%94/Codex/Gate5_Part2_Chapter4.pdf.

[16] UN PRI signatories, both in responses to the OECD ESG survey and in the UN PRI data, have reported to be fully aligned with its guidelines and to already integrate ESG criteria in their investment decisions, apart from those that only recently joined the UN PRI and are still implementing the integration of these criteria in their decision-making process.

[17] EIOPA plans to launch a similar stress test to assess ESG risks in the insurance sector, starting 2020.

[18] NEST is the national employment savings trust, i.e. the occupational pension provider set up by the United Kingdom government to ensure all employers are able to offer their employees an occupational pension in line with regulatory requirements. NEST covers over 880 000 employers, over 8.6 million members, and GBP 10 billion of retirement assets https://www.nestpensions.org.uk/.

[19] Detailed ESG rating methodologies are generally not publicly available. The FTSE4Good Index inclusion criteria of 2016 included a parameter linked to the distance between the highest responsibility for ESG and sustainability topics and the board, https://blog.metu.edu.tr/sascigil/files/2016/02/FTSE4Good_Inclusion_Criteria.pdf.

[20] https://www.allianz.com/en/sustainability/strategy-governance/governance.html.

[21] The UN SDGs address global challenges, including poverty, inequality, climate change, environmental degradation, peace and justice. The Paris Agreement includes the target of reducing global warming to well below 2 degrees Celsius. Other initiatives include the UN Asset Owner Alliance, which is formed of investors who aim net zero emissions in their portfolios by 2050.

[22] https://www.bnpparibas-am.com/en/sustainability/.

[23] https://english.pfa.dk/news-archive/2020/02/02/19/54/introduces-climate-focused-pension-solution/.

[24] https://www.ipe.com/news/atp-resorts-to-dkk13m-divestment-after-mexican-mining-giant-fails-to-engage/10043476.article.

[25] However, it should also be noted that other passive investors see engagement as an important tool for promoting ESG as they cannot easily divest from certain companies. https://www.blackrock.com/uk/individual/blackrock-client-letter.

[26] https://www.ft.com/content/9b228d14-1c34-11ea-97df-cc63de1d73f4.

[27] https://www.otpp.com/investments/investment-teams/teachers-infrastructure-and-natural-resources/greenfield-investments-and-renewables, https://www.unisuper.com.au/investments/investment-options-and-performance/super-performance-and-option-holdings/global-environmental-opportunities, https://www.swissre.com/dam/jcr:acec5faf-4ea3-46f9-9605-ef8299fb885b/SwissRe-ESG-highlights.pdf.

[28] https://www.generali.com/our-responsibilities/our-commitment-to-the-environment-and-climate.

[29] https://www.australiansuper.com/campaigns/socially-aware.

[30] https://www-axa-com.cdn.axa-contento-118412.eu/www-axa-com/cf61ff6c-ee1d-4dcb-92ba-ed243ae7f2fb_2018+tcfd+full+report+-+final+-+b.pdf.

[31] https://www.asrnl.com/-/media/files/asrnederland-nl/investor-relations/jaarverslagen/2019/2019-annual-report-asr-nederland.pdf?la=en.

[32] Some of the larger institutional investors have in-house investment teams that perform ESG analysis internally (e.g. CPPIB, GPIF).

[33] https://www-axa-com.cdn.axa-contento-118412.eu/www-axa-com%2Fcf61ff6c-ee1d-4dcb-92ba-ed243ae7f2fb_2018+tcfd+full+report+-+final+-+b.pdf.

[34] The OECD Guidelines for Multinational Enterprises are adhered to by 49 countries. National Contact Points for responsible business conduct are established by adhering countries to promote the Guidelines and handle cases of alleged non-observance of the Guidelines by companies. The list of countries can be found at http://mneguidelines.oecd.org/ncps/.

[35] The UN Global Compact involves 12 840 active signatories in over 160 countries. https://www.unglobalcompact.org/participation on 20 May 2020.

[36] https://www.iso.org/standards.html.

[37] ACSI's members include 41 Australian and international asset owners and institutional investors, collectively managing over AUD 2.2 trillion in assets, and owning on average 10 per cent of each of the 200 largest Australian listed equities by market capitalisation (S&P ASX200 index). https://acsi.org.au/.

[38] The Red Line Voting campaign is based on the ten principles of the United Nations Global Compact, and on the UK Corporate Governance Code. http://redlinevoting.org/what-is-red-line-voting/.

[39] Examples of such initiatives include the Global Reporting Initiative, the Carbon Disclosure Project, the GreenHouse Gas Protocol, the Climate Disclosure Standard Board, and the International Integrated Reporting Council. https://www.globalreporting.org/Pages/default.aspx, https://www.cdp.net/en, https://ghgprotocol.org/, https://www.cdsb.net/, https://integratedreporting.org/.

[40] https://ec.europa.eu/info/sites/info/files/business_economy_euro/banking_and_finance/documents/200309-sustainable-finance-teg-final-report-taxonomy_en.pdf.

5. Promoting responsible lending in the banking sector: The next frontier for sustainable finance

This chapter explains why strengthening ESG integration in corporate lending practices should be a key objective of sustainable finance initiatives and provides an overview of drivers for ESG in the commercial lending activities of banks. It examines the current practices of banks in integrating sustainability considerations into their corporate lending activities, the challenges they face in doing so and how policy makers can facilitate scaling up responsible lending practices.

5.1. Introduction

Sustainable finance, as a practice and policy concept, is on the rise globally. The volume of "responsible" or "sustainable" financial products and strategies has grown exponentially in the past 10 years, driven largely by increased demand from beneficiaries, as well as policy signals that the financial sector should be a driving force in achieving global sustainability agendas. To date, the focus of these initiatives has largely been on the role of institutional investors and asset owners.[1] Less attention has been paid to how banks can drive sustainability through corporate lending although this represents a significant source of global capital.

While corporate debt has always been an important source of finance for enterprises, recent years have seen unprecedented growth in the volume of debt stocks. In March 2020, the Economist reported that non-financial corporate debt had reached USD 74 trillion (Economist, 2020[1]). At the end of 2019, the global outstanding stock of non-financial corporate bonds, a sub-set of global corporate non-financial debt, reached an all-time high of USD 13.5 trillion in real terms (Celik, Demirtas and Isaksson, 2020[2]).[2] As debt has ballooned, the relative quality of new debt stocks has diminished. Research by the OECD published in early 2020 found that "compared with previous credit cycles, today's stock of outstanding corporate bonds has lower overall credit quality, higher payback requirements, longer maturities and inferior covenant protection. These are features that may amplify the negative effects that an economic downturn would have on the non-financial corporate sector and the overall economy" (Celik, Demirtas and Isaksson, 2020[2]).[3] See also (Economist, 2020[1]).

Credit from banking institutions continues to be a dominant source of finance globally. In the European Union it represents around two thirds of investment and in 2017 the banking share of total debt of non-financial corporations stood at 82% (European Banking Federation, 2017[3]). However, competition from non-bank lenders such as private capital firms and fintechs is on the rise (Deloitte, 2020[4]).[4]These platforms have the potential to harness and analyse large amounts of data, potentially accelerating and simplifying financing transactions, but also putting pressure on commercial banks to keep pace.

Growing global debt, diminishing quality, and competitive pressures can have important implications for promoting ESG in corporate finance. On the one hand, ESG integration into lending activities may contribute to higher quality debt stocks and more resilience in the financial sector. For example, early evidence from the period of the COVID-19 pandemic is showing that companies which perform better on ESG have also been slightly more financially resilient in the face of disruptions wrought by the crisis (see below). However, competition from peers and new entrants to the sector threaten to put banks that conduct thorough environmental and social due diligence at a disadvantage in attracting clients, who may be able to access financing more quickly from other sources.

Additionally, challenges with respect to in-house capacity of practitioners, quality and availability of ESG data and barriers to collaboration also hinder banks from meaningfully integrating ESG in their lending processes. While there has been significant progress in terms of practice, many banking practitioners are still in early stages of understanding and managing ESG types of risks.

As the world braces itself against the current disruptions caused by the COVID-19 crisis, policy makers should also consider how to build back more resilient systems to cope with future shocks, including those predicted to manifest from climate impacts in the near future. Global leaders have regularly underscored that private finance will be needed to achieve many global goals (United Nations, 2015[5]) (G20, 2017[6]). An estimated USD 5-7 trillion a year is needed to realise the 2030 Sustainable Development Agenda (UNEPFI, 2018[7]), and an additional USD 83 billion in energy related investments is needed per year from the period 2016-2050 to limit global warming to 1.5 degrees Celsius (IPCC, 2018[8]). However, such goals do not appear to be fully reflected in many commercial and investment banking practices. For example, research by the European Central Bank has found that corporate lending is less likely to promote lower CO2 emissions than equity capital (Popov, 2019[9]). (See also Chapter 4).

Given the scale and significance of this part of the sector, strengthening ESG integration in corporate lending practice will be necessary to meet global sustainability goals as well as enhance resiliency in the financial sector. This chapter explores current practices of banks in integrating sustainability considerations into their corporate lending activities, the challenges they face in doing so and how policy makers can facilitate scaling up responsible lending practices.

5.2. What is driving ESG in corporate lending transactions?

As in other parts of the financial sector described in Chapter 1, consideration of ESG issues is on the rise in the context of corporate finance. Various drivers are behind this trend including demand from investors, pressure from civil society, and increasing understanding of the material impact of ESG on the financial performance of corporates.

From May to June 2020, the OECD Secretariat conducted interviews with 17 of the largest banks headquartered in OECD countries to understand current drivers, practices and challenges facing practitioners in integrating ESG consideration in lending transactions (see Annex 5 for more information). According to the banks interviewed, demand from investors, as reflected in investor position statements such as BlackRock CEO's letter to companies, was a leading driver for ESG integration in lending practices.

rA 2019 S&P survey of 194 credit risk professionals working in banks and other financial institutions found that 86% agreed that heightened investor demand is making it critical to consider ESG factors more fully in credit risk analysis (S&P Global Market Intelligence, 2019 ESG Survey[10]). The same survey found that 83% of respondents noted that ESG factors are integral to the credit risk area.

Considering the impact of environmental and social issues on creditworthiness has become commonplace in recent years driven primarily by concerns about physical and transition risks related to climate change. In seven of the last ten years, the global costs of natural disasters have exceeded the 30-year average of USD 140 billion per year. In 2017 alone natural disasters cost the US economy USD 307 billion (Reuters, 2018[11]). Such impacts can pose a risk to financial stability broadly as well as to individual banks. For example, analysis by the European Systemic Risk Board (ESRB) has found that costs associated with climate change are inevitable and that to date financial markets only price this risk in a limited way. It found that while diversified exposures should shield the banking sector from large losses, if high-emitting firms within sectors at risk of climate change are downgraded, losses for selected exposures would still be significant (ESRB, 2020[12]). On the flip side, various studies have shown that sustainable lending can decrease risks of default. For example, research has found that Chinese banks with higher ratios of green lending have lower non-performing loan (NPL) ratios (Cui, 2018[13]).

Early evidence also suggests that companies with strong ESG performance have been more resilient in withstanding shocks associated with the COVID-19 crisis. For example, in the months following the introduction of confinement measures in OECD countries, sustainable debt and green bonds have been more resilient than mainstream corporate debt. According to Bloomberg/Barclays, the US Green Bond Index has outperformed S high-grade corporate index by 261 bps (Climate-kic, 2020[14]). This trend will need to be re-evaluated at a later date to take into account time lags in arrangement, issuance, and trading in secondary markets.

Beyond the potential impact of ESG issues on creditworthiness, pressures on investors to integrate and report on ESG in their processes may be cascading down to banks in corporates. In April of 2019, the European Parliament approved Regulation 2019/2088 on Sustainability-Related Disclosures in the Financial Services Sector ("Sustainable Finance Disclosures Regulation"). The Regulation introduces transparency rules for financial institutions involved in investment management on the integration of sustainability risks and impacts in their processes and financial products, including reporting on adherence to internationally recognised standards for due diligence (Official Journal of the European Union, 2019[15]).[5] Subsequently, investor pressure on banks as well as corporates to engage in ESG risk management and reporting is increasing. For example, in 2020 a group of 105 international investors, representing over USD 5 trillion in assets under management, called on governments to put in place regulatory measures requiring companies to conduct and report on human rights due diligence (Investor Alliance for Human Rights, 2020[16]).

Social expectations and pressure from civil society on the banking sector to consider environmental and social risks more carefully is also growing. Data from Sigwatch, an organisation which tracks NGO campaigning activity globally has found that the number of campaigns targeting the financial sector have nearly doubled over the last 8 years (Sigwatch, 2019[17]). Such campaigns can represent significant reputational and financial risk to banks. For example, as part of protests against the construction of the Dakota Access Pipeline (DAPL) in the United States, several campaigns targeting banks providing financial support to the project were launched, inviting clients of these banks to close their accounts. The Defund DAPL website reported total account closures valued at USD 4.4 billion. This figure includes 150,000 personal account closures valued at USD 86.2 million and city divestment valued at USD 4.3 billion (Fredericks, 2018[18]).

International instruments, such as the OECD Guidelines for Multinational Enterprises and UN Guiding Principles for Business and Human Rights, also recognise that enterprises, including banks, should prevent and mitigate any adverse impacts to society and the environment arising from their activities (OECD, 2011[19]). In recent years there has been a rise of submissions involving the financial sector to OECD National Contact Points, the grievance mechanism attached to the OECD Guidelines for Multinational Enterprises.[6] For the past three years (2016-2019) 15% of all new submissions target the financial sector (compared to less than 10% in 2000-2015) (See Box 5.1).

Box 5.1. Examples of submissions filed with OECD National Contact Points involving the financial sector

Australian and New Zealand Banking Group Limited (ANZ Group) financing of Phnom Penh Sugar: In 2014, NGOs Equitable Cambodia (EC) and Inclusive Development International (IDI) submitted a case on behalf of 681 families in relation to ANZ's involvement with Phnom Penh Sugar (PPS), the developer of a sugar plantation and refinery project in Cambodia. The project is alleged to have forcibly displaced the families and dispossessed them of their land and productive resources. The NCP concluded that in this case it was difficult to reconcile ANZ's decision to take on PPS as a client with its own internal policies and procedures—which appear to accord with the OECD Guidelines—as the potential risks associated with this decision would likely have been readily apparent. The NCP also recommended a series of actions to strengthen ANZ's due diligence and remediation mechanisms. In February 2020, the parties reached an agreement in which ANZ Bank agreed to compensate the impacted families by paying them the profits it earned from the loan, setting a precedent for provision of remedy in the banking sector.

ING climate risk management and disclosure: In 2017, the NGOs Oxfam Novib, Greenpeace, BankTrack and Friends of the Earth Netherlands submitted a case to the Dutch NCP concerning ING, a Dutch bank. Specifically, the submitters argued that the bank does not report the levels of greenhouse gas emissions caused by its lending activities and has not yet announced whether it intends to do so in the near future. In addition, they argued that the bank has not set a target to reduce greenhouse gas emissions in its lending. Their submission requested the NCP to examine ING's climate policy and to urge ING to align its climate and other policies with the Guidelines. In April 2019, the case was concluded and the parties reached an agreement, in which ING committed to align its portfolio with the Paris Agreement. Additionally, ING and the NGOs called directly on the Dutch government to request the International Energy Agency (IEA) to develop two 1.5 degrees scenarios, one with and without the use of Carbon Capture and Storage (CCS), that provide a 66% chance to limit global warming to below 1.5 degrees.

Credit Suisse relationship with companies involved in the North Dakota Access Pipeline: In April 2017, the Swiss NCP received a submission from the Society for Threatened Peoples (STP) concerning the business relationship of Credit Suisse with companies involved in the construction of the Dakota Access Pipeline ("DAPL") in the United States. The submitter claimed that despite international criticism about the project, Credit Suisse has increased its business relations with enterprises involved in the construction of the DAPL. On September 2019, the parties reached an agreement on several points. One outcome from the agreement includes the inclusion of Free Prior Informed Consent (FPIC) in Credit Suisse's internal sector specific policies for Oil & Gas, Mining and Forestry & Agribusiness.

Source: OECD Database of Specific Instances

Unlike institutional investors, banks in OECD countries have been under less regulatory pressure to integrate ESG into their lending processes and to date have largely used voluntary industry standards to guide their ESG strategies (see below). However, policy makers have been recognising in recent years that initiatives in the banking sector should be scaled up, and therefore regulation may become a stronger driving force in promoting ESG in this sector in the near future.

5.3. Current practices in ESG integration and due diligence in corporate lending

5.3.1. Moving beyond project finance

Consideration of ESG issues has long been common practice for banks in the context of project finance transactions, specifically those concerning large-scale infrastructure or extractive projects. Immobile assets, potentially significant environmental and social footprints, large upfront costs and long repayment terms heighten the significance of ESG risks associated with these type of projects. For example, research on the costs of company-community conflict, a major source of disruption in mining and other infrastructure projects, has found that lost productivity due to temporary shutdowns or delay would cost a **major, world-class mining project with capital expenditure of between USD 3-5 billion roughly USD 20 million per week of delayed production in Net Present Value** (NPV) (Franks, 2014[20]).

Box 5.2. Terminology: RBC, ESG, and ESR

Under the OECD Guidelines for Multinational Enterprises "responsible business conduct" (RBC) means that business should: i) make a positive contribution to economic, environmental, and social progress with a view to achieving sustainable development; and ii) should avoid and address adverse impacts through their own activities and seek to prevent or mitigate adverse impacts directly linked to their operations, products, or services by a business relationship (OECD, 2011[19]). "Environmental, social, and governance" (ESG) criteria or "Environmental and social risk" (ESR) is the term normally used by financial institutions to describe the set of criteria they use when assessing the sustainability performance of a company.

The scope of RBC and ESG/ESR criteria are highly related. Both relate to understanding and quantifying the impacts of business activities on environmental and social issues. However RBC is specific to the standards and recommendations set out in the MNE Guidelines and pertains primarily to impacts to the environment and society, independent of financial materiality. While no formal, widespread definition exists for "ESG" and there is diversity with respect to how these concepts are instrumentalised by financial institutions and intermediaries, they often pertain primarily to environmental and social risks which also pose financial risks.

In this respect some banks have adhered to and implement the Equator Principles (EPs). The EPs are an industry-developed standard for managing environmental and social risks associated with project finance transactions for commercial banks. They have been adopted by 105 financial institutions in 38 countries and include specific benchmarks and requirements with respect to the ESG performance, rooted in recommendations of the International Finance Corporation (IFC) performance standards (see Box 5.2).

Box 5.3. Overview of the Equator Principles (EP)

The Equator Principles (EP) were first introduced in 2003 and most recently updated (EP4) in 2019. The EP are a risk management framework for determining, assessing and managing environmental and social risk in projects, including in sectors such as mining, infrastructure and oil and gas, which are funded by financial institutions.

Equator Principle Financial Institutions (EPFIs) commit to implementing the EP in their internal environmental and social policies, procedures and standards for financing projects and also commit to not extend financing where a prospective client will not, or is unable to, comply with the EP.

Broadly, the EP require its members to categorise projects "based on the magnitude of potential environmental and social risks and impacts" based on the IFC's environmental and social categorisation. Based on the project's risk categorisation, EPFIs are required to conduct appropriate due diligence, and assessment documentation must include both an Environmental and Social Impact Assessment (ESIA) and an assessment of human rights and climate risks and impacts.

For certain projects EPFIs also commit to requiring clients to engage in effective stakeholder engagement, establish environmental and social management systems and grievance mechanism, and incorporate expectations into financing covenants.

EPFIs are also required to publically report annually on transactions covered by the EP framework that reach financial close.

The EP apply to transactions in all industries and sectors that meet the below thresholds:

1. **Project Finance Advisory Services** where total Project Capital Costs are USD 10 million or more.
2. **Project Finance** with total Project Costs of USD 10 million or more.
3. **Project-Related Corporate Loans** where all the following three criteria are met:
    a. The majority of the loan is related to a Project over which the client has Effective Operational Control (either direct or indirect).
    b. The total aggregate loan amount and the EPFI's individual commitment (before syndication or sell down) are each at least USD 50 million.
    c. The loan tenor is at least two years.
4. **Bridge Loans** with a tenor of less than two years that are intended to be refinanced by Project Finance or a Project-Related Corporate Loan that is anticipated to meet the relevant criteria described in 2 and 3 above.
5. **Project-Related Refinance and Project-Related Acquisition Finance**, where all of the following three criteria are met:
    a. The underlying Project was financed in accordance with the Equator Principles framework.
    b. There has been no material change in the scale or scope of the Project.
    c. Project Completion has not yet occurred at the time of the signing of the facility or loan agreement.

Source: Equator Principles (2020), https://equator-principles.com/wp-content/uploads/2020/05/The-Equator-Principles-July-2020-v2.pdf

Although the EP provide a strong framework for assessing and responding to certain ESG risks, only a small amount of global corporate lending transactions fall within their scope (see Box 5.4). Indeed many leading banks have noted that they conduct minimal project finance transactions and/or that this line of businesses is decreasing. For example, during the 2018 reporting period, the total number of transactions reported, including project finance advisory services, project related corporate loans, and project finance transactions across all EP adherents, was 1 031 by 102 financial institutions.[7] The largest number of transactions reported among the institutions which have adopted the EPs was 88 by Sumitomo Mitsui Banking Corporation, followed by 87 by MUFG Bank, and 55 by Société Générale. In terms of other leading banks, only 2 transactions were reported by Bank of America, 4 by Wells Fargo, 8 by JP Morgan, 22 by BNP Paribas and 26 by HSBC Holdings. By comparison, all banks interviewed by the OECD noted that they each carry out thousands of corporate lending transactions annually, for some institutions even tens of thousands. Several banks interviewed by OECD noted they applied the standards of the EPs beyond transactions falling within their defined threshold for application. Nonetheless the vast majority of bank's lending portfolios are currently not subject to the EPs.

Box 5.4. OECD Due Diligence for Responsible Corporate Lending and Securities Underwriting

The guidance outlines how banks can carry out a due diligence process to identify and respond to environmental and social risks and impacts associated with the activities of clients or prospective clients. The guidance is organised according to a six step framework:

1. **Embedding RBC into policies and management systems**: describe approaches to due diligence and assign roles to relevant business units.
2. **Identifying actual and potential adverse RBC impacts**: develop a *first* screen and *second* screen for enhanced identification, and develop a process for assessing a bank's involvement with an adverse impact.
3. **The cessation, prevention, and mitigation of such impacts**: for corporate lending transactions, incorporate RBC expectations in contractual documents or written agreements, engaging with clients, and well as collaborating to address systemic issues.
4. **Tracking implementation and results**: request clients to report on issues and in high risk cases, require third party review of compliance.
5. **Communicating how impacts are addressed**: publicly communicate on RBC policies and number of corporate lending transactions subjected to enhanced due diligence.
6. **Providing for or cooperating in remediation when appropriate**: seek to use leverage to encourage clients to provide for or co-operate in remediation and enable access to remediation by establishing a bank-level grievance mechanism.

The guidance was developed in close consultation with a multi-stakeholder advisory group of over 50 organisations, including leading global banks, governments and expert stakeholders. It was also approved by the 49 governments that adhere to the OECD Guidelines for Multinational Enterprises.

Source: OECD (2019), Due Diligence for Responsible Corporate Lending and Securities Underwriting, https://mneguidelines.oecd.org/due-diligence-for-responsible-corporate-lending-and-securities-underwriting.htm.

Until very recently, no broadly recognised environmental and social standards existed for general corporate lending or underwriting transactions, although they represent the vast majority of banking finance activities. This changed in 2019 with the publication of the *OECD Due Diligence for Responsible Corporate Lending and Securities Underwriting* (OECD, 2019[21]) and, separately, the UNEP FI Principles for Responsible Banking (UNEP-FI, 2019[22]) (see Box 5.5 and Box 5.6). Both standards provide frameworks for ESG risk management for lending transactions beyond project finance. However, as they have only recently been introduced, awareness and implementation of these standards are in their initial stages and many banks have only recently began incorporating ESG considerations into general corporate lending transactions. For the most part, such processes are generally less developed and thorough than processes undertaken for project finance activity. However, they are also quickly evolving and in interviews conducted by the OECD most banks have signalled a willingness to be more ambitious with respect to ESG due diligence processes in general corporate lending transactions. Nonetheless, several challenges were identified by banks interviewed by the OECD to enhancing ESG practices in the context of these transactions, including issues around resources, constraints to collaboration and transparency, and quality of data. These are further discussed in the following section.

Box 5.5. The UNEP Finance Initiative Principles for Responsible Banking

In September 2019, the United Nations Environment Programme Finance Initiative (UNEP FI) Principles for Responsible Banking were launched with the objective of providing guidance on sustainability across all business areas of banks. These principles provide a six-point framework for sustainable banking:

1. **Alignment:** with social goals, such as with the SDGs and Paris Climate Agreement
2. **Impact and Target Setting:** publish targets related to most significant impacts
3. **Clients and Customers:** encourage sustainable practices with clients and customers
4. **Stakeholders:** engage stakeholders
5. **Governance and Culture:** implement effective governance and culture of responsible banking
6. **Transparency and Accountability:** review individual and collective implementation of the principles and be transparent and accountable for positive and negative impacts

The principles represent a multi-stakeholder partnership between UNEP FI and the banking industry to help banks implement these principles through guidance and reporting frameworks. They are open for banks to sign on. Signatory banks are required to report on their self-assessment within 18 months of becoming a signatory. Within a maximum of four years, banks are expected to have implemented their targets.

Source: UNEP FI Principles for Responsible Banking, https://www.unepfi.org/banking/bankingprinciples.

5.3.2. Current practice in lending transaction

ESG policies

In OECD interviews with banks, nearly all noted that they had an environmental and social (E&S or ESG) policy, and that most of the policies covered E&S practices in general corporate lending.[8] Generally, the banks' E&S policies outline the framework and governance of E&S risk management, including the responsibilities and mandates of various group functions. All banks interviewed also noted that their policies referenced international standards or frameworks, including one or more of the following: the UN Guiding Principles for Human Rights, OECD Guidelines for Multinational Enterprises, OECD due diligence standards, UN Global Compact, IFC Performance Standards, Equator Principles, Principles for Responsible Investment, and the Paris Agreement. Many of the banks interviewed by the OECD also noted that they are now studying their policies' alignment with the OECD guidance on *Due Diligence for Responsible Corporate Lending and Securities Underwriting*.

Research by Fitch Ratings has also found that the influence of ESG-related policies spans beyond major banks that formally adhere to them (i.e. through signing onto them or explicitly referencing them in their policies). According to the study, almost half the 182 surveyed banks' stock of lending assets and new lending flows are affected by ESG policies. (Fitch Ratings, 2020[23])

5.3.3. ESG incorporation in Risk Management

Banks have displayed diversity and variation in how they apply international standards in their E&S due diligence.

All banks interviewed by the OECD noted that they screen their lending portfolios against specific ESG risks. However, banks reported a broad range of practice with respect to the degree of ESG due diligence that is carried out. For example, most banks noted that they normally undertake several thousand corporate lending transactions per year, including revolving credit facilities and new loans. Several of the banks noted they would undertake enhanced due diligence processes for only around ten general corporate lending transactions per year, while one bank reported it undertook enhanced due diligence on 281 general corporate lending transactions in the previous year. All banks reported that enhanced ESG due diligence was more common for project finance transactions, as it was required by the Equator Principles.

A recent study by Fitch Ratings surveying 182 global banks found that 64% of them incorporated ESG into their risk management processes 'always' or 'most of the time'. (Fitch Raings, 2019[24]) The study found that banks based in Africa and Asia-Pacific were more likely to integrate ESG into risk management frameworks than European (particularly Eastern European) and North American banks. This discrepancy was particularly pronounced with respect to climate risk management, where North American banks significantly lagged behind those in Africa and Asia; 77% of African banks integrated climate-related consideration into their risk framework, compared to only 18% of North American banks. This discrepancy was partially attributed to fewer ESG-related regulatory standards in Europe and North American companies (see below).

Research by Fitch also concluded that ESG screening would in most cases lead to enhanced due diligence and further checks on clients rather than a restriction on financing. Only in limited cases where significant human rights impacts were identified or where a bank committed to stop financing of specific types of assets (i.e. new thermal coal-mines or coal-fired power station projects) was financing not extended (Fitch Ratings, 2020[23]). Similarly, in OECD interviews with banks, all noted that rescinding or suspending existing credit lines due to ESG issues was extremely uncommon.

According to interviews with OECD banks, ESG integration in annual credit reviews appeared to be the main systematic monitoring process for general corporate lending. In this respect some banks noted that they require an update on ESG issues for all clients, while other banks include such criteria only for select clients prioritised by risk if reputational issues or if allegations of adverse impacts have arisen, or on a client-sector basis. Beyond annual credit reviews, the monitoring of clients on ESG issues appeared limited when not required by specific criteria integrated in covenants, risk prioritisation by sector or geography as outlined in a bank's policy.

Most interviewed banks noted that they would like to scale up their ESG integration processes and that ESG processes related to corporate lending transactions could be further enhanced. Many also recognised that their peers felt the same way. However almost all interviewed banks noted that syndicated transactions currently posed challenges to ESG integration. Specifically, they noted that it is difficult to ensure that participating banks carry out the same level of due diligence or require the same standard of conduct from their clients, particularly when they are working with banks operating in different geographies. Information asymmetries between the lead arranger bank and participants can also pose challenges. Some banks have pointed out that integration of ESG expectations into template lending covenants, such as those developed by the Loan Markets Association (LMA), could be useful in establishing a baseline for ESG expectations of clients and due diligence processes of lenders. LMA template covenants do not currently include any conditions related to environmental and social performance and as such it is very rare for banks to include these types conditions in lending contracts (except in the context of project finance transactions covered by the Equator Principles, see above).

Human Resources for ESG analysis

Human resources for ESG analysis in finance department of banks is currently limited. The reported number of staff ranged from two dedicated staff to 13, with an average of 7.5. Many interviewed banks noted that capacity remained a challenge, especially when considering the volume of lending transactions handled and the complexity and variety of ESG issues that banks are exposed to. However 13 out of the 17 interviewed banks noted that their staff resources have grown over recent years. An additional three banks responded that they are or were planning to commit further resources to these issues. Many banks also noted that in addition to a dedicated ESG team they are working to mainstream ESG related functions by enhancing capacity on ESG issues amongst relationship managers, credit officers and other front office roles.

Where ESG functions sit within a bank can also vary significantly and may impact to what extent ESG issues are considered in lending decisions.

Among interviewed banks the most common location of the team responsible for undertaking ESG due diligence was in the risk function category (See Figure 1.1). This includes teams hosted in a global E&S risk management unit or linked to the credit risk function or group. While a number of banks did not formally locate their E&S risk management teams in a risk function, the large majority of the banks interviewed noted that E&S risk assessments and due diligence are formally embedded in the credit approval process for general corporate lending transactions.

Figure 5.1. Location of E&S due diligence teams of banks interviewed

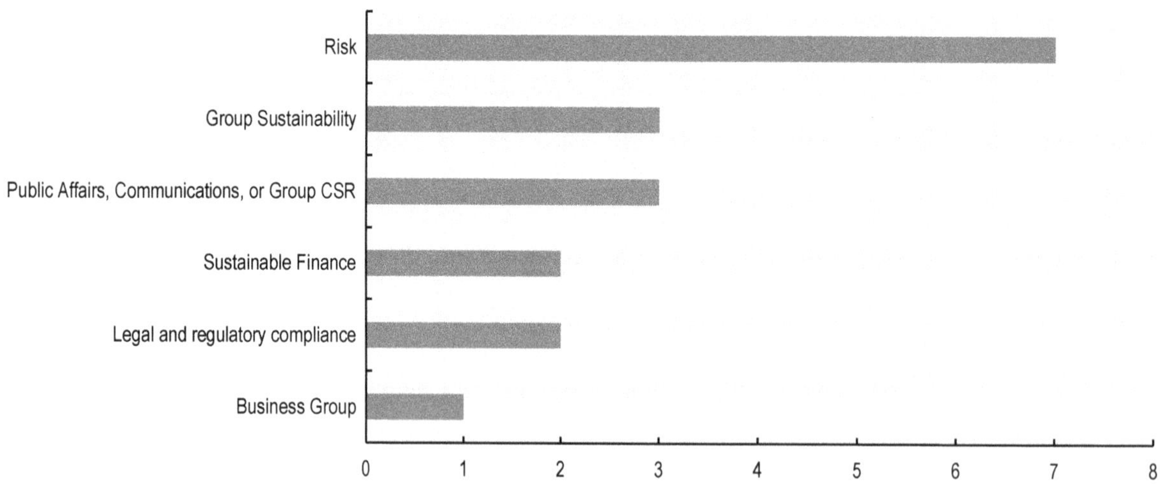

In this respect, some banks noted that E&S teams provide advisory support to credit committees on an ad hoc basis and do not have decision-making power with respect to approval of a transaction, whereas others responded that the consent of E&S teams is required for transaction approval.

Most banks responded that they have formal escalation channels where a more senior ranking committee can take a decision on a transaction if there is a difference of opinion at the credit committee level. A number of financial institutions noted that it is important for deal teams to have a strong understanding of the bank's ESG/RBC policy so that transactions that do not comply with the policy do not reach a formal credit approval process, as this would result in lost time and efforts by transaction teams.

Sustainability Reporting

Most banks interviewed noted that they produce sustainability reports and that they base their disclosures on sustainable reporting standards. These include recommendations of the Task Force on Climate-related Financial Disclosures (TCFD), Global Reporting Initiative (GRI), Sustainability Accounting Standards Board (SASB), and Carbon Disclosure Project (CDP). However, quality ESG reporting continues to be a challenge globally, and particularly in the banking sector.

A KPMG study of sustainability reporting in the banking sector found that banking is one of the sectors least likely to set targets for material ESG issues in public disclosures. Over a quarter (27%) of banks do not set any targets at all, compared to the global average of 17%. Additionally, fewer than half of banks report in detail on the social and environmental impacts of their products and services (47%). Additionally, less than a quarter of banks (23%) currently report on the financial impacts associated with ESG risks related to their products or services (KPMG, 2016[25]). In the context of climate impacts the European Central Bank has likewise noted that insufficient granularity and breadth of corporate disclosures had resulted in the ESG ratings of banks being driven by traditional corporate social responsibility considerations, such as operational carbon emissions, rather than lending activity to carbon-intensive companies (Responsible Investor, 2020[26]).

Likewise a study of sustainably reporting across banks in 5 ASEAN countries[9] found that though there have been noticeable improvements over recent years, disclosure practices of banks are still uneven within and across ASEAN countries. In this respect only five out of 29 banks assessed disclose statistics on the implementation of their E&S policies (e.g. number of transactions assessed, or declined based on E&S considerations) (WWF, 2019[27]).

As in other parts of the financial sector, data gaps on ESG continue to be a challenge to banks in accurately measuring and tracking ESG risks. For example, a lack of historical performance data related to ESG issues makes it difficult to assess and quantify related financial risk. A study by the European Systemic Risk Board (ESRB) notes that there are considerable uncertainties around amplifying dynamics regarding physical risks associated with climate change, and their impact on financial institutions (ESRB, 2020[12]).

While the capacity to measure impact of climate, governance and some other environmental impacts is growing, understanding the financial risks associated with social issues such as human rights and labour violations is still at a very early stage, even though these issues can also have a financially material impact. In the wake of COVID-19, ESG-related conditions have reportedly become a bigger priority for banks and investors (Wall Street Journal, 2020[28]).[10]

ESG impacts associated with loans for general corporate purposes are even more difficult to assess as they have a weaker link to a specific project or activity (Network for Greening the FInancial System, 2020[29]). For example, a study by UNEP FI found that with respect to climate risks, banks lack data on the locations and production characteristics and facilities of commercial borrowers, making it difficult to assess climate risk in a general corporate lending transaction (UNEP FI, n.d.[30]). The same study found that additional in-house technical capacity to understand climate risks would be useful to help banks better identify and assess these risks in lending transactions.

A lack of adequate sustainability reporting within banks can pose risks both to investors relying on such disclosures and to the banks themselves. In recent years, activist groups have started targeting banks with insufficient sustainability disclosure. For example, shareholders of the Commonwealth Bank of Australia brought a lawsuit against the bank in 2016 alleging that it violated local company law by failing to disclose climate change risks related to a proposed investment in a controversial coal mine in its annual report (Guardian, 2017[31]). In 2017, a complaint was brought to the OECD NCP of the Netherlands alleging that

ING bank did not observe the OECD MNE Guidelines by failing to report levels of greenhouse gas emissions associated with its lending activities and to set targets for reducing such emissions in its lending (see Box 5.2).

During the development of the OECD paper *Due Diligence for Responsible Corporate Lending and Underwriting*, banks identified client confidentiality obligations as a barrier to sustainability reporting and due diligence more broadly. Many jurisdictions have legal frameworks that recognise that a bank has a legal duty to keep its clients' affairs confidential. The scope of the duty differs from one country to another[11], however where it exists, a bank's duty of client confidentiality generally covers more than just financial information (e.g. the state of the client's account) and extends to all information received in the course of the relationship. It may also require the bank to keep confidential the existence of the client relationship itself. Such confidentiality obligations can prevent sustainability reporting related to specific clients and issues, which can make disclosures less useful for investors and other stakeholders. It can also limit opportunities for collaboration and tracking on ESG performance across a bank's business units, in syndicated transactions and at an industry level.

5.3.4. "Green" and sustainable lending

Beyond integrating ESG into risk management systems, sustainable or green lending (see Box 5.7) has also been on the rise in recent years.

Box 5.6. Classifications of sustainable loans

Green loans – The funds are committed to environmental or climate projects, such as recycling of plastic.

Social loans – The funds are committed to social impact projects, such as training people with disabilities to improve employability.

Sustainability loans – The funds are committed to green and social impact projects, such as providing people with disabilities employment opportunities in a plant that recycles plastic.

Source: Sustainalytics, https://www.sustainalytics.com/sustainable-finance/2019/08/15/sustainable-finance-green-bonds-green-loans-sustainability-linked-loan/.

Global green and sustainability-linked loans have risen to over USD 99 billion starting in 2018 (Linklaters, n.d.[32]). According to the Financial Times and based on data from Refinitiv, the issuance of sustainability-linked loans increased by nearly 250%in 2019 with similar growth expected in 2020 (Financial Times, 2020[33]).

The majority of banks interviewed by the OECD highlighted the growth of sustainability-linked loans as a positive development and opportunity. However, some banks noted that whilst there has been a great deal of attention placed on green loans (as well as bonds), these products primarily focus on climate impacts and limited attention has been dedicated to other social issues such as labour rights, biodiversity, and human rights.

Others noted that classifying what may qualify as "sustainable" or "green" and ensuring that such products actually reflect strong ESG performance can be challenging. According to Reuters, "increasing issuance of sustainability-linked loans by top investment-grade companies is boosting lenders' reliance on independent ratings agencies to score and monitor firms' environmental, social and governance (ESG) performance [...]" (Reuters, 2019[34]). Reliance on ESG performance ratings can be problematic as the quality and consistency of ESG ratings services vary, and methodologies evaluating ESG performance are likely to evolve. These issues are discussed in more detail in Chapter 2 of this publication. Credit raters such as S&P and Moody's have in recent years also begun integrating ESG ratings into credit worthiness assessment, in addition to issuing separate ESG ratings. Unlike ESG performance ratings, credit ratings of companies across agencies have been found to match 99% of the time (Florian Berg, 2020[35]). However the reason for this might at least partially be due to "credit rating shopping" by companies (Florian Berg, 2020[35]). [12]

In 2019, the Loan Syndications and Trading Association, Loan Market Association and Asia Pacific Loan Market Association developed Sustainability-Linked Loan Principles to guide lending of this nature. (see Box 5.8). Such principles provide a good starting point on minimum guidelines for sustainable lending but remain relatively high level and aspirational. In May 2020 the EBA also published guidelines on Loan Origination and Monitoring which include binding requirements for environmentally sustainable lending. These guidelines call on banks to develop policies and processes defining eligibility for products and activities as well as evaluating the use of proceeds of these loans. They also call for the establishment of indicators to assess the contribution of the products or activities to environmental sustainability (European Banking Authority, 2020[36]). Additional technical guidance on benchmarking performance such as taxonomies developed by the EU and China and more concrete reporting expectations could be useful to banks seeking to enhance the use of sustainability linked loans. This is discussed further below.

Box 5.7. Sustainability-Linked Loan Principles

In March 2019, the LMA with the Loan Syndications and Trading Association and the Asia Pacific Loan Market Association, launched the Sustainability Linked Loan Principles (SLLP). In May 2020, a Guidance on Sustainability Linked Loan Principles was published.

The SLLP "aim to facilitate and support environmentally and socially sustainable economic activity and growth" and define sustainability-linked loans as "any types of loan instruments and/or contingent facilities (such as bonding lines, guarantee lines or letters of credit) which incentivise the borrower's achievement of ambitious, predetermined sustainability performance objectives."

The SLLP contain four core components which aim to guide market participants on the characteristics of a sustainability linked loan

1. **Relationship to Borrower's Overall Sustainability Strategy:** borrowers are encouraged to communicate how a sustainability linked loan aligns with the borrower's sustainability performance targets (SPT) and sustainability strategy, policy, or processes.
2. **Target Setting – Measuring the Sustainability of the Borrower:** loan terms should be linked to the borrower's sustainability performance.
3. **Reporting:** borrowers should be encouraged to publically report information on their STPs.
4. **Review:** it is recommended that a borrower seek external review of its performance against STPs, such as an auditor, environmental consultant, and/or independent rating agency.

Source: https://www.icmagroup.org/assets/documents/Regulatory/Green-Bonds/LMASustainabilityLinkedLoanPrinciples-270919.pdf.

Box 5.8. Spotlight on ESG and underwriting

While this paper has primarily focused on E&S due diligence and risk management integration in corporate lending, debt and equity underwriting also represent two important pillars of bank financing and associated services and thus merit mention here.

Debt underwriting

The first green bond was issued by the World Bank in 2008, and since then more than USD 500 billion worth of bonds have been issued. Additionally, in recent years, sustainable and SDG linked bonds have been introduced by banks and other enterprises. In 2019, Enel issued the first general-purpose SDG linked bond raising USD 1.5 billion. Investor demand continues to grow for these products, as they allow for investment in activities aligned with global sustainability agendas and meet growing demands of beneficiaries.

Banks that underwrite such bonds are in a unique position to encourage clients to identify, assess and disclose important information on ESG issues, which investors are increasingly demanding. However, in the context of underwriting activities banks face the same challenges related to data as those faced in the provision of sustainability linked loans. (See above) Furthermore, "green" or "SDG" bonds are often designated as such by the issuer rather than the bank. These classifications are not currently based on agreed classifications or benchmarks, which may increase the risk of greenwashing and undermine this growing industry.

Equity underwriting: IPOs

Banks also have large potential to increase E&S risk factor integration and disclosure in IPOs. However, often prospectus material contains only highly general or superficial treatment of ESG issues.

For example, in the prospectus materials of the largest IPO of 2019, Saudi Aramco, climate change is recognised as a major risk factor, noting "[c]limate change concerns manifested in public sentiment, government policies, laws and regulations, international agreements and treaties and other actions may reduce global demand for hydrocarbons and propel a shift to lower carbon intensity fossil fuels such as gas or alternative energy sources." It is also notes that climate change concerns "including physical impacts to infrastructure" will have a "material adverse effect" on the company. However, only three paragraphs out of the 658-page prospectus deal with this topic. Furthermore, no information is provided about the company's GHG emissions, reduction targets or climate transition plans.

This example also reflects a general trend of prospectus materials describing ESG risks as externalities rather than issues linked to the business model or operations of a company itself. For example, OECD analysis of seven of the ten largest IPOs of 2019[1] revealed that where ESG risks were mentioned, 87% of the time they were presented as potential systemic or external issues threatening the profitably of the enterprise, rather than risks related to the actual operations or business model or culture of the enterprise itself.

Considering the growing demand for ESG disclosure and data by investors, governments, and the public, the depth of elaboration in company prospectuses on ESG risk factors may not be sufficient.

[1] Seven out of the ten largest IPOs' prospectuses were assessed and analysed, while three IPO prospectuses were omitted due to their unavailability in English or online access. The 10 largest IPOs were determined according to data by FactSet, a data provider, and reported by CNBC, https://www.cnbc.com/2019/12/29/saudi-aramco-alibaba-among-biggest-ipos-of-2019.html.

Source: World Bank (2019), https://www.worldbank.org/en/news/immersive-story/2019/03/18/10-years-of-green-bonds-creating-the-blueprint-for-sustainability-across-capital-markets , UN Global Compact, https://www.unglobalcompact.org/news/4471-09-06-2019 , Saudi Aramco IPO Prospectus, https://www.saudiaramco.com/-/media/images/investors/saudi-aramco-prospectus-en.pdf?la=en&hash=8DE2DCD689D6E383BB8F4C393033D8964C9F5585, Uber IPO Prospectus, https://www.sec.gov/Archives/edgar/data/1543151/000119312519103850/d647752ds1.htm#toc647752_2, S&P (2019), Banks face scrutiny for underwriting Aramco IPO amid climate change concerns, https://www.spglobal.com/marketintelligence/en/news-insights/latest-news-headlines/banks-face-scrutiny-for-underwriting-aramco-ipo-amid-climate-change-concerns-55641656.

5.4. Select policy initiatives to enhance ESG in corporate lending

The past ten years have seen a dramatic increase in ESG regulation and policy in the financial sector. The amount of policy instruments that require or encourage ESG integration across the intermediation chain in finance doubled between 2013 and 2016 and has only increased since (PRI, 2016[37]).

Although corporate lending represents a significant source of global capital, policy responses to promote sustainable finance have to date largely not focused closely on this part of the sector. As of December 2019, the Green Financial Measure Database has mapped 391 national and sub-national policy and regulatory measures in place related to sustainability in the financial sector. Of those already implemented, nearly half (47%) focus exclusively on the investment sector. Measures relating to the banking sector accounted for approximately 16% (Green Growth Knowledge Platform, 2019[38]). See Table 5.1 and Figure 5.2 for a break-down of the measures in the database for banks by geography and theme.

Table 5.1. Policy and regulation related to sustainability in the banking sector by geography

Geography	Number of policy and regulations related to sustainability in the banking sector
Africa	
Kenya	1
Morocco	2
Nigeria	1
South Africa	3
Asia & Middle East	
Bangladesh	5
Cambodia	1
China	8
India	1
Indonesia	7
Japan	6
Kazakhstan	2
Lebanon	3
Malaysia	2
Nepal	1
Pakistan	2
Singapore	4
Thailand	1
United Arab Emirates	2
Vietnam	2
Europe	
Austria	2
Belgium	1
Bulgaria	1
Croatia	1
Czech Republic	1
Denmark	1
EU	14
Finland	1
France	9
Germany	4
Greece	1
Hungary	2
Ireland	1

Geography	Number of policy and regulations related to sustainability in the banking sector
Italy	2
Luxembourg	1
Netherlands	5
Portugal	1
Russia	3
Spain	1
Sweden	5
United Kingdom	6
Americas	
Argentina	2
Brazil	10
Canada	6
Colombia	1
Costa Rica	1
Mexico	2
Mongolia	2
Peru	1
United States of America	8
Oceania	
Australia	9
Fiji	1
New Zealand	2

Note: The above table includes mandatory regulation as well a non-binding guidance and policy on sustainability issues related to the banking sector as collected by the Green Finance Platform. It is not an exhaustive compilation of measures. It is not limited to regulation and policy specific to lending activity.
Source: (Green Growth Knowledge Platform, 2019[38]) Accessed 15 September 2020.

Figure 5.2. Focus areas of policy and regulation related to sustainability in the banking sector

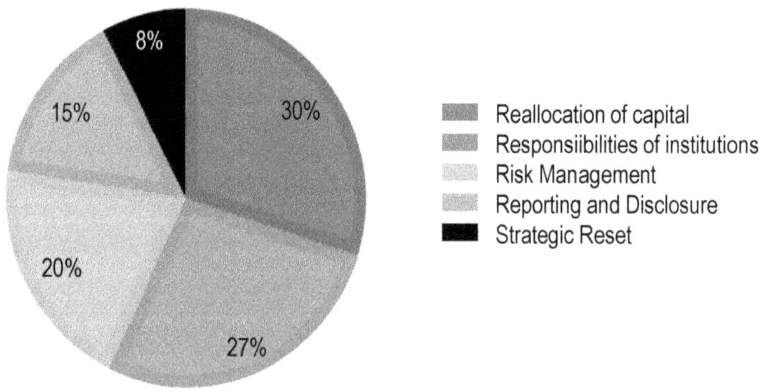

Notes: The above table includes mandatory regulation as well a non-binding guidance and policy on sustainability issues related to the banking sector as collected by the Green Finance Platform. It is not an exhaustive compilation of measures. It is not limited to regulation and policy specific to lending activity.
Reallocation of capital refers to promoting capital allocation to green sectors; Risk management refers to strengthening environmental risk management practices within institutions; Responsibility refers to clarifications of banks responsibilities regarding environmental factors in capital markets; Reporting and disclosure refers to strengthening flows of information related to environmental factors within the financial system; Reset refers to measures to align banks with environmental and sustainability objectives.
Source: (Green Growth Knowledge Platform, 2019[38]). Accessed 15 September 2020.

To date many of these interventions have been principle-based, voluntary or are in the early stages of development. Policy makers broadly agree that further action in this area is necessary.

In the context of the EU Sustainable Finance Action Plan, legislators agreed on three actions aimed at integrating ESG considerations into EU banking regulation:

- a mandate for the European Banking Authority (EBA) to assess whether a dedicated prudential treatment of exposures related to assets or activities associated substantially with sustainability objectives would be justified.
- a mandate for the European Banking Authority (EBA) to assess and possibly issue guidelines regarding the inclusion of ESG risks in the supervisory review and evaluation process;
- a requirement for large, listed institutions to disclose ESG risk (European Commission, 2020[39]).[13]

As discussed further below in 2019 the EU adopted a banking package making concrete progress on several of these elements (European Commission, 2019[40]). However, the consultation document developed for the revision of the EU Sustainable Finance Strategy notes that "[g]iven the new objectives under the European Green Deal, it can be argued that the efforts in this area need to be scaled up in order to support a faster transition to a sustainable economy and increase the resilience of physical assets to climate and environmental risks" (European Commission, 2020[39]).

Broad categories of policy responses are considered in more detail in the next section. The following analysis does not represent a comprehensive analysis of global regulatory approaches to promote sustainable lending but rather provides illustrative examples of the initiatives in select jurisdictions.

5.4.1. Macro-prudential responses

Central banks and supervisors are increasingly recognising climate impacts as a potential risk to financial stability and the economy. In this respect, the Network for Greening the Financial System (NGFS)[14] has stressed the importance for regulators of including climate related risks in prudential agendas. (NGFS, 2020[41]) (see also Chapter 2). However, in most jurisdictions such approaches are relatively nascent. A survey by the Basel Committee of its 27 member countries and observers found that the majority of these countries have not yet factored the mitigation of climate related financial risks into their prudential capital frameworks, or considered doing so, and none had short-term plans of applying Pillar 1 or Pillar 2 capital requirements to climate risks (Basel Committee on Banking Supervision, 2020[42]).

Some emerging market central banks have used prudential policies in order to encourage lending to low-carbon activities. For example, Banque du Liban differentiates reserve requirement ratios according to the amount of bank lending flowing to renewable energy and energy efficiency projects (Banque du Liban, 2010[43]) (Campiglio, 2018[44]). However, this is not yet common practice.

One challenge to integration of climate issues into capital requirements is the lack of sufficient evidence of a risk differential associated with "green" or sustainable products. Alternatively, the idea of introducing a "brown penalty", which would require enhanced capital reserves for activities that are not in line with climate objectives, has not gained political traction. While proponents believe this would help capture and account for climate risks currently not adequately priced into lending transactions, critics point out that it could penalize major economic sectors and create disincentives to greening those sectors.

Adjusting capital requirements to better capture ESG risk and drive sustainable finance can be a powerful tool for policy makers. However, further study on risk differentials associated with sustainability and climate risks will be needed before this becomes widespread practice.

5.4.2. ESG risk management frameworks for lending activity

Policy makers can promote ESG risk management at firm level by encouraging banks to enhance ESG integration in governance and risk management. In the context of the revision of its Sustainable Finance Strategy, the EU has recognised that "[i]ntegrating sustainability considerations in banks' business model requires change in culture which their governance structure need to effectively reflect and support" (European Commission, 2020[39]).

In this respect, various jurisdictions have introduced policies requiring that banks integrate sustainability issues in their corporate governance models. For example, the Reserve Bank of India has been issuing circulars and guidance on the Role of Banks in Corporate Social Responsibility, Sustainable Development and Non-Financial Reporting since 2007 (Chakrabarty, n.d.[45]). The Bank of England Prudential Regulation Authority has also released guidance asking that boards of banks understand and manage financial risks posed by climate change (Bank of England Prudential Regulation Authority, 2019[46]) and the German Federal Financial Supervisory Authorities has issued guidance on how sustainability risks should be managed through responsible corporate governance frameworks (BaFin, 2019[47]). The European Central Bank also recently published a Guide on climate-related and environmental risks noting that a bank's "management body is expected to consider climate-related and environmental risks when developing the institution's overall business strategy, business objectives and risk management framework and to exercise effective oversight of climate-related and environmental risks" (European Central Bank, n.d.[48]). In May 2020, EU Commissioner Reynders likewise announced that the European Union would consider a revision to EU regulation on director duties to incorporate sustainability considerations.

As discussed above, to date banks in OECD countries have broadly relied on industry-led guidelines to define their ESG risk management approaches and, until recently, such standards were limited to defining environmental and social due diligence for project finance transactions. Expectations from policy makers to integrate ESG considerations into lending transactions, where they exist, have largely taken the forms of voluntary guidelines rather than mandatory regulations. For example, in a survey of 27 Basel members, three fifths of respondents noted that they have not issued supervisory guidance related to governance, strategy or risk management of climate-related financial risks by banks. The remainder noted that they have or are in the process of issuing such guidance, but that guidance was not necessarily legally binding but principle-based or interpretations of existing rules (Basel Committee on Banking Supervision, 2020[42]). Under the 2019 banking package adopted by the EU the European Banking Authority has been mandated to develop two reports: one on how to incorporate environmental, social and governance (ESG) risks into the supervisory process and one on the prudential treatment of assets associated with environmental or social objectives (European Commission, 2019[40]).

Mandatory approaches calling for ESG risk management in lending transactions have been more common in developing and emerging economies (Campiglio, 2018[44]). For example, the Central Bank of Nigeria requires financial institutions to formalise their ESG policy and monitors performance of financial institutions against principles for responsible finance it has issued (Sustainable Banking Network, n.d.[49]). In Vietnam credit institutions are required to formalise their E&S risk management policies and report to the central banks (State Bank of Vietnam, 2015[50]). Banco Central do Brazil requires commercial banks to incorporate environmental and social risk factors into their governance framework and demonstrate how these risks are evaluated when calculating their capital needs (Banco Central do Brasil, 2011[51]) (Campiglio, 2018[44]).

In order to enhance practice but also to help banks overcome coordination issues in the context of syndicated transitions, regulators may consider clarifying minimum expectations for ESG risk management or due diligence in lending transactions and monitoring compliance with these expectations. Introducing common standards, drawing from existing internationally agreed benchmarks, can also provide a common reference point or baseline of expectations for financial institutions and mitigate the risk of a multiplication of varying expectations across jurisdictions and initiatives. In this respect policy makers may wish to build on international standards already being implemented by banks. See Boxes 1.4, 1.5 and 1.6.

5.4.3. Sustainability disclosure

Sustainability reporting has been a key regulatory tool for policy makers looking to promote ESG integration as well to ensure that institutional investors, shareholders and other stakeholders have access to necessary information about corporate conduct. In this respect studies have found that mandatory sustainability reporting can have a meaningful impact on socially responsible management practices (Serafeim, 2014[52]).[15] Likewise, a lack of quality disclosures continues to be a key barrier to understanding and managing ESG risks in lending transactions and more broadly. This has been particularly underscored in the context of climate issues. For example, the ESRB has noted that improving disclosures on climate risks to address current information gaps will be a crucial step to better understanding systemic risks and performance differentials associated with climate impacts (ESRB, 2020[12]).

As discussed in other chapters of this publication, few countries have introduced mandatory sustainability reporting requirements for banks.[16] However, reporting in response to these expectations is often still not of sufficient quality. For example, study of 1 000 reports filed in response to the EU Directive found that on average less than a quarter of companies report on specific environmental risks that may affect their business model, strategy, and financials, only 14% report on human rights risks in this respect, and only 0.5% provide information on sustainability challenges supported by financial amounts (Corporate Alliance for Transparency, 2019[53]). The same study found that across sectors companies from the financial sector were least likely to disclose climate related targets (20.5%). Likewise a relatively low percentage of financial companies reported on strategies to manage risks and impacts of climate change (25.2%), and on exposure of their lending, investment and underwriting activities to sectors contributing to climate change (13.4%).

Sustainability reporting requirements which provide more specificity and require reporting on specific sustainability risks, strategies and targets, as well as performance against those targets would be useful in promoting more useful disclosures. This would also align with reporting recommendations of the TCFD, updated GRI universal reporting standards and OECD due diligence reporting standards.

There is also an emerging consensus on the need for standardised benchmarks and definitions related to ESG impacts and performance both to respond to various expectations of shareholders and stakeholders as well as to ensure that materiality and risk information that is tied to that can be better construed (see also Chapters 1 and 2). In this context international standards such as the OECD Guidelines for Multinational Enterprises could provide a useful foundation.[17] "Double materiality" reporting which would call for disclosure of ESG information that is deemed to be financially material as well as information about significant ESG performance and impacts (i.e. climate performance or linkage to human rights impacts) independent of the financial impact of those issues to the reporting entity could also be useful, especially as financial impacts of ESG are currently not well understood and can be expected to continue evolving.

The EU has already called for considering and reporting in line with a concept of double materiality in its recently agreed Sustainable Finance Disclosures Regulation (Official Journal of the European Union, 2019[15]). Additionally, the concept of double materiality reporting has received strong support in the context of the revision of the EU non-financial reporting directive from leading ESG standards bodies including SASB (SASB, 2020[54]) the UN Global Compact, the Social Value Initiative and the World Benchmarking Alliance (IMP Structured Network, 2020[55]).

Policy makers should also ensure that there is alignment between reporting obligations of corporates, banks and investors. In the context of the EU this would mean aligning expectations of the Sustainable Finance Disclosures Regulation, Non-Financial Reporting Directive and any future legislation mandating environmental and social due diligence for corporate actors. Comprehensive and quality ESG reporting by non-financial corporates will be a prerequisite for banks and other financial institutions to use such information in risk processes, ESG financial products, and their own sustainability reporting.

Lastly, policy makers should consider whether client confidentiality obligations (discussed above) are creating barriers to meaningful disclosure and how these could be overcome. For example, by creating exemptions in existing laws or helping to make client consent processes systematic. Working with industry associations such as the Loan Markets Association to encourage inclusion of client consent to disclose the existence of the client relationship in template covenants can also be helpful to overcoming some of the associated challenges.

5.4.4. Agreeing on metrics and benchmarks

In addition to strengthening and aligning disclosure expectations, in order to help banks better identify and report on risks associated with ESG impacts, specifically with respect to climate, forward looking methodologies are needed. A core aspect of the recommendations of the TCFD relates to reporting on climate metrics and targets and taking into consideration different climate-related scenarios. (TCFD, 2017[56]). In the context of climate issues industry actors have requested policy makers to prioritise the development of common scenarios and assumptions to facilitate banks' scenario analysis and enhancement of their own stress testing frameworks (European Banking Federation, 2017[3]). Some central banks and supervisory authorities have attempted to undertake climate stress tests to assess risks on the financial system more broadly (in equity and debt portfolios).[18] Notably, DNB (Netherlands) did the first climate stress test two years ago and central banks of England, France and Japan currently have stress tests ongoing. Although central bank level stress tests have different objectives to bank level scenario analysis (respectively, measuring risks to financial stability vs demonstrating resilience to investors), they provide a useful reference.

Stronger benchmarks and taxonomies to assess ESG performance of clients and specific activities can also help facilitate green and sustainable lending and avoid some of the issues involved in reliance on ESG rating and research providers. Common taxonomies have also been identified by practitioners as essential for efficient allocation of financial resources to green products and assets (European Banking Federation, 2017[3]).

Both China and the EU have developed green taxonomies to assess the environmental performance of activities. While the EU taxonomy is voluntary and does not currently apply to lending activities it can still provide a useful framework for banks (see also Chapter 2). Over time, policy makers may also consider developing further taxonomies for other leading ESG impacts such a human rights and labour issues.[19] In order to do so, impact measurement methodologies and data collection on social risks will need to also be improved.

5.5. Conclusions

Expectations of banks to integrate ESG considerations – with an emphasis on climate issues – is growing amongst investors and society. Until recently ESG standards for general corporate lending transactions did not exist and sustainability considerations did not feature prominently in the context of these transactions. Bank themselves have signalled that they would like to scale up ESG integration in lending transactions but have noted that challenges associated with capacity, competition and co-ordination, and data continue to hamper their efforts.

Despite the significance of lending transactions in global capital flows, to date this part of the sector has been largely overlooked by sustainable finance policy initiatives that focus more prominently on the role of institutional investors. In this respect policy makers should allocate more attention to scaling up sustainability in lending transactions and may consider:

- Developing guidance for integration of sustainability considerations within the governance frameworks and introducing minimum expectations for ESG risk management or due diligence in lending transactions in line with international standards.
- Promoting sustainability reporting that encourages disclosure on sustainability (including disclosure on ESG performance and impacts in addition to the potential financial risk related to that performance and those impacts), strategies and targets, as well as performance against targets; this reporting should be streamlined across banks, corporates and investors.
- Leading development of necessary metrics and methodologies to facilitate measurement of risk associated with ESG issues (at a macro and firm level), and overtime, expanding such metrics and methodologies beyond climate environmental performance to other significant ESG issues such as human rights and labour.

Policy makers should also be mindful of new entrants to this sector and ensure that any expectations imposed on banks should likewise apply to non-bank enterprises providing lending services.

In the coming year, responding to disruptions wrought by the COVID-19 crisis will be a priority for policy makers globally. In this respect, it is important that the momentum of the sustainable finance agenda is not lost. Enhancing sustainability throughout the financial sector can strengthen resilience and better prepare economies for future shocks. But more importantly, it can contribute to channelling global capital towards activities that avoid negative impacts to society and the environment and thus potentially lessens shocks related to climate impacts or pandemics.

References

BaFin (2019), "BaFin Guidance Note on", http://file:///C:/Users/Bljelic_B/Downloads/dl_mb_Nachhaltigkeitsrisiken_en.pdf. [47]

Banco Central do Brasil (2011), *Circular 3, 547 of July 7, 2011: Establishes Procedures and Parameters Related to the Internal Capital Adequacy Assessment Process (ICAAP).* [51]

Bank of England Prudential Regulation Authority (2019), *Enhancing banks' and insurers' approaches to managing the financial risks from climate change*, https://www.bankofengland.co.uk/-/media/boe/files/prudential-regulation/supervisory-statement/2019/ss319.pdf?la=en&hash=7BA9824BAC5FB313F42C00889D4E3A6104881C44. [46]

BankTrack (2020), "Fossil Banks, No Thanks", last accessed 30 June, 2020, https://www.fossilbanks.org/. [60]

Banque du Liban (2010), *Intermediate Circular 236.* [43]

Basel Committee on Banking Supervision (2020), *Climate-related financial risks: a survey on current initiates*, https://www.bis.org/bcbs/publ/d502.htm. [42]

Campiglio, E. (2018), *Climate change challenges for central banks and financial regulators*, https://doi.org/10.1038/s41558-018-0175-0. [44]

Celik, Demirtas and Isaksson (2020), "Corporate Bond Market Trends, Emerging Risks and Monetary Policy", *OECD*, http://dx.doi.org/www.oecd.org/corporate/Corporate-Bond-Market-Trends-Emerging-Risks-and-Monetary-Policy.htm. [2]

Chakrabarty, K. (n.d.), *Non-financial reporting – what, why and how – Indian perspective*, https://www.bis.org/review/r110621e.pdf. [45]

Climate-kic (2020), “Implications of the COVID-19 Pandemic for Global Sustainable Finance: An initial framwork for response strategies”, https://www.climate-kic.org/wp-content/uploads/2020/05/eb1f0b_8f85048725a54699b97faa88ac6761c1.pdf. [14]

Corporate Alliance for Transparency (2019), *2019 Research Report: An analysis of the sustainability reports of 1000 companies pursuant to the EU Non-financial Reporting Directive*, https://www.allianceforcorporatetransparency.org/assets/2019_Research_Report%20_Alliance_for_Corporate_Transparency-7d9802a0c18c9f13017d686481bd2d6c6886fea6d9e9c7a5c3cfafea8a48b1c7.pdf. [53]

Cui, Y. (2018), “The Impact of Green Lending on Credit Risk in China. Sustainability”. [13]

Deloitte (2020), “2020 banking and capital markets outlook”, https://www2.deloitte.com/us/en/insights/industry/financial-services/financial-services-industry-outlooks/banking-industry-outlook.html. [4]

Economist (2020), “Corporate bonds and loans are at the centre of a new financial scar” 12 March, https://www.economist.com/finance-and-economics/2020/03/12/corporate-bonds-and-loans-are-at-the-centre-of-a-new-financial-scare. [1]

ESRB (2020), “Postively green: Measuring climate change risks to financial stability”, https://www.esrb.europa.eu/pub/pdf/reports/esrb.report200608_on_Positively_green_-_Measuring_climate_change_risks_to_financial_stability~d903a83690.en.pdf. [12]

European Banking Authority (2020), “Guidelines on Loan Origination and Monitoring”. [36]

European Banking Federation (2017), “Towards a Green Finance Framework”, https://www.ebf.eu/wp-content/uploads/2017/09/Geen-finance-complete.pdf. [3]

European Central Bank (n.d.), “Guide on climate-related and environmental risks: Supervisory expectations relating to”, https://www.bankingsupervision.europa.eu/legalframework/publiccons/pdf/climate-related_risks/ssm.202005_draft_guide_on_climate-related_and_environmental_risks.en.pdf. [48]

European Commission (2020), *CONSULTATION ON THE RENEWED SUSTAINABLE FINANCE STRATEGY*, https://ec.europa.eu/info/sites/info/files/business_economy_euro/banking_and_finance/documents/2020-sustainable-finance-strategy-consultation-document_en.pdf. [39]

European Commission (2019), “Adoption of the banking package: revised rules on capital requirements (CRR II/CRD V) and resolution (BRRD/SRM)”, https://ec.europa.eu/commission/presscorner/detail/en/MEMO_19_2129. [40]

Financial Times (2020), *Green loans catch on in push for companies to clean up*, https://www.ft.com/content/d649cf78-35f8-11ea-a6d3-9a26f8c3cba4. [33]

Fitch Raings (2019), *Banks Risk Management Embraces ESG*, https://www.fitchratings.com/research/banks/banks-risk-management-embraces-esg-04-12-2019. [24]

Fitch Ratings (2020), *ESG Bites into Banks 'Lending to Corporates Screening for Environmental and Social Risks Is Widespread, but Outright Prohibition Is Rare*, https://www.fitchratings.com/research/banks/esg-bites-into-banks-lending-to-corporates-07-01-2020. [23]

Florian Berg, J. (2020), *Aggregate Confusion: The Divergence of ESG Ratings*, MIT School of Management, https://papers.ssrn.com/sol3/papers.cfm?abstract_id=3438533. [35]

Franks, R. (2014), *Costs of Company-Community Conflict in the Extractive Sector*, https://www.shiftproject.org/resources/publications/costs-company-community-conflict-extractive-sector/. [20]

Fredericks, M. (2018), *Social Cost and Material Loss: The Dakota Access Pipeline*, https://www.colorado.edu/project/fpiep/sites/default/files/attached-files/social_cost_and_material_loss.pdf. [18]

G20 (2017), *G20 Hamburg Climate and Energy Action Plan for Growth*,, http://unepinquiry.org/wp-content/uploads/2017/07/Climate_and_Energy_Action_Plan_for_Growth.pdf. [6]

Green Growth Knowledge Platform (2019), *Nearly 400 Policy and Regulatory Measures Mapped in New Green Finance Measures Database*, https://www.greengrowthknowledge.org/news/nearly-400-policy-and-regulatory-measures-mapped-new-green-finance-measures-database. [38]

GRI and CSR Europe (2017), *Member State Implementation of Directive 2014/95/EU*, https://www.globalreporting.org/resourcelibrary/NFRpublication%20online_version.pdf. [59]

Guardian (2017), *Commonwealth Bank shareholders sue over inadequet disclosure of climate change risks*, https://www.theguardian.com/australia-news/2017/aug/08/commonwealth-bank-shareholders-sue-over-inadequate-disclosure-of-climate-change-risks. [31]

IMP Structured Network (2020), *IMP Structured Network submission to consultation on revision of the EU Non-Financial Reporting Directive*, On file with the OECD. [55]

Investor Alliance for Human Rights (2020), *Investors with US$5 trillion call on governments to institute mandatory human rights due diligence measures for companies*, https://investorsforhumanrights.org/news/investor-case-for-mhrdd. [16]

IPCC (2018), "Summary for Policymakers. In: Global Warming of 1.5°C. An IPCC Special Report on the impacts", https://www.ipcc.ch/sr15/chapter/spm/. [8]

KPMG (2016), *Corporate Responsibility in the Banking Sector*, https://assets.kpmg/content/dam/kpmg/pdf/2016/07/corporate-responsibility-in-the-banking-sector.pdf. [25]

Linklaters (n.d.), *The rise of green loans and sustainability linked lending*, https://www.linklaters.com/en/insights/thought-leadership/sustainable-finance/the-rise-of-green-loans-and-sustainability-linked-lending. [32]

Network for Greening the FInancial System (2020), *A Status Report of Financial Institution's Experiences from working with green, non green and brown financial assets and a potential risk differential*, https://www.ngfs.net/sites/default/files/medias/documents/ngfs_status_report.pdf. [29]

NGFS (2020), *Guide for Supervisors: integrating climate-related and environmental risks into prudential supervision*, https://www.ngfs.net/en/liste-chronologique/ngfs-publications. [41]

OECD (2019), "Due Diligence for Responsible Corporate Lending and Underwriting", https://www.oecd.org/daf/inv/mne/due-diligence-for-responsible-corporate-lending-and-securities-underwriting.htm. [21]

OECD (2011), "OECD Guidelines for Multinational Enterprises", http://www.oecd.org/daf/inv/mne/48004323.pdf. [19]

Official Journal of the European Union (2019), *REGULATION (EU) 2019/2088 OF THE EUROPEAN PARLIAMENT AND OF THE COUNCIL of 27 November 2019 on sustainability-related disclosures in the financial services sector*, https://eur-lex.europa.eu/legal-content/EN/TXT/PDF/?uri=CELEX:32019R2088&rid=1. [15]

Official Journal of the European Union (2014), *Directive 2014/95/EU of 22 October 2014 amending Directive 2013/34/EU as regards disclosure of non-financial and diversity information by certain large undertakings and groups*. [58]

Popov, R. (2019), "FInance and carbon emissions, ECB Working Paper Series No. 2318". [9]

PRI (2016), *Global Guide to Responsible Investment Regulation*, https://www.unpri.org/download?ac=325. [37]

Responsible Investor (2020), *ECB warns 'regulatory competition undermining' the EU Action Plan, calls for brown taxonomy*, https://www.responsible-investor.com/articles/ecb-warns-regulatory-competition-undermining-the-eu-action-plan-calls-for-brown-taxonomy. [26]

Reuters (2019), *Growth in sustainability-linked loans boosts ESG ratings firms*, https://www.reuters.com/article/growth-in-sustainability-linked-loans-bo/growth-in-sustainability-linked-loans-boosts-esg-ratings-firms-idUSL2N27615Y. [34]

Reuters (2018), "Weather disasters cost U.S. record $306 billion in 2017: NOAA", https://www.reuters.com/article/us-usa-climatechange/weather-disasters-cost-u-s-record-306-billion-in-2017-noaa-idUSKBN1EX1XC. [11]

S&P Global Market Intelligence (2019 ESG Survey), , https://pages.marketintelligence.spglobal.com/ESG-Survey.html. [10]

SASB (2020), *EU Directive can lay the foundation for a Global ESG DIsclosure Standard*, https://www.sasb.org/blog/eu-directive-can-lay-the-foundation-for-a-global-esg-disclosure-solution/. [54]

Serafeim, I. (2014), *The Consequences of Mandatory Corporate Sustainability Reporting*, London Business School, Harvard Business School, https://sustain.pata.org/wp-content/uploads/2014/12/The-Consequences-of-Mandatory-Corporate-Sustainability-Reporting.pdf. [52]

Sigwatch (2019), *Data from Sigwatch internal database. Shared with OECD on 7 January 2019.*. [17]

State Bank of Vietnam (2015), *Decision on issuance of Action Plan of banking sector to implement the National Strategy on Green growth towards 2020.* [50]

Sustainable Banking Network (n.d.), *Country Progress Report: Nigeria*, https://www.ifc.org/wps/wcm/connect/6c9b6a8b-4809-4570-9a33-2c11cc10e802/SBN+Country+Progress+Report+-+Nigeria.pdf?MOD=AJPERES&CVID=m746LEj. [49]

TCFD (2019), *2019 Status Report: Task Force on Climate-related Financial Disclosures: Status Report*. [57]

TCFD (2017), *Recommendations of the Task Force on Climate-related Financial Disclosures: Final Report*. [56]

UNEP FI (n.d.), *Navigating a New Climate*, https://www.unepfi.org/wordpress/wp-content/uploads/2018/07/NAVIGATING-A-NEW-CLIMATE.pdf. [30]

UNEPFI (2018), *Rethinking Impact to Finance the SDGs*, https://www.unepfi.org/wordpress/wp-content/uploads/2018/11/Rethinking-Impact-to-Finance-the-SDGs.pdf. [7]

UNEP-FI (2019), "Principles for Responsible Banking", https://www.unepfi.org/banking/bankingprinciples/. [22]

United Nations (2015), *Paris Agreement*, https://unfccc.int/sites/default/files/english_paris_agreement.pdf. [5]

Wall Street Journal (2020), *Corona Virus Pandemic Could Elevate ESG Factors*, https://www-wsj-com.cdn.ampproject.org/c/s/www.wsj.com/amp/articles/coronavirus-pandemic-could-elevate-esg-factors-11585167518. [28]

WWF (2019), *Sustainable Banking Regulations in ASEAN: Raising the Bar*, https://d2ouvy59p0dg6k.cloudfront.net/downloads/wwf_sustainable_banking_regulations_in_asean___raising_the_bar__dec_2019_.pdf. [27]

Annex 5.A. Questionnaire on current practices in E&S bank policies on corporate lending

From May to June 2020, the OECD Secretariat conducted phone interviews with key E&S risk management practitioners in 17 leading banks headquartered in OECD countries. The banks were asked eight questions (see Annex Table 5.A.1), including on current practices in E&S bank policies on corporate lending, E&S risk management incorporation in credit approval and committee processes, and what challenges and opportunities practitioners currently foresee in this work. The scope of the interviews was limited to general corporate lending, also known as general corporate purpose loans. Practices in credit or equity underwriting were out of the scope of the interviews. The list of participating banks is located in Table 5.A.2.

Annex Table 5.A.1. Questionnaire on E&S integration in corporate lending in leading banks in OECD countries

1	Do you have an E&S policy, and if so, does it cover general corporate lending transactions?
2	On average, approximately how many corporate lending transactions does your bank handle annually? Approximately how many of these transactions are screened for E&S risks and how many undergo an enhanced E&S screen?
3	How large is your E&S team? Where is it located in the bank's structure? Are you planning to grow the team or resources?
4	Is an E&S risk assessment and due diligence formally embedded in the credit approval process for general corporate lending transactions?
5	To what extent does your bank consider E&S criteria or conditions in the provision of finance (e.g. client commitment to E&S industry standards and international standards, exclusionary criteria, action plans)? Does the bank engage in E&S performance monitoring of a client once a loan has been disbursed?
6	Does your institution have or participate in any grievance mechanism for issues resulting from activities of companies you provide financing to?
7	Does your policy commit to international standards or instruments? What standards or frameworks, if any, do you use for your non-financial reporting (e.g. GRI, SASB, TCFD)?
8	What are the biggest challenges and opportunities you see for integrating E&S due diligence into general corporate lending transactions?

The banks that accepted to participate in the phone interviews conducted by the OECD Secretariat feature in the top 60 largest banks headquartered in OECD countries as measured by Assets Under Management (AUM) by S&P in 2019.[20]

Annex Table 5.A.2. List of banks who participated in the phone interviews

Name	Country	Total Assets in 2019 (USD Billion)
Mitsubishi UFJ Financial Group	Japan	3 069.20
JPMorgan Chase	United States	2 622.53
BNP Paribas	France	2 336.66
Wells Fargo	United States	1 895.88
Deutsche Bank	Germany	1 543.55
Barclays	United Kingdom	1 444.39
ING Group	Netherlands	1 015.61
UBS	Switzerland	958.49
Goldman Sachs	United States	931.8
Credit Suisse	Switzerland	781.45
Standard Chartered	United Kingdom	688.76
Australia and New Zealand Banking Group	Australia	681.3
Westpac	Australia	636.69
Bank of Montreal	Canada	613.56
National Australia Bank	Australia	583.79
ABN AMRO Group	Netherlands	436.56
KBC Bank	Belgium	324.95

Notes

[1] ESG practices and policy for institutional investors was explored in OECD (2019), "Trust and financial markets", in OECD Business and Finance Outlook 2019: Strengthening Trust in Business, OECD Publishing, Paris, https://doi.org/10.1787/4d7c9b81-en, and is also discussed in further detail in this year's publication in Chapters 1, 2 and 4.

[2] This record amount is the result of an unprecedented build-up in corporate bond debt since 2008 and a further USD 2.1 trillion in borrowing by non-financial companies during 2019.

[3] According to The Economist, two-thirds of non-financial corporate bonds in America are rated "junk" or "bbb", the category just above junk. Outside America the figure is 39%.

[4] According to the 2020 Deloitte Banking and Capital Markets Outlook report, "[d]emand for real-time liquidity and funding is expected to grow. [...] There could very well be greater competition from insurance companies, private equity firms, traditional asset managers, and fintechs in the corporate lending space. Thus, the corporate bank over the next decade could look very different than the one today, as it redefines its role in the new financial ecosystem."

[5] The Regulation also notes that when reporting on due diligence, practitioners "should consider the due diligence guidance for responsible business conduct developed by the Organisation for Economic Cooperation and Development."

[6] National Contact Points (NCPs) are set up by governments that have adhered to the OECD Guidelines for Multinational Enterprises (the Guidelines). NCPs have two main objectives: to promote the Guidelines and handle enquiries, which means that NCPs: 1) organise and participate in events related to RBC to raise awareness of the Guidelines and respond to questions about the Guidelines; and 2) provide a grievance mechanism to resolve cases (known as "specific instances") relating to non-observance of the recommendations of the Guidelines. To date over 500 specific instances have been filed with NCPs.

[7] Figure developed based on NGO BankTrack's database collection of public reporting by Equator Principle member banks, https://docs.google.com/spreadsheets/d/1K0qTCeioe9epPjwcKnGSZ7OOwslmnuoHzWgZmiUjX3Q/edit?ts=5bc5ceea (accessed 10 June 2020).

[8] One bank noted it was currently developing such a policy.

[9] Indonesia, Malaysia, Singapore, Thailand, Vietnam.

[10] According to Citigroup, investors are asking more questions about issues such as employee benefits and mortgage relief, and COVID is affecting priorities in ESG, making temporary workers and stock buybacks the new focus for corporate governance.

[11] For example, while this duty does not exist in the United States, it is recognised in the United Kingdom and most European countries under civil law. In Switzerland and Singapore, violating obligations of client confidentiality can be a criminal offence.

[12] The authors of the study have noted that this rate can be attributed to the fact that 1) credit worthiness is clearly defined as likelihood of default while ESG performance is currently not clearly defined, 2) ESG performance ratings are often based on corporate sustainability disclosures which are not standardised, and 3) companies, rather than investors, pay for credit ratings which may result in in "rating shopping".

[13] A vast array of policy instruments exist or have been proposed to promote sustainable finance. This chapter does not treat them all in detail but provides a broad outline of recent developments with respect to prudential association, ESG integration, and reporting and measurement of ESG issues.

[14] The Central Banks and Supervisors Network for Greening the Financial System (NGFS) is a group of Central Banks and Supervisors willing, on a voluntary basis, to exchange experiences, share best practices, contribute to the development of environment and climate risk management in the financial sector, and to mobilise mainstream finance to support the transition toward a sustainable economy.

[15] A study by Professor Ioannis Ioannou of London Business School and Geoge Serafeim of Harvard Business School found that where mandatory sustainability reporting was introduced, sustainable development and employee training become a higher priority for companies and corporate governance improved. The study also found that companies implemented more ethical practices, reduced bribery and corruption and increased managerial credibility. The effects were larger for countries with stronger law enforcement and more widespread assurance of sustainability reports.

[16] For example, Austria in 2003, Malaysia in 2007, Sweden in 2009, China in 2020, Spain in 2012, Belgium in 2016 and Hungary and Singapore in 2017.

[17] 17% of financial statements filed in response to the EU NFRD in 2019 specify that they rely on the OECD Guidelines for Multinational Enterprises or OECD due diligence guidance. Furthermore, OECD due diligence standards will be incorporated in GRI universal report standards, relied on in 54% of financial statements filed. See (Corporate Alliance for Transparency, 2019[53]).

[18] A stress test is a "projection of the financial condition of a firm or economy, under a specific set of severely adverse conditions. This may be the result of several risk factors over multiple periods of time, or one risk factor that is short in duration." A sensitivity analysis is the "effect of a set of alternative assumptions regarding a future environment. A scenario used for sensitivity testing usually represents a relatively small change in these risk factors or their likelihood of occurrence."

[19] Although the current taxonomy includes minimum safeguards related to human rights and labour issues (see Box 1.1) it does not include technical guidance and benchmarks for assessing performance related to social issues.

[20] The world's 100 largest banks, S&P Global Market Intelligence. 5 April 2019, https://www.spglobal.com/marketintelligence/en/news-insights/trending/t-38wta5twjgrrqccf4_ca2.

6. State-owned enterprises, sustainable finance and resilience

State-owned enterprises (SOEs) account for a growing share of the global corporate landscape, and the trend is likely to continue. SOEs' commitment to sustainable development matters because of their sheer size, because they tend to be located in high-impact sectors and because SOEs enable the state to set the "tone at the top" in the business sector. This chapter analyses national approaches to environmental, social and governance concerns in the state-owned sector. Overall, SOEs' commitment to sustainability is higher than among other firms but the trend is far from uniform, with some sectors and geographic regions clearly lagging behind. The chapter further highlights some challenges arising from increasing state ownership, including a large state involvement in sectors that continue to rely on fossil fuels, and a generally higher risk of corruption and other irregular practices in SOEs than in other firms.

Finding proper balance between corporate and governmental approaches toward sustainability inevitably becomes more complex when governments themselves are enterprise owners. This issue has come to the forefront in recent years, reflecting the growing importance of state-owned enterprises (SOEs) in the global marketplace. According to OECD calculations, around a fourth of the largest global companies are entirely or largely owned by the state (OECD, 2019). Among the world's listed companies, public sector[1] ownership comprises of 14% of global market capitalisation (OECD, 2019), and in the OECD-plus area[2] alone their value exceeds 2.4 trillion USD (full or majority ownership) (OECD, 2017). In a number of emerging and post-transition economies the share of state-ownership across the globe is estimated to be even higher.

Taking into account the numerous government support measures to tackle the COVID-19 induced economic crisis, those numbers may be set to grow in the OECD area and beyond (Abate et al., 2020). Moreover, in OECD and other economies that may have relatively small SOE sectors, SOEs continue to exercise an impact that exceeds their share of the national productive economy. This is because they tend to be unusually large and concentrated in economic activities (e.g. infrastructure; network industries; finance) that are of disproportionate importance to the performance and productivity of the rest of the business sector (OECD, 2017).

Table 6.1. State-owned enterprises among the world's largest 500 companies

	2019	2000
World total	**132**	**34**
Asia total	**100**	**16**
China	90	8
India	4	1
Japan	2	5
Other Asia	4	2
Europe total	**20**	**15**
France	9	6
Russia	3	1
Germany	3	2
Italy	3	2
Other Europe	2	4
Rest of the world	**12**	**3**
Brazil	4	1
United States	3	1
Mexico	2	0
Middle East	3	1

Note. A broad definition of an SOE has been applied whereby any enterprise where the state is the beneficiary owner of more than 10% of the voting shares is considered an SOE.
Source: OECD calculations based on Fortune Global 500.

Where state ownership prevails the issue of sustainable finance is defined more broadly than in the private sector. Private investors may decide to define sustainability in terms of the risk-weighted returns on portfolios of assets, but the ultimate beneficiary owners of SOEs are the population at large. In this sense the state officials involved in the oversight of SOEs are arguably subject to obligations toward the public that are not unlike the fiduciary duties that a private company's board and management owe to their shareholders. They need to ensure that the financial and non-financial dispositions of their portfolio of SOEs serve not only long-term profit maximisation but also the fulfilment of widely held public policy priorities.

At the same time, the distinction (mentioned in earlier chapters) between political and corporate responsibilities still applies. First, SOEs are usually subject to ordinary company law. This implies limitations to how the state may dispose over their assets and free cash flow – especially where minority investors are invited into their shareholder structure. Second, if the financing of important public policy objectives are delegated to a corporation, great care must be taken to ensure fiscal transparency and accountability, competitive neutrality, and to sheltering governing bodies from undue interference. Third, SOEs have, or should have, corporate forms that are designed with a view to ensuring an efficient operation of commercial operations; where the state wishes to carry out purely public policy objectives (e.g. the provision of health, social and educational services) then other types of public agencies or policy measures are typically more suitable delivery vehicles. The remainder of the chapter focuses on SOEs that are mainly, or largely, concerned with the pursuit of commercial objectives.

6.1. The quest for environmental, social and governance (ESG) performance

From the perspective of an inclusive approach to sustainability in the state-owned sector, the ESG nexus also needs to be more broadly interpreted. For starters, it would hardly suffice for the state owner of a well-run SOE to apply ESG criteria to its investment as a means to maximising returns. In most cases other public (and political) priorities for environmental and social performance are integrated into its operational goals. For example, state-owned "green banks" like the UK Green Investment Bank (since privatised) are set up with the explicit mandate to further environmental goals through project level financing. In cases like these, high standards of governance rather than being a goal in themselves are – from the owners' perspective – an essential ingredient in companies' ability to deliver a satisfactory environmental, social as well as financial performance.

At the same time, the E, S and G dimensions remain closely interrelated. The extent to which SOEs are expected to incorporate societal and environmental concerns into their business models will depend on the state's various roles as policymaker, regulator, owner and shareholder. It is also worth noting that a recent OECD study finds that the effectiveness of a country's sustainable development practices in the SOE sector largely depends on institutional arrangements for SOE governance, legislative, regulatory or policy requirements and different incentive mechanisms for encouraging such practices (OECD, 2020 forthcoming). The issue of proper incentivisation of the corporate agents involved in the process is also increasingly recognised (OECD 2020d).

Clear distinction between each of these roles is necessary to ensure that the state does not exercise undue influence on the governing bodies of the company while also exercising proportionate influence on the company as its owner/shareholder. For this reason, explicit public policy objectives should be expressed in the form of policies or regulations[3]; in its role as owner the responsible ownership entity might formulate "owner's expectations" to be taken into consideration by the governing bodies of the company in view of managing and mitigating reputational and other risks.

The state might also exert its influence through its role as shareholder. These various roles should be carefully balanced, keeping in mind that this involves not only the governing bodies of SOEs themselves but also the state ownership function which normally monitors the companies in real time. SOEs are in most cases overseen by elected politicians and are normally more risk averse than the average private firm. Politicians are kept informed on a "no surprises" basis.

6.1.1. The governance challenge: Companies with a credible commitment to sustainable development

The goal setting and performance of SOEs depend both on the corporate governance of the enterprises themselves and, to an important degree, on the quality of public governance in their home jurisdiction.

Government officials entrusted with exercising the ownership of SOEs must be held accountable. They should act as active and informed enterprise owners, communicating objectives and owner expectations to the SOEs that are fully aligned with the public interest such as expressed through their nation's democratic choices.

There would also be expectations that SOEs themselves are held accountable and operate according to high standards of transparency and disclosure in areas relevant to ESG. This means striking a balance between intervention in the management of the SOE and hands-off ownership that can, in some cases, provide a smokescreen for inappropriate conduct amongst SOEs.

Box 6.1. OECD Guidelines on Corporate Governance of State-Owned Enterprises

I. Rationales for state ownership

The state exercises the ownership of SOEs in the interest of the general public. It should carefully evaluate and disclose the objectives that justify state ownership and subject these to a recurrent review.

II. The state's role as an owner

The state should act as an informed and active owner, ensuring that the governance of SOEs is carried out in a transparent and accountable manner, with a high degree of professionalism and effectiveness.

III. State-owned enterprises in the marketplace

Consistent with the rationale for state ownership, the legal and regulatory framework for SOEs should ensure a level playing field and fair competition in the marketplace when SOEs undertake economic activities.

IV. Equitable treatment of shareholders and other investors

Where SOEs are listed or otherwise include non-state investors among their owners, the state and the enterprises should recognise the rights of all shareholders and ensure shareholders' equitable treatment and access to corporate information.

V. Stakeholder relations and responsible business

The state ownership policy should fully recognise SOEs' responsibilities towards stakeholders and request that SOEs report on their relations with stakeholders. It should make clear any expectations that the state has in respect of responsible business conduct by SOEs.

VI. Disclosure and transparency

SOEs should observe high standards of transparency and be subject to the same high quality accounting, disclosure, compliance and auditing standards as listed companies.

VII. The responsibilities of the boards of directors of state-owned enterprises

The boards of SOEs should have the necessary authority, competencies and objectivity to carry out their functions of strategic guidance and monitoring of management. They should act with integrity and be held accountable for their actions.

The OECD has issued recommendations in this respect through the OECD Guidelines on Corporate Governance of State-Owned Enterprises ("SOE Guidelines"), which were developed in 2005 and last revised in 2015 (Box 1). Implementation of the SOE Guidelines can help governments align their sustainable development priorities while ensuring that internationally accepted good standards of corporate governance related to state ownership entities and separation of functions are respected.

6.1.2. Key elements of national governance frameworks: Transparency and risk management

By way of illustration, transparency and risk management figure prominently among the elements of corporate governance that investors monitor, and consequently are included in most ESG ratings. In addition to being important to safeguard the sustainability of the equity invested in the SOEs, these aspects of corporate governance also have important ramifications for sustainable finance. A government commitment to public policy goals is only truly credible when the public is availed of the necessary information to monitor it. And risk management is integral to both the corporate compliance function and to the board's and management's duties to monitor corporate behaviour and safeguard corporate reputation.

Transparency and disclosure

At the level of the individual SOEs, reporting on financial and other performance does not differ radically from general corporate practices. Most state-owned enterprises are incorporated joint stock or limited liability companies and hence subject to general accountancy and audit rules. The SOE Guidelines recommend that SOEs implement IFRS reporting or equivalent national accounting standards, and according to recent evidence a growing number of jurisdictions implement this recommendation (OECD, 2018).

Where SOEs do differ is with respect to the disclosure and transparency commitments of their state owners. The SOE Guidelines recommend that the ownership entity develop aggregate reporting that covers all SOEs, making it a key disclosure tool directed to the general public. To facilitate transparency and disclosure, around 65% of the 52 countries surveyed in a recent study produce, and make available online, some form of aggregate reporting on SOEs (OECD, 2018). Most of them include all, or the majority of, SOEs in the reports (Figure 6.1). However, only 17% of the countries include information on the costs related to SOEs' public policy objectives and the related funding provided from the state budget.

Figure 6.1. Types of information included in aggregate ownership reporting (number of countries)

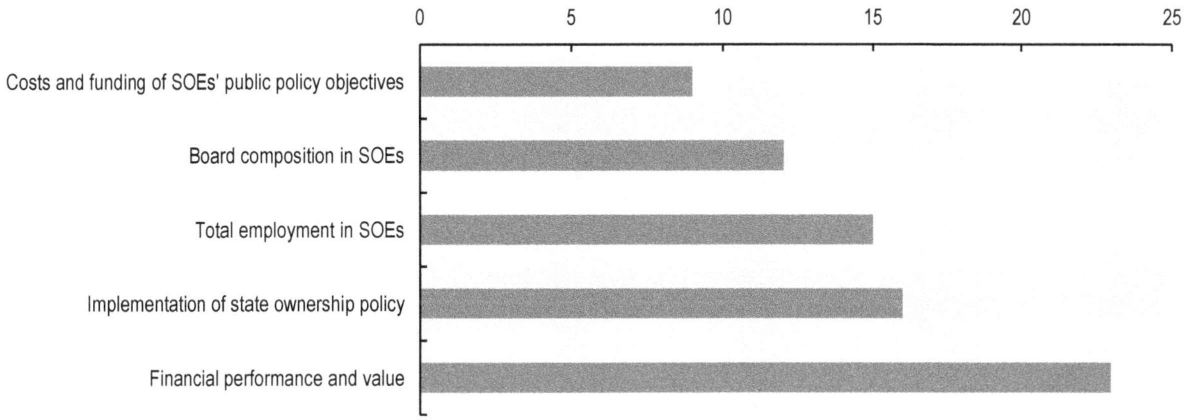

Note: Data is based on a sample of 52 countries
Source: OECD (2018) and OECD (forthcoming)

The implications of Figure 6.1 for ESG in the state-owned sector are important. While most governments engage in some form of aggregate reporting, less than half provide detailed financial data and important ESG relevant indicators such as board composition and public policy objectives are covered only by a small minority of such reports. As mentioned elsewhere in this report, ESG ratings are uncertain in part because of lack of comparable data and a dearth of reporting by state enterprise owners can only aggravate this problem. Governments might argue against this that the SOEs themselves disclose detailed information, but OECD experience shows that such data are often incomplete or inconsistent across companies. The reliability of available information can be raised – and the cost for market participants of obtaining information can be lowered – when states engage in proper aggregate reporting consistent with OECD's recommendations.

An important additional consideration arises when SOEs act as investors – as is the case where the state owns financial institutions or investment vehicles that may, or may not, be incorporated. In this case the state should normally be expected to act as a responsible "ESG investor". However, it will then face the same information and methodological constraints as the ones of private investors identified elsewhere in this report.

Risk management

The SOE Guidelines indicate that financial and operational risks should be understood, managed, and when appropriate, communicated. A key responsibility of boards of directors relates to the management and, where needed, mitigation of these risks to ensure the sustainability and resilience of SOEs. Around two-thirds of the 32 participating countries in a 2016 survey apply SOE-specific risk rules that either complement or supersede rules applicable only to private companies. The most common practice among these countries is including risk-specific guidance within the broader legal, regulatory and policy framework for SOE governance (i.e. SOE governance laws, SOE codes of corporate governance, state enterprise ownership policies or guidelines, or other SOE strategic planning documents) (OECD, 2016).

Significant progress has also been made in terms of establishing regulations or code recommendations on internal control and risk management systems. More than 70% of the respondents in the same survey reported that they undertake some forms of review of SOEs' internal risk management systems. Countries may employ more than one method for undertaking such reviews. The most common means for ownership entities' review of SOEs' risk management systems included: assessments via reviews of SOEs' activity reports; reviews undertaken by the ownership function; via participation in or engagement with the board; and/or via the Annual General Meeting.

6.1.3. The environmental and social dimensions

The OECD has a host of instruments that promote social and environmental values in SOEs, tackling relevant responsibilities at the level of the state and SOEs. They supplement and reinforce each other, hence providing guidance which enables countries to pursue corporate governance aligned with international standards for social and environmental issues.

The SOE Guidelines assign the state an important role with respect to sustainability and systemic stability in SOEs. Since their revision in 2015 they incorporate a chapter on 'Stakeholder relations and responsible business'. This asks governments to ensure that the state ownership policy fully recognises SOEs' responsibilities towards stakeholders, and that they make their expectations about responsible business conduct clear to SOEs. The SOE Guidelines also encourage boards to observe high standards of responsible business, a key element of sustainability. They promote reporting by SOEs on their relations with stakeholders, including labour and affected communities. The OECD Guidelines for Multinational Enterprises (the "MNE Guidelines" referenced in other chapters in this report) provide recommendations addressed by governments to businesses on responsible business conduct. They apply to all entities within the enterprise in all sectors, whether of private, state or mixed ownership.

Box 6.2. OECD recommendations on social and environmental responsibilities in SOEs

Recommendation:

SOEs should observe high standards of responsible business conduct. Expectations established by the government in this regard should be publicly disclosed and mechanisms for their implementation be clearly established. (SOE Guidelines Chapter V item D)

Implementation guidance:

SOEs should observe high standards of responsible business conduct, including with regards to the environment, employees, public health and safety, and human rights. Their actions should be guided by relevant international standards, including: the OECD Guidelines for Multinational Enterprises, which have been adopted by all OECD member countries and reflect all four principles contained in the ILO Declaration on Fundamental Principles and Rights at Work, and the UN Guiding Principles on Business and Human Rights. [...] SOE boards and management should ensure that [owners' expectations] are integrated into the corporate governance of SOEs, supported by incentives and subject to appropriate reporting and performance monitoring.

SOEs should not be required to engage in charitable acts or to provide public services that would more appropriately be carried out by the relevant public authorities. The state's expectations regarding the responsible business conduct of SOEs should be disclosed in a clear and transparent manner.

Source: OECD (2015), Guidelines on Corporate Governance of State-Owned Enterprises.

The MNE Guidelines and the SOE Guidelines both suggest that state ownership entities should give due regard to the content of the other when communicating their expectations for responsible business conduct to the SOEs under their purview. Adherents to the MNE Guidelines currently 48 countries, are required to set up a National Contact Point (NCP) for the Guidelines (for further reference to the instrument, see OECD, 2011). NCP are agencies established by adhering governments to promote and implement the Guidelines. The NCPs assist enterprises and their stakeholders to take appropriate measures to further the implementation of the Guidelines. They also provide a mediation and conciliation platform for resolving issues that may arise. Based on the Guidelines, the OECD has developed guidance on due diligence in a number of sectors, namely minerals, extractive industries, garment and footwear, agriculture and the financial sector.

6.2. ESG performance by SOEs: a snapshot of the evidence

It follows from the previous section that the OECD consensus would have SOEs operate at least at par with best-practice private sector companies in terms of their commitment to sustainability. Two questions however arise: first, to what extent do governments across the globe share this aspiration and, second, do inherent institutional, corporate governance or other challenges make it difficult to reach this goal in practice.

To assess the differences among different categories of companies, ESG ratings have been collected based on Thompson-Factset's rating of around 6,600 listed companies. This index can be said to be, on the one hand, encompassing in the sense that it covers all important economies around the globe. However, it must be cautioned that it includes only companies traded in regulated markets and hence cannot automatically be assumed to be representative of the majority of SOEs that are closely held by the state[4]. State ownership has been identified in 494 of the companies (with SOEs being defined broadly to include firms with more than 10% state ownership)[5]. A sectoral background of SOEs and private companies is provided in Figure 6.2.

Figure 6.2. Average ESG ratings by main sectors

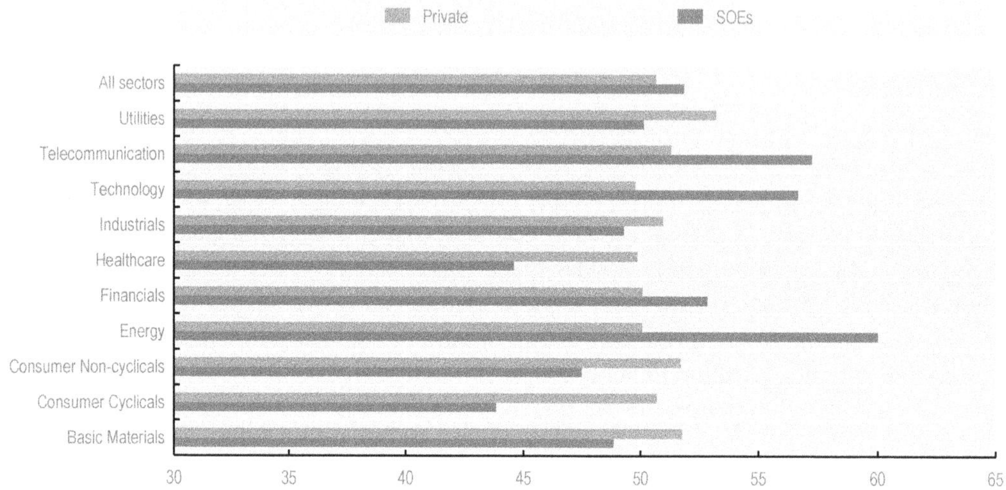

Source: Author calculations based on Thompson-Reuters.

It follows from the figure that SOEs do indeed, on average, have higher ESG ratings than private firms. However, the overall difference is not very big, and there are major underlying sectoral variations. In sectors such as energy, telecommunication, (other) technology and to some extent finance, SOEs have clearly higher ESG ratings than private firms. Conversely, in most of the traditional industries and the service sector SOEs tend to score worse than their private sector counterparts. A perhaps tempting interpretation could be that SOEs that are active in sectors generally perceived to operate in the "public interest" are subject to greater scrutiny and a higher level of reputation risk and therefore strive to raise their commitment to good governance and sustainability. It is, however, also likely that part of the explanation is national difference, since SOEs have different sectoral distributions across countries.

Figure 6.3. Average ESG ratings for SOEs, by geographic region

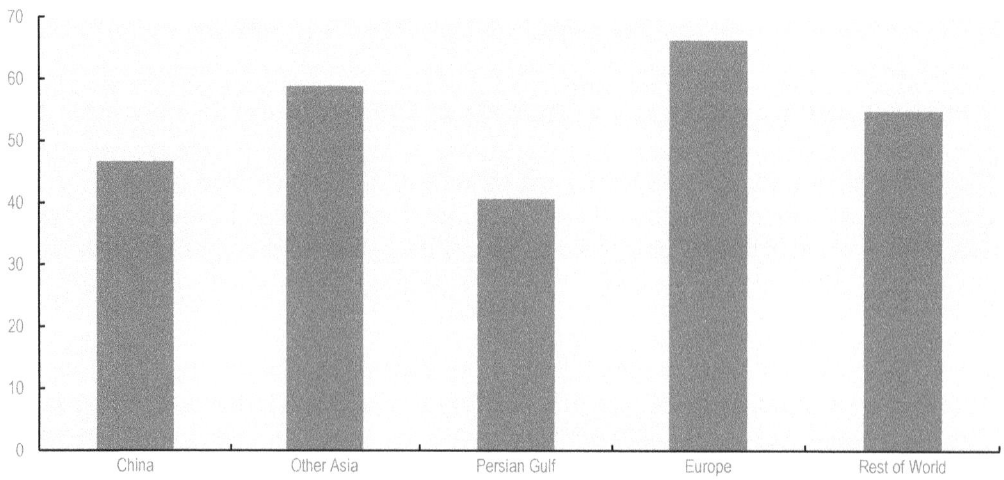

Source: Author calculations based on Thompson-Reuters.

To further examine the point about national difference, Figure 6.3 provides an overview of average ESG ratings of SOEs located in five regions of the world[6]. It occurs that SOEs owned by European governments score significantly higher than any others, followed by "other Asia" (which encompasses two Asian OECD member countries, Singapore and a handful of other economies in South and South East Asia). One interpretation would be that countries that are signatory to OECD good practices in areas such as SOE governance and responsible business conduct have indeed taken steps to implement these practices in the companies that they own[7]. A supplementary reason might be that these countries are mostly high-income economies and have relatively small portfolios of SOEs. Where remaining state ownership of a few companies are perhaps "a matter of policy choice" the authorities can be expected to implement high standards of governance and sustainability in those companies.

6.3. Integrating sustainability considerations into state ownership policy

OECD countries' efforts to enhance corporate governance and state ownership practices in the state-owned sector (the "G" component of ESG) is well documented[8]. Recent OECD research moreover sheds light on governments' efforts to raise standards of sustainable development in the companies they control. According to the 2020 OECD report on "Implementing the OECD Guidelines on Corporate Governance of State-Owned Enterprises," two-thirds of the 28 countries surveyed have made material progress in recent years in national practices concerning the integration of sustainability-related values into government policies, requirements and expectations with regard to the SOE sector (OECD, 2020). Some examples of national practices in this regard are provided below.

It is also notable that one fifth of the countries surveyed have newly put in place SOE board obligations to establish ethics and compliance programmes or measures. This demonstrates the importance given to RBC as a core business issue in recent years and indicates that the increasing pressure for accountability and transparency of corporate behaviour is supporting innovations and improvements in practices by SOEs.

Figure 6.4. How countries have promoted responsible business in the SOE sector, 2013-18

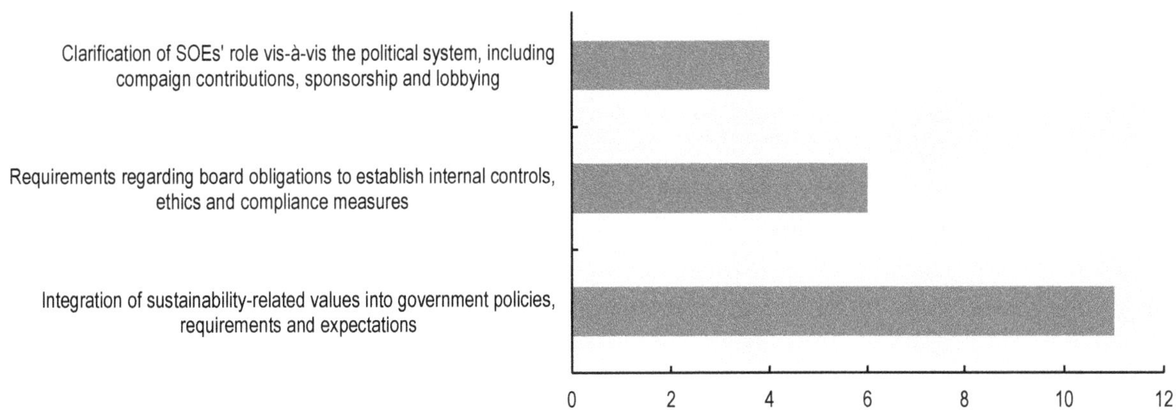

Note: The data is based on a sample of 28 countries. It indicates the material policy changes made by governments on responsible business in the SOE sector.
Source: OECD (2020)

In particular, many OECD Member countries seem to think that SOEs can – and should – play a leading role in their sector to motivate virtuous behaviour from all market participants. An increasing number of these governments are incorporating sustainable development goals into their ownership policies to allow for public disclosure of expectations for sustainability and establishing mechanisms for their implementation. In addition, as a regulator, the state can further encourage positive behaviour by playing a leading role itself in terms of social and environmental responsibility. In these cases, ensuring co-ordination between general sustainability policy and SOE-specific objectives and creating a level-playing field among private players are important to ensure efficiency. A few examples of national practices (without prejudice to whether they can be considered "best practice") are the following:

- Finland's ownership policy ["Government Resolution on State Ownership Policy of 13 May 2016"] clearly expects companies to set an example in value leadership and corporate social responsibility as part of the company values and requires that they "contribute to the long-term development and renewal of society".
- In 2018, the Korean government designated "public institutions as a driving force for achieving social values" and included them as one of 100 major national tasks of the government's five-year administrative plan. The government has defined a set of indicators to monitor the performance of SOEs and new public institutions with respect to human rights, ethical management, occupational safety, environment conservation and social integration.
- In Switzerland, the Federal Council published in 2015 an official position paper on corporate social responsibility ["*RSE - Position et Plan d'Action du Conseil Fédéral*"]. It states that the Swiss Confederation should act as a role model in particular when performing ownership rights over state owned companies.
- In New Zealand, the SOE Act requires every SOE to exhibit a sense of social responsibility by having regard to the interests of the community in which it operates and by endeavouring to accommodate or encourage these when able to do so. SOEs are expected to formulate and report on CSR objectives on an equal footing with financial objectives.

More detailed national information regarding France, Norway and Sweden are provided in boxes Box 6.3 and Box 6.4.

Box 6.3. France's Global strategy on corporate social responsibility

The strategy covers the entire SOE portfolio of the state as well all the administration that manages SOEs in general. It consists of several tiers, some of which are cross-cutting while other are more specific to certain sectors or enterprises. The global strategy is being finalised through a charter, with three main pillars:

1. **Integrating CSR in the SOEs' strategy, in particular in their purpose ("raison d'être")**. Concretely, SOEs are required to explicitly state their own objectives in terms of CSR and vis-à-vis stakeholders in their individual strategies.
2. **Improving gender equality.**
3. **Reducing greenhouse gas emissions**. This particular pillar consists in assessing SOEs' progress on reducing greenhouse gas emissions by establishing SOE's carbon footprint (globally and individually) and by setting a target to reduce emissions. The latter is done individually by SOEs which have to establish an action plan aimed at reaching their respective target

To date, the French state's ownership agency APE has observed a certain disparity between SOEs in terms of individual practices, with some relatively more advanced than their peers. This includes most notably the French Public Investment Bank, Bpifrance, which is finalising a "climate plan" to assess its carbon footprint and direct its actions towards sustainable finance, as well as EDF (the national electricity producer and distributor) which aims to double renewable energy production by 2030 and to triple energy storage capacity by 2035. Other examples include the railway company SNCF which has ordered 100 trains that consume 20% less energy than the current fleet, and the postal company (La Poste) which is increasingly using electric vehicles.

As the adaptation of environmental and social responsibility practices in SOEs gains momentum worldwide, it should be kept in mind that some of the most basic elements of good governance can also have direct impact on sustainability goals. Peru, for example, which is considered as one of the countries most vulnerable to climate change, is making high SOE governance standards a centrepiece of its efforts. When the central ownership unit was established, the need to tackle sustainability issues (including the SDGs) was explicitly cited as one of the reasons. Within the broader ownership framework, the ownership unitg provides: 1) impact analysis of SOEs' sustainability programmes; 2) a framework for project development to enhance the sustainability of SOEs; and 3) technical assistance to SOEs for developing their sustainability programmes.

Box 6.4. Recent changes to the state ownership policy in Norway and Sweden: A focus on value creation

Sustainability

The Norwegian state expects individual SOEs to have an agenda for sustainable value creation stating how the company plans to create value overtime. A similar expectation features in Sweden's new ownership policy (2019) according to which SOEs have to contribute (through their business models) to value creation in a way that promotes long-term sustainable development.

More concretely, the Norwegian government expects from companies that their respective sustainable value creation agendas are specified in terms of clear goals and strategies and that companies report on them. This presupposes that individual companies identify and address material opportunities and risks for their business and those affected by their activities. A similar case is made in Sweden where SOEs, in light of their respective industries and markets in which they operate, have to identify and minimise the risk of negative impact of their operations while also taking advantage of new business opportunities for sustainable value creation. Hence since 2013, boards of directors are officially responsible for setting strategic targets for sustainable business in their business models.

Responsible business conduct (RBC)

The new Norwegian state ownership policy introduces clear expectations in terms of Responsible Business Conduct. More specifically, SOEs are expected to lead the field on RBC, which entails, amongst other aspects, that companies identify main risk areas for stakeholders affected by their operations (including in the supply chain), and incorporate RBC into their goals and strategy and follow internationally agreed standards and principles such as the OECD Guidelines for Multinational Enterprises (MNE Guidelines). As companies differ in business, size and risk exposure, the RBC-related work needs to be adapted on an individual basis.

Additional specific expectations for SOEs include work to protect human rights and labour rights, to reduce their climate and environmental footprints, and prevent economic crime including corruption and money laundering. SOEs are expected to conduct due diligence for their RBC based on recognised methods. Similar expectations exist in Sweden where SOEs are expected to follow MNE Guidelines as well as the UN Guiding Principles on Business and Human Rights, amongst other standards.

6.4. But SOEs are not just a force for good: Challenges arising from state ownership

6.4.1. Managing costs, protecting the competitive environment

State-owned enterprises' commitment to sustainable development can, even where fully implemented, give rise to some policy challenges. A basic commitment to responsible business conduct (RBC) along the lines of private companies is unproblematic, as such strategies are commonly assumed to serve the goal of long-term corporate value creation. Some governments, however, have gone further and broadened the concept of RBC to encompass demands that their SOEs shall carry out a number of public policy function. Recent examples from Asia include SOEs being instructed to dedicate a percentage of their earnings to acts of corporate charity, or to carry out public services including education, housing and health for their employees or local communities (OECD, 2020 forthcoming). While the provision of such public functions is indeed important, mostly it is better carried out either by dedicated government agencies or sourced from private sector providers, and funded from public budget rather than imposed on the state-owned enterprises themselves.

The state may nevertheless decide to charge SOEs with certain public policy objectives that would not be expected from private firms in like circumstances – and the presence of such objectives may be integral to the rationale for state ownership. In the context of sustainable development, recent examples of such "non-commercial" objectives have included demands that SOEs invest in green technology to a greater extent than imposed by the markets; and, through their staffing decisions, play a stabilising role in labour markets during times of economic crisis. Some governments attach great value to the policy leverage arising from SOEs public policy objectives, and *inter alia* for this reason they actively support the relevant SOEs and shield them from competition and takeover.

This in turn gives rise to two twin policy challenges related to (i) the balancing of commercial and non-commercial objectives; and (ii) maintaining a level playing field in markets where SOEs and private firms coexist. According to the SOE Guidelines and previous studies conducted by the OECD[9], in order to ensure a balance between commercial and non-commercial priorities, an important challenge for policy makers is to ensure that SOEs receive an adequate and transparent compensation for the public policy priorities they are asked to undertake. They should neither be put at a competitive disadvantage nor have their competitive activities effectively subsidised by the State.

To maintain a level playing field (commonly referred to as "competitive neutrality") a high level of transparency is called for. Any obligations and responsibilities that an SOE is required to undertake in terms of public services beyond the generally accepted norm should be clearly mandated by laws or regulations. The SOE Guidelines recommend that such obligations and responsibilities be disclosed to the general public and related costs should be covered in a transparent manner. A number of governments have in the past chosen to compensate SOEs for their public policy roles not through carefully targeted subsidies, but rather through in-kind benefits (e.g. preferential access to land or inputs), preferential tax treatment, soft loans, favourable public procurement framework, and a general relaxation of any rate-of-return requirements imposed on the companies. This is not recommended since such measures have adverse effects on competition and generally do not reflect accurately the cost of the public policy objectives imposed on the SOEs.

Good practices in the Guidelines also call on SOEs to separate the accounts of commercial and non-commercial activities. OECD Member countries are increasingly adopting such practices. In the case of EU countries (as well as members of the EEA) the rules guiding the Single Market impose accounting separation to all undertakings (public or private) receiving public funds or benefiting from special or exclusive rights (the methods used to calculate costs are also subject to specific requirements). In the

OECD area more generally, such rules are commonly applied in certain sectors (e.g. the public utilities and energy sectors) where significant public service obligations are in place.

6.4.2. Ensuring coherence between policy and practice

As noted in above sections, ownership entities around the world are actively integrating environment, social and governance goals for their SOE portfolios. This goes hand in hand with broader international commitments and an increasing awareness that governments as enterprise owners should "lead by example." However, a challenge arises from a lack of coherence between stated public policy goals and the corporate objectives pursued by individual SOEs in a number of countries. The SOE Guidelines – as well as the OECD Best Practice Principles on the Governance of Regulators (OECD, 2014) – recommend a strict separation of the state's roles as enterprise owner and economic regulator, as well as the appointment of professional and autonomous boards of directors in each SOE to ensure that the companies act according to their corporate objectives rather than in response to ad-hoc political intervention.

The energy sector provides a useful illustration of this point. Although there has been considerable market liberalisation, state ownership remains prevalent in the energy sector with energy SOEs representing almost a quarter of the total equity value of the state-ownership portfolios of 39 OECD and partner countries; and 37% of the total equity value of publicly traded SOEs where the state remains a prominent shareholder (10 per cent or more).[10] (OECD, 2017)

These SOEs represent almost 40% of energy investments globally (IEA, 2020a) across all sub-sectors of the energy sector including the most polluting ones (Figure 6.5). As a result of their power generation capacity, SOEs are among the world's largest emitters of greenhouse gasses at both the country and global levels, owning over half of the world's coal power plants (Prag *et* al, 2018). In the aggregate, SOEs emit over 6.2 gigatonnes of carbon dioxide equivalent per year in energy sector in greenhouse gasses, which by some calculations (Benoit, 2019), represent more emissions than every country except China.

Figure 6.5. Share of government/SOE ownership in energy investment (percent, 2015-2019)

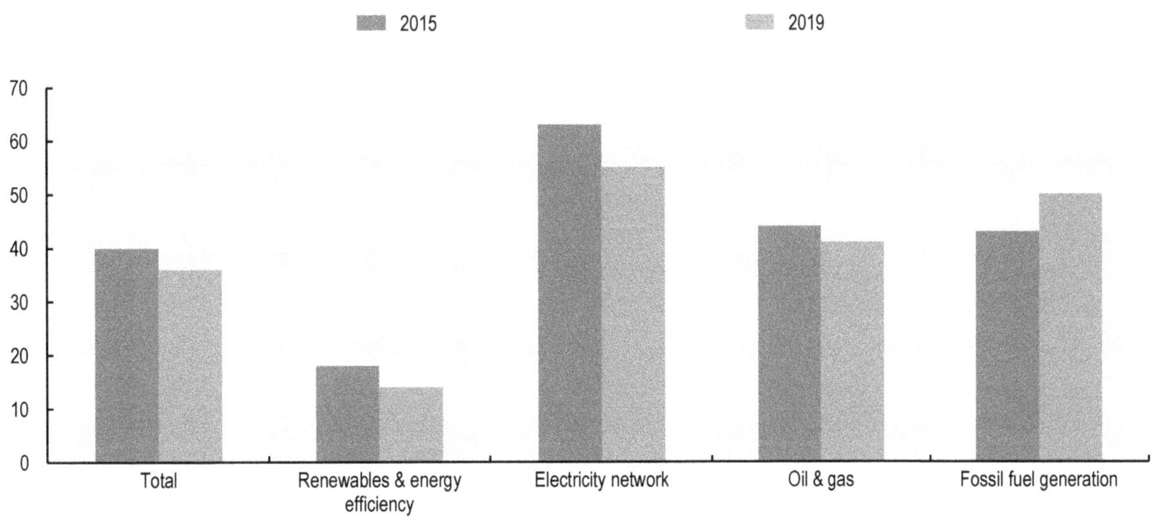

Source: IEA (2020a), Share of state-owned energy investments by economy type and sector, 2019, IEA, Paris https://www.iea.org/data-and-statistics/charts/share-of-state-owned-energy-investments-by-economy-type-and-sector-2019

At the same time, many SOEs are responsible for a growing share of investment in low-carbon alternatives, such as renewables power, and importantly, they are incentivised to expand these investments by their government owners as part of societal expectations to meet ambitious energy transition targets set according to international, multilateral or national commitments. These two policy realities often co-exist: one where the government is actively promoting a low carbon transition; and one where SOEs continue to invest in high carbon assets.

An example can be made of coal power plants. Globally, SOEs are on average investing in new coal plants at a higher rate than their non-state counterparts - as of 2017, more than half of all coal power plants planned and under construction were built by SOEs (Prag *et al.,* 2018). This trend raises two potential issues, the first relates to the economic and financial risk management of SOEs that are carrying out these investments, and the second relates to coherence of policy goals by governments acting as owners of enterprises.

Regarding economic and financial risk management of SOEs, investments currently in the pipeline will, if built and fully operated as planned, continue to be "locked in" to produce significant carbon dioxide emissions far into the future – especially as governments and other investors are increasingly moving away from these types of investments. Current SOE investors in coal face a risk of having their assets economically stranded.[11] According to Prag *et al.* (2018), by allowing these investments to go ahead, governments are potentially creating a future dilemma between placing SOE assets under financial risk or locking-in greenhouse gas emissions.

Arguably, a number of governments have not focused enough on "stranded asset risks" in their approach towards SOE portfolio management. Such an approach relates to company level financial returns that may drive private sector investors, rather than the broader economic returns that motivate government owners (Benoit, 2019). This is consistent with the approach that would (and should) be taken by the government agencies responsible for ownership. The challenge is to enshrine, on a whole-of-government basis, an approach toward enterprise ownership that focuses on maximising long term "value for society" and incorporates sound economic and financial management.

The second issue relates to the policy goals of government owners, where the case for a policy reorientation is strong. The ability to change investment behaviour of SOEs depends heavily on their mandates. Unlike private firms, SOEs often have to mind more than the bottom line. Mandates to ensure energy security and affordability or to support employment in the sector could act as barriers to more climate-friendly investment decisions (Prag, et al., 2018). SOEs, and in many cases the policy makers that own them, are positioned to directly influence climate-relevant decisions in the power market which should act in favour of reducing and eventually eliminating coal power plants not increasing them. Unfortunately, the impact of the COVID-19 induced economic crisis may weaken the ability of many companies to invest in new capacity – which will depend heavily on the financial sustainability and strategic choices of these SOEs and their government owners. There is a risk that some state actors fall back on familiar levers for economic development (e.g. expansion of activities in sectors that rely on fossil fuels heavily, such as steel and other basic metal sectors), pushing up coal use and emissions. (IEA, 2020b)

Encouragingly, OECD research has demonstrated that SOE ownership may also have a positive effect on investment in the renewable electricity generation sector in OECD and G20 countries[12]. This effect could be due to a number of reasons, including government mandates to advance their decarbonisation strategies, preferential financing terms potentially available to SOEs, the existence of explicit or implicit state guarantees (which translate into lower costs of capital), and incumbency advantages in the market place. As many governments develop incentives to promote a low carbon transition they might consider how such incentives are applied to the SOE sector. While such schemes can be necessary, especially in the case of clear market failures, they should also not distort the competitive landscape nor hinder the entry of new market players that may also facilitate the low carbon transition. Applying the principles of competitive neutrality and good state ownership practices, as elaborated above, can help to address such concerns.

6.4.3. *Fighting corruption in the state-owned sector*

Integrity and anti-corruption safeguards are crucial for sustainable development and the long-term resilience of SOEs. If proper anti-corruption and integrity measures are in place, SOEs will less likely suffer from financial losses due to sanctions or misuse of funds, or from reputational damages[13]. Conversely, the acceptance of corruption practices in SOEs tends to weaken their corporate governance (the "G" of ESG, again) to the point where their contribution to sustainability and resilience becomes significantly impaired.

However, corruption continues to impede the successful performance of SOEs across the globe. Alleged corruption in some of the world's biggest SOEs has been investigated and prosecuted in a number of countries in recent years. The charges have included procurement-related passive bribery (38 persons were indicted in a scheme involving the French state-owned EDF in 2019), and active foreign bribery and related money-laundering offences (the Brazilian state-owned Banco do Brasil is under investigation for possible money-laundering scheme for bribery payments)[14]. The financial losses incurred by SOEs because of corruption-related sanctions have also grown considerably over the years. Mere allegations of corrupt conduct involving SOEs have had an immediate economic impact, with the announcements of probes leading to falls in share price of the SOEs involved.[15]

In response to these and other SOEs-related corruption scandals, many countries have recognised the need to take action by introducing various anti-corruption and integrity measures into the exercise of their state ownership. For example, Denmark, Sweden, Norway and Finland have included anti-corruption and integrity expectations into their ownership policies, along with those for sustainability and responsible business conduct. Other countries have included effective anti-corruption and integrity measures into the guidelines for their SOEs. For example, Chile's Corporate Governance Guidelines for the SOEs, developed by its ownership entity, inter alia cover internal and external audit, risk management, conflicts of interest, codes of conduct, and transparency. France, through its ownership entity, is providing ethics and integrity advice through a dedicated ethics advisor, under the supervision of the Ethics Committee. Similar advice is available in Canada.

Some countries have stepped up co-operation and coordination between their ownership entities and anti-corruption authorities in order to prevent corruption in SOEs. For example, Argentina has set up an "Integrity task-force" involving Argentina's co-ordination council of SOEs, the anticorruption agency and the state control body. Italy's Ministry of Economy and Finance and anti-corruption authority set up a dedicated working group to create guidelines for partly or wholly owned SOEs, at the central and local level, to properly address anti-corruption and integrity issues.

Individual SOEs are also putting anti-corruption and integrity measures in place more actively. By now, most of the large SOEs in OECD countries have adopted ethics codes or similar instruments, and have set up compliance programmes. Both the sanctions, as well as government requirements, have encouraged SOEs to build anti-corruption programmes, which would go beyond simple declarations and formalities. In France, large companies, including SOEs, are required by law to introduce eight key elements ensuring that anti-corruption and integrity measures are effective. Consequently, all nine of the French largest SOEs have adopted both the Code of Ethics and anti-corruption programmes and widely publicised their policy of zero tolerance to corruption.

An OECD initiative against SOE corruption

The initiatives summarised above are contributing to stamping out corruption in the state-owned sector, but it is commonly agreed that more needs to be done. In this spirit, OECD countries made a joint high-level commitment by adopting the Guidelines on Anti-Corruption and Integrity in State-Owned Enterprises (ACI Guidelines) in 2019. The ACI Guidelines are the first international instrument to offer states, in their role as owners of enterprises, support in promoting integrity and fighting corruption in enterprises they own.

They represent a widely held international consensus and underline the importance for action in this regard, making this instrument an important milestone. The ACI Guidelines complement various international commitments and standards on anti-corruption in the private sector and highlight the importance of levelling the playing field for all market actors – private and state-owned. They also clearly place responsibility for integrity of SOEs both with the state and SOEs management.

OECD countries have reaffirmed their commitment to implementing the ACI Guidelines by mandating the OECD to "develop, through an inclusive process, an implementation guide that helps Adherents implement the Recommendation" (OECD, 2019). The Implementation Guide will provide guidance to support state owners in implementing the provisions of the ACI Guidelines. It will cover all four pillars of the recommendations (Figure 4.6). Like the ACI Guidelines, the Implementation Guide will be a tool for the state as owner, but will provide insights that may be additionally useful for all entities engaging with SOEs and for SOEs. As the Guide is implemented , new good practices will emerge to offer responses to corruption in SOEs.

Figure 6.6. Main elements of the Guidelines on Anti-Corruption and Integrity in State-Owned Enterprises

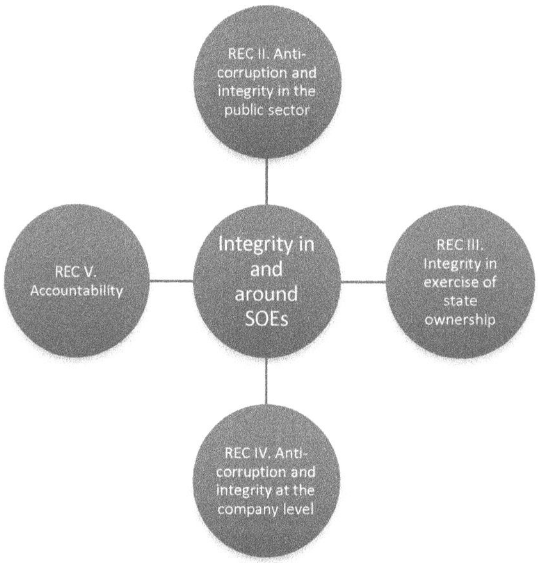

The COVID-19 pandemic has exposed new potential vulnerabilities of SOEs to corruption risks. Transport and logistics is already one of the sectors of the economy most impacted by COVID-19. This sector has also been found among the most susceptible to corruption (OECD, 2018b). As government support to SOEs grows, with large injections of funds through extra-ordinary expedited procedures, opportunities for graft and other forms of corruption will multiply. At the same time, as national budgets shrink, the public will watch the appropriation of state support even more closely. The state will need to demonstrate that the scarce funds have not been lost to corruption and other misappropriation. Similarly, SOEs will need to demonstrate that their anti-corruption and integrity measures function well to prevent any misconduct. This can be done, inter alia, by rigorous implementation of the ACI Guidelines and other related legal instruments of the OECD.

6.5. State ownership, sustainability and resilience after the COVID-19 crisis

Going forward, a key question is how the state owned sector may contribute to creating a more sustainable and resilient corporate sector. A growing number of companies could end up in state ownership in consequence of the current crisis. A number of companies deemed "strategic" or systemically important have been rendered virtually insolvent and may have to rely on government – or government-supported – equity injections to survive. The pressure on balance sheets is further exacerbated by the fact that a number of countries had record-high levels of corporate indebtedness already prior to the crisis.

Table 6.2. Government support for the airline industry announced or implemented since the outbreak of the COVID-19 pandemic

Country	Target	Measures implemented/announced	Equity investment by state?
Company specific interventions			
Austria	Austrian Airlines	Loan guarantees	No
Belgium	Brussels Airlines	State loan	No
Finland	Finnair	Loan guarantees plus a rights issue to all shareholders underwritten by the state	Potentially
France[1] and the Netherlands	Air France-KLM	Mostly loan guarantees, plus a state loan	No
Germany	Condor	Loans by federal and regional government	No
	Lufthansa	Equity, loans and convertible debt	Yes
Hong Kong, China	Cathay Pacific Airways	A combination of share and warrant purchases and a bridge loan	Yes
Israel	El Al	Loan guarantee and stock issuance.	Yes
Italy	Alitalia	Nationalisation	Yes
Korea	Korean Air	Bond purchases	No
Latvia	Air Baltic	Recapitalisation	Yes
New Zealand	Air New Zealand	State loan convertible to equity	Potentially
Norway	Norwegian Air	Loan guarantees (conditional on a debt equity swap with the private creditors)	No
Portugal	TAP	Loan and capital injection	Yes
Singapore	Singapore Airlines	Equity and convertible debt issuance. The state acts as investor of last instance	Potentially
South Africa	South African Airways	Recapitalisation by the state owner	Yes
Sweden[2] and Denmark	Scandinavian Airlines SAS	Loans, loan guarantees, hybrid notes and stock issuance.	Yes
Switzerland	Swiss	Loan guarantees (sureties)	No
Industry-wide programmes[1]			
United Kingdom	Three airline companies	State loans	No
United States	Airline industry	Mix of grants, redeemable loans and warrants	Potentially

Notes. This table lists company-specific interventions. The countries included are OECD member countries and partner countries that have engaged actively with the OECD Working Party on State Ownership and Privatisation Practices.

1. Not including certain narrowly targeted measures, such as deferral of tax payments in some jurisdictions.

2. Additional support has been pledged by the government of the Netherlands.

3. This is part of a broader industry-wide support programme.

Source: OECD calculations based on press sources between 1 March and 15 July 2020.

The effects of the crisis on state enterprise ownership will continue to evolve over the coming years. The most immediate effects have been seen in the air transportation sector, which is both one of the most directly affected sectors and also widely perceived by governments as systemically important due to the externalities that national flag-carriers are believed to confer on the rest of the business sector. Table 2 provides an overview of some of the recent measures to provide balance sheet support (whether equity, loans, guarantees and donations) to troubled air carriers.

To this point relatively few governments have taken equity stakes in previously private firms, but the likely outlook is for an increase over time. First, several rescue packages include convertible debt, which over the medium term could be transformed into voting shares. Second, the debt instruments and loan guarantees are redeemable, so unless the recipients achieve a financial turnaround after the crisis, the government creditors will at a later stage have to consider either debt forgiveness or a debt-equity swap that could then lead to state ownership of the companies.

In addition to the company specific measures reviewed in the table a majority of OECD countries have announced broader economy-wide programmes (or in some cases having a sectoral focus). These programmes are presented as aimed at staving off corporate failure as a the specific consequence of the COVID-19 crisis[16], but there is some evidence of national initiatives assisting firms that were in trouble prior to the crisis and/or targeting "strategic" concerns unrelated to COVID-19. The onus of these programmes is mostly on debt instruments such as loans and loan guarantees, but a number of governments have indicated that government share ownership is not excluded. Moreover, a few national initiatives announced so far – including notably Germany's Economic Stabilisation Fund – have as a specific goal to support companies through share purchases.

Again, most of the support measures are unlikely to lead to equity ownership by the state, but some of them will and it is hard to escape the conclusion that the world is headed for a growing government involvement in the corporate economy. The European Union has responded to this by imposing on EU member countries – which in the near term have been granted sweeping exemptions from the Union's Single Market rules – restrictions on longer-term share ownership by the state.[17] Where rescue operations involve equity investment exceeding 20% of a company's equity, the government must present an exit plan detailing how it will divest from the company over a five-year period.

6.5.1. The quest for "building back better": What role for the SOEs?

Equity support by the state to individual companies should normally come with a clearly defined exit plan detailing how and when the state plans to divest.[18] However, in some cases governments may conclude that a rescued company should remain part of the state's SOE portfolio. The post-COVID-19 corporate environment could have changed significantly, creating new rationales for state ownership. For instance, the outlook is for a growing concentration among fewer enterprises in a number of sectors, which might induce the government to stay involved as an owner to protect the integrity of the marketplace.

The crisis has further highlighted a situation where the quest for corporate profitability, for example via the reduction of corporate inventories associated with "just-in-time" supply management, left many firms with shortages of vital supplies when confronted with an unexpected surge in demand. Going forward this will lead to a stronger state involvement in corporate activities deemed to be of overriding societal importance. This should preferably take the form of independent market regulation, but where this is not feasible a continued state ownership of certain companies may be the outcome.

The challenge to "build back better" includes two main elements: (i) making the economy more resilient, both with regard to avoiding future corporate crises and to limit the risk of supply shortages and disruptions to value chains; (ii) ensuring that crisis resolution and mitigation measures are supportive of broader sustainability and other societal goals.

Regarding the first point, the crisis has brought to the fore the need to ensure the resilience of supply-chains of key essential goods[19]. This requires that both governments and firms carefully re-assess the strengths and fragilities of key supply chains, avoiding quick assumptions on what can increase resilience when making sourcing decisions. This will require revisiting procurement strategies and introducing relevant criteria going beyond economic efficiency. It may also require re-examining redundancy capacity and inventory stocks. If governments impose new public service obligations on firms (e.g. stockpiling certain goods) to further ensure essential supplies, these would need to be appropriately and transparently reimbursed.

Some argue for a greater reliance on domestic production, which may have a role to play in increasing resilience, but which also has drawbacks. Important production activities should clearly not depend on supply chains in which one single producer is indispensable, but the best remedy against this is a diversified production with adequate competition. Sovereign governments and regulatory authorities can achieve this outcome without relying on SOEs – or on nationally owned producers, for that matter.

However, as demonstrated during the early stages of the COVID-19 crisis, the presence of multiple suppliers may not prevent acute shortages during period of booming demand. It is simply not commercially viable for private producers to maintain a supply capacity sufficient to deal with all eventualities. If the authorities, in the public interest, want to maintain a particularly large delivery capacity they basically have three options: (i) compensate existent private suppliers; (ii) maintain large precautionary stocks (which is only possible for some kinds of produce); or (iii) assume control over the production process via SOEs (or state-linked private firms). If the third option is chosen, it is imperative that measures are taken to ensure competitive neutrality so that in terms of their normal (non-crisis related) commercial activities the SOEs compete with the private sector on an entirely level playing field. This is further important in the context of ensuring that the allocation of resources remains essentially guided by market signals rather than dictated by government planning.

The state may further want to involve itself in the corporate economy where, on the one hand, certain activities are deemed systemically important, while on the other hand no viable option for private supply exists[20]. A current example is the airlines industry where governments perceive important economic externalities arising from maintaining a "flag carrier" and an important airline hub within the country. Going forward similar action might occur when doubts arise about the viability of companies that retain important proprietary technologies and/or economies of scale.

The OECD takes no position on whether the ownership of commercial enterprises is better placed with the private or public sector, but in the countries where the state does decide to assume an enlarged ownership role good practices need to be respected. The state should exercise its role as an enterprise owner in accordance with the OECD Guidelines on Corporate Governance of State-Owned Enterprises. This implies, among other things, a corporate governance that is up to private sector best practices; high standards of transparency and accountability; and a continued effort to ensure a level playing field in competitive markets.

Also, the state needs to clearly accentuate the rationale for owning commercial enterprises and regularly review the rationale. The highest standards of transparency and accountability should be applied, including explaining ex-ante why the government chooses to favour equity stakes, as opposed to other policy and financial instruments, to deliver its policy objectives. Such information should be disclosed to the public via well structured annual aggregate reporting by the state ownership entities, covering all relevant aspects of ESG in accordance with OECD recommendations. Going forward the OECD will work toward raising standards of disclosure by SOEs and their owners. This will involve cooperation with other standard-setting organisations to clarify the system of standards and reporting tools that exist and how they complement each other, including via joint initiatives such as the Impact Management Project[21].

If the state assumes a significant position as a company owner it needs to pay even greater attention to broader policy priorities in the area of responsible business conduct. The state will effectively be setting "the tone at the top" within the business sector. As such, it is well placed to use its shareholding position to encourage environmental, social and governance standards in line with its international policy commitments, including the MNE Guidelines. It will also be in a position to step up the fight against corruption, in which irregular payments to SOEs have in the past often played a role, in accordance with OECD's Anti-Corruption and Integrity Guidelines for State-Owned Enterprises.

In addition to a heightened emphasis on RBC and integrity, the state might want to take a further step toward ensuring long-term sustainable development. As an important enterprise owner it could integrate broader objectives such as, for instance, climate, inclusion and digital transformation considerations in its ownership practices. The effect can be magnified by integrating such objectives into SOEs' procurement criteria, as well as their supply chains more generally. However, if governments choose to go in this direction care must be taken to avoid conflicts with commonly agreed good practices for public procurement, competition and non-discrimination in international trade and investment.

References

Abate, C., A. Elgouacem, T. Kozluk, J. Stráský and C. Vitale (2020), "State ownership will gain importance as a result of COVID-19", policy paper issued by VoxEU and CEPR, 7 July 2020, https://voxeu.org/article/state-ownership-will-gain-importance-result-covid-19.

Benoit, P. (2019), "Engaging State-Owned Enterprises in Climate Action," Centre on Global Energy Policy, Colombia SIPA. https://energypolicy.columbia.edu/research/report/engaging-state-owned-enterprises-climate-action.

Christiansen, H. (2013), "Balancing Commercial and Non-Commercial Priorities of State-Owned Enterprises", *OECD Corporate Governance Working Papers, No. 6*, OECD Publishing. http://dx.doi.org/10.1787/5k4dkhztkp9r-en.

Hodges, C. (2016), "Ethical Business Regulation: Understanding the Evidence", UK Department for Business Innovation & Skills, Monograph.

IEA (2020a), Share of state-owned energy investments by economy type and sector, 2019, IEA, Paris https://www.iea.org/data-and-statistics/charts/share-of-state-owned-energy-investments-by-economy-type-and-sector-2019

IEA (2020b), World Energy Investment 2020, IEA, Paris https://www.iea.org/reports/world-energy-investment-2020

IMF (2019), *IMF Working Paper WP/19/253,* "Governance and State-owned enterprises: How costly is corruption?" https://www.imf.org/en/Publications/WP/Issues/2019/11/22/Governance-and-State-Owned-Enterprises-How-Costly-is-Corruption-48800.

OECD (2020a), *Implementing the OECD Guidelines on Corporate Governance of State-Owned Enterprises: Review of Recent Developments,* OECD Publishing, Paris, https://doi.org/10.1787/4caa0c3b-en.

OECD (2020b) "Equity injections and unforeseen state ownership of Enterprises during the COVID-19 crisis", Paris. https://read.oecd-ilibrary.org/view/?ref=131_131932-wj071ujbxy&title=Equity-injections-and-unforeseen-state-ownership-of-enterprises-during-the-COVID-19-crisis.

OECD (2020c), "Shaping Government interventions for a faster and more resilient economic recovery", Statement by the OECD Secretary-General [link to be provided].

OECD (2020d), *Behavioural Insights and Organisations: Fostering Safety Culture,* http://www.oecd.org/gov/regulatory-policy/behavioural-insights-and-organisations-e6ef217d-en.htm.

OECD (2020 - forthcoming), Responsible business conduct in state-owned enterprise sector: Stocktaking of national practices, OECD Publishing, Paris.

OECD (2020- forthcoming), “Transparency and Disclosure Practices of State-Owned Enterprises and their Owners,” OECD Publishing, Paris.

OECD (2019), *Guidelines on Anti-Corruption and Integrity in State-Owned Enterprises,* Paris www.oecd.org/corporate/oecd-guidelines-anti-corruption-integrity-state-owned-enterprises.htm..

OECD (2018a), *Ownership and Governance of State-Owned Enterprises: A Compendium of National Practices*, http://www.oecd.org/corporate/ca/Ownership-and-Governance-of-State-Owned-Enterprises-A-Compendium-of-National-Practices.pdf.

OECD (2018b), *State-Owned Enterprises and Corruption: What Are the Risks and What Can Be Done?* Paris, https://doi.org/10.1787/9789264303058-en.

OECD (2017), The Size and Sectoral Distribution of State-Owned Enterprises, OECD Publishing, Paris, https://doi.org/10.1787/9789264280663-en.

OECD (2015), *OECD Guidelines on Corporate Governance of State-Owned Enterprises*, 2015 Edition, OECD Publishing, Paris, http://dx.doi.org/10.1787/9789264244160-en.

OECD (2014), *The Governance of Regulators*, https://www.oecd.org/gov/regulatory-policy/the-governance-of-regulators-9789264209015-en.htm.

OECD (2012a), *Competitive Neutrality: Maintaining a level playing field between public and private business,* https://www.oecd.org/competition/competitiveneutralitymaintainingalevelplayingfieldbetweenpublicandprivatebusiness.htm.

OECD (2012b), Recommendation of the Council on Regulatory Policy and Governance, https://www.oecd.org/governance/regulatory-policy/49990817.pdf.

OECD (2011), Guidelines for Multinational Enterprises, http://www.oecd.org/daf/inv/mne/48004323.pdf.

Prag, A., D. Röttgers and I. Scherrer (2018), "State-Owned Enterprises and the Low-Carbon Transition", OECD Environment Working Papers, No. 129, OECD Publishing, Paris, https://doi.org/10.1787/06ff826b-en.

Notes

[1] Public sector ownership is defined as ownership through direct government ownership or through sovereign wealth funds, public pension funds and state-owned enterprises.

[2] OECD plus is defined as 39 countries, including the portfolios of large G20 countries such as India, Brazil, Saudi Arabia.

[3] OECD (2012b) provides insights on OECD’s position regarding good standards for regulatory policies.

[4] The concerns about the methodology applied to ESG scorecard methodologies expressed elsewhere in this Outlook. However, in the present chapter the purpose of the exercises is more narrowly defined as monitoring public perceptions of different companies’ performance.

[5] The geographic distribution of the SOEs is: China 242; Persian Gulf 48; other Asia 80; Europe 87; rest of the world 37.

[6] One might ideally want to analyse a breakdown of SOEs both by regions and sector, but the underlying sample (494 state-owned companies) is too limited to allow meaningful conclusions.

[7] This is further supported by the school of thought referred to as "Ethical Business Regulation" (for further details, see Hodges, 2016).

[8] As mentioned elsewhere this body of evidence is summarised in OECD (2018).

[9] An early such study was conducted by Christiansen (2013).

[10] The 39 countries cover: Argentina, Australia, Austria, Brazil, Canada, Chile, Colombia, Costa Rica, Czech Republic, Denmark, Estonia, Finland, France, Germany, Greece, Hungary, Iceland, India, Ireland, Israel, Italy, Japan, Korea, Latvia, Lithuania, Mexico, the Netherlands, New Zealand, Norway, Poland, Saudi Arabia, the Slovak Republic, Slovenia, Spain, Sweden, Switzerland, Turkey, the United Kingdom and the United States.

[11] The risk relates to the fact that investors cannot recoup their investment in such assets because climate or other related policies and market forces will curtail the economic life or otherwise limit the operations of the facility to the point of preventing a sufficient financial return.

[12] Prag et al. (2018).

[13] Moreover, research suggests that profitability tends to be higher in countries and economic sectors with less corruption and the impact appears more pronounced for SOEs. In a low corruption environment, SOEs can be as, or more, productive than private firms and reforms aimed at improving integrity and government oversight improve their performance underscoring the importance of anti-corruption and integrity initiatives (IMF, 2019).

[14] Moreover, large SOEs including German Deutsche Telekom, Norwegian Equinor (Statoil), Swedish and Finnish Telia, Italian ENI have all been sanctioned for violating Foreign Corrupt Practices Act in the last decade.

[15] In October 2019, the shares of Banco do Brasil fell 3.4 percent in one day, after the Brazilian press reported that it was being investigated as part of the anti-corruption operation "Car wash" and was accused of laundering bribes.

[16] Among the early beneficiaries of these schemes, alongside with the airlines, have been the automobile industries in some countries. This is discussed in OECD (2020b).

[17] Subsequently the Union issued a white paper detailing its approach to foreign governments' approach to subsidising SOEs, linking these to the application of European state aid rules to companies facing competition from such foreign SOEs (https://ec.europa.eu/commission/presscorner/detail/en/ip_20_1070).

[18] In terms of sound fiscal practices there should also be transparent and comprehensive reporting in the government's balance sheet showing any difference between the government's interventions cost (including borrowing) and the value of the assets these interventions create (loans or equity stakes).

[19] This point was developed in OECD (2020c).

[20] This is a variation of the argument for government interventions during the COVID-19 crisis: some activities were seen as "too important to be allowed to fail".

[21] For further information on the Project, see https://impactmanagementproject.com/.

7. ESG and institutional investment in infrastructure

The quality and design of infrastructure play a key role in shaping how we live, what we do, and how we interact in almost every aspect of life. It determines economic structures and outcomes, social systems, personal well-being, and environmental impact, as well as development pathways. Policy makers are increasingly aware of the contribution environmental, social and governance (ESG) and broader sustainability factors make in ensuring quality infrastructure investment.

As institutional investors gain exposure to infrastructure through their portfolio investments, there is increasing recognition that ESG factors are relevant for their infrastructure investments. However, there are challenges in implementation, due in part to the particularities of infrastructure markets. This chapter analyses the growing use of ESG criteria in institutional investment in infrastructure, including investor motivations and objectives, as well as ESG frameworks and tools and related implementation issues. It concludes by offering options for the way forward.

7.1. Introduction

As the COVID-19 crisis has highlighted, infrastructure systems such as healthcare, power, water and sanitation, transport, and telecommunications provide essential services, contributing to economic and social activity and promoting broader economic and social resilience. Yet they can be vulnerable to shocks and stresses, particularly as they are often organised in complex networks through which even small local shocks can propagate quickly (OECD, 2019c). Disruptions to, and stresses on, infrastructure can amplify chronic infrastructure challenges such as underfunding, poor maintenance, and mismanagement.

Extreme weather, water and other climate-related events are increasing in frequency and severity, and a focus on trying to limit their impact through adaptation measures has become essential.[1] According to a recent study, the frequency of coastal flooding is set to rise by around 50% over the next 80 years and could threaten human lives and habitat, in addition to affecting assets worth 20% of global gross domestic product (Kirezci, E. et al., 2020). These developments will have implications for infrastructure assets, which may be impacted.

Institutional investors have been increasingly seeking to make allocations to infrastructure, largely driven by a search for enhanced diversification and yield. This has occurred while governments have – given limits on public investment – made efforts to mobilise institutional capital for sustainable and resilient infrastructure investment, to address the need to renew or build infrastructure, especially in emerging markets. From an investor point of view, particularly institutional investors who typically have long investment horizons, the long-lived nature of infrastructure assets exposes them to risks of disruption over time, often arising from environmental, social and governance (ESG) factors. If not managed and mitigated, these risks may ultimately impact the performance of an asset and the rate of return for investors.

Chapter 4 concludes that pension funds and insurance companies are increasingly choosing to integrate ESG factors in their investment decisions but that major challenges remain. Major barriers to ESG integration are also obstacles to the elaboration of better risk management strategies for investors and the allocation of finance to infrastructure investments. As infrastructure investing exhibits different characteristics from other asset classes, this chapter looks at specific barriers to ESG investment and analysis.

ESG factors often lie beyond the time horizons of investors and policy misalignments or market failures (such as the disconnection of risk pricing) do not provide correct market signals.[2] Specific to private markets and infrastructure, further complications include the capabilities and expertise of investors, potential short termism due to market structures (for example, the principal-agent issue between asset owners and asset managers), and a lack of financial data and track records on the financial and ESG performance of infrastructure projects.

ESG factors can present risks across the infrastructure lifecycle – from the pre-construction phase through to the operational phase – for financing providers, from banks to asset managers and institutional investors. Furthermore, the central role of infrastructure in economic and social activity, and its broader environmental and social impacts, may serve to accentuate ESG risks, by introducing policy, regulatory, and reputational risks. While focusing on the financing of infrastructure by institutional investors, this chapter leverages the expertise and views of different stakeholders (engineering, academic and policy) beyond the investor community.

The first section discusses the growing relevance of ESG for quality infrastructure investment and the increasing role of institutional investors in infrastructure investment. The second section analyses the range of motivations for institutional investors to consider the adoption of an ESG lens for their infrastructure investments. The third section describes the large number of ESG frameworks and tools applicable to infrastructure that can assist institutional investors. The final section describes sustainable investment strategies for infrastructure being adopted by institutional investors, with a focus on large pension funds and their "green" investments and low-carbon infrastructure investments. Selected directions for the way forward are provided at the end, including further research, data, and policy actions.

7.2. The relevance of ESG factors and institutional capital in sustainable and quality infrastructure investment

7.2.1. Sustainable and quality infrastructure investment

The quality and design of infrastructure[3] play a key role in shaping how we live, what we do, and how we interact in almost every aspect of life. These aspects determine economic structures and outcomes, social systems, personal well-being, environmental impact as well as development pathways. Investment in sustainable and quality infrastructure, implemented through appropriate delivery mechanisms, and managed efficiently over the life cycle, contribute to economic development, and enable the achievement of ESG objectives and the Sustainable Development Goals (SDGs). In fact, goal 9 of the SDGs calls for the development of "quality, reliable, sustainable and resilient infrastructure, including regional and trans-border infrastructure, to support economic development and human well-being, with a focus on affordable and equitable access for all."

In developed economies, a significant share of existing infrastructure is reaching the end of its life cycle and is outdated or does not adequately meet today's requirements. This could be the result of obsolescence, economic growth, demographics, shifts in values, or environmental sustainability. In less developed economies, infrastructure investment needs to be scaled up, in some instances massively, in order to provide access to basic services like energy or drinking water, and to enable the flow of goods and people. Recent estimates show that emerging markets will invest an average of USD 2.2 trillion, or 3.9% of GDP, annually in infrastructure to 2040, close to double the aggregate spent in advanced markets over the same period (Swiss Re, 2020). Numerous estimates of the needs for global infrastructure investment all point to the need to increase investment in order to meet growth and sustainability targets.

Responses to the COVID-19 shock for economies and societies are expected to include renewed infrastructure investment as a stimulus measure. This presents an opportunity to steer the infrastructure sector onto a more resilient and sustainable path, avoiding a 'lock-in' of fossil fuel infrastructure and carbon-intensive assets. The IEA estimates that an additional USD 1.1 trillion will need to be invested annually in both supplying power and altering how end users consume power between now and 2040 to meet the IEA Sustainable Development Scenario (IEA, 2018).

While serving as a key means to achieve sustainable development, infrastructure, in both its construction and operation, needs to consider changing community expectations, the increasing power of civil society and social connectivity, as well as potential new legal requirements, all of which add to the complexity of delivering infrastructure projects (Valenzuela et al., 2016; Watkins et al., 2017). Strong community opposition – often due to ESG considerations – can result in delays and cause changes in project scope,[4] and prove costly – and potentially be material – for investors. In May 2020, work on the upgrade of the A49 road in Germany was halted due to environmental concerns. Turkey's megaproject Canal Istanbul has hit a major roadblock over environmental and economic concerns. In July 2020, the works on the expansion of Lisbon's airport and the conversion of the Montijo airbase in Portugal were halted due to strong opposition.[5] In February 2020, as part of a judicial review, the Court of Appeal of England and Wales ruled that the British government's decision to expand Heathrow was "unlawful", on climate change grounds, following a legal challenge.[6]

The importance of ESG and broader sustainability objectives and elements in infrastructure investment is increasingly being recognised at the international level by policy makers, as part of a broader consensus on the ingredients of quality infrastructure investment. Notably, the recently adopted *G20 Principles for Quality Infrastructure Investment* set out a set of voluntary, non-binding principles that reflect a common strategic direction and aspiration for quality infrastructure investment within the G20, which are: (i) Maximising the positive impact of infrastructure to achieve sustainable growth and development; (ii) Raising economic efficiency in view of life-cycle cost; (iii) Integrating environmental considerations in infrastructure investments (iv) Building resilience against natural disasters and other risks; (v) Integrating social considerations in infrastructure investment; and (vi) Strengthening infrastructure governance[7]. This increasing consensus at the policy level may translate into reputational risks and pressures for investors expected to meet heightened ESG expectations.

7.2.2. Institutional investors' investment in infrastructure

As governments make efforts to promote sustainable and quality infrastructure investment, they are also seeking to mobilise private capital to meet large infrastructure investment needs, and thereby achieve more ambitious development, sustainability, and resiliency objectives. While infrastructure investment is generally dominated by the public sector, public budgets are limited and private capital is needed to compliment public investment. Over the years, institutional investors (which include pension funds, insurers, and sovereign wealth funds) have been making allocations to infrastructure, largely driven by a search for enhanced diversification and yield. The infrastructure financing market has in fact gone through a radical transformation since 2005. A number of factors, such as a changed macroeconomic environment, more stringent regulations on financial intermediaries, and a modified appetite for long-term asset investments, have led to a reallocation of flows from the banking sector to the institutional investors sector.

Shifting market trends and growing demand for infrastructure across developed and emerging markets, have resulted in increased private sector participation through both debt and, increasingly, direct equity investment to supplement public capital. Unlisted equity investments have created pathways to directly influence infrastructure project development and outcomes. In public markets, investors can typically access infrastructure through the equity of companies which are exposed to infrastructure such as utilities, energy or transport companies. In recent years, new investment vehicles (e.g. indices, mutual funds, ETFs) have been created for those not able or willing to make their own investment.

When looking at specific infrastructure allocation, it has been through unlisted equity vehicles that the characteristics of the infrastructure asset class have been formulated. As of December 2019, the infrastructure fund industry holds USD 631 billion in infrastructure assets, up from just USD 129 billion at the end of 2009 (see (Preqin (2020) and (Figure 7.1). Totals in 2018 and 2019 both approached USD 100 billion – a substantial increase compared with full-year fundraising of USD 17 billion back in 2009. This is causing major challenges and highlighting structural issues in the market, including competition for limited quality assets and overconcentration of the largest infrastructure funds.

Figure 7.1. Private capital assets under management by asset class, 2009 - 2019

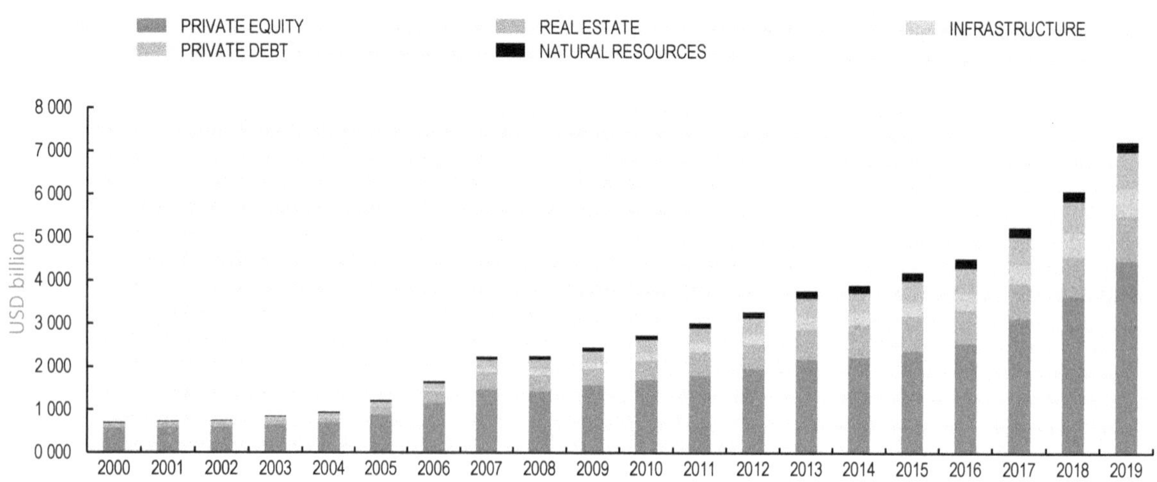

Source Preqin (2020).

In private markets, direct investment is a common method for pension funds to gain exposure to infrastructure, especially amongst large funds that have the size and expertise to manage assets directly. However, as the overall pension market is highly fragmented, many smaller funds do not possess the staff or expertise to directly manage assets. Hiring external consultants and asset managers to manage infrastructure investment is the preferred route to access this asset class. Principal-agent issues between short-term private equity asset managers and long-term asset owners could create disincentives for the adoption of ESG factors in the investment process. This is particularly relevant for the unlisted infrastructure equity market where a number of infrastructure funds have adopted the private equity incentive structure that usually only allows for an investment holding period of 4-5 years in order to make the most of the financial rewards of this vehicle (Clark, G.L. and A.H.B. Monk, 2017 and Bennon M. and R. Sharma, 2018).

The momentum toward greater involvement of institutional investors in infrastructure investment continues. For instance, at the start of 2020, with over 250 infrastructure funds collectively seeking more than USD 200 billion from investors - double the total capital targeted at the start of 2015 - strong growth in infrastructure AUM is expected to continue (Preqin, 2020). Ultimately the primary concern for institutional investors **is the investment performance** in the context of their specific objectives (such as paying pensions and annuities). Infrastructure can keep growing as an alternative asset class for private investors provided that investors can access bankable projects and an acceptable risk/return profile is offered.

7.3. ESG and institutional investment in infrastructure

The growth of institutional investment in infrastructure in recent years has been accompanied by an increased effort to apply ESG considerations from other portfolio investments (e.g. investments in publicly traded companies) to infrastructure assets, for those investors with ESG investment decision-making processes in place. The 2019 edition of the EDHEC/GIH survey of over 300 infrastructure investors revealed that close to half of the surveyed investors (asset owners, asset managers) are at least somewhat aware (48%) or very aware (42%) of the ESG characteristics of their infrastructure investments, leaving just under 10% unaware. The ESG approaches followed by investors will vary depending on how the infrastructure investment is accessed. Infrastructure investments can be undertaken in public markets through investment in the stocks and bonds of infrastructure corporates, or in listed infrastructure funds, and through the private markets through direct investments or unlisted funds, and through equity and debt.

In the absence of an understanding in the industry of how ESG factors affect infrastructure returns (see further below), it appears that infrastructure investors use these factors as a tool for ***managing ESG-related risks***, in particular to obtain downside protection. As shown in Figure 7.2 below, ESG factors feature as key sources of risk for infrastructure projects, for instance through the channel of social acceptance, the governance and management of projects, and environmental characteristics and impacts. The long lifespan of infrastructure assets, the central role of infrastructure in economies and societies, and its impact on the environment and communities, mean that ESG factors can present risks across the infrastructure lifecycle and can generate political, regulatory, and reputational risks (e.g. adverse change in regulation). The growing support for ESG and sustainability factors in quality infrastructure investment at the policy level may heighten expectations in regard to infrastructure projects from an ESG perspective.

As investors with a typically long-term horizon, institutional investors have a particular incentive to consider ESG risks in infrastructure, which may materialise in the medium to long-term. This long-term horizon stems from the generally long-dated nature of pension fund and life insurer liabilities, which they seek to match with investments with similar duration, which unlisted (brownfield) infrastructure investments can offer due to their long-term and often stable cash flows. Yet the long holding period creates a long-term exposure to investment risks, requiring investors to consider all long-term risk factors, financial or non-financial (including ESG), that can impact the performance of their portfolios over time and the delivery of payouts. An example of an ESG risk matrix for infrastructure investment can be found in Figure 7.3 below which presents a matrix used by an asset manager to identify "material ESG risks and opportunities" at the sectoral level, a tool complemented by a customised asset-level questionnaire.

Figure 7.2. Classification of risks linked to infrastructure assets

<table>
<tr><th>Risk Categories</th><th>Development Phase</th><th>Construction Phase</th><th>Operation Phase</th><th>Termination Phase</th></tr>
<tr><td rowspan="8">Political and regulatory</td><td>Environmental review</td><td>Cancellation of permits</td><td rowspan="3">Change in tariff regulation</td><td>Contract duration</td></tr>
<tr><td rowspan="3">Rise in pre-construction costs (longer permitting process)</td><td rowspan="3">Contract renegotiation</td><td>Decommission</td></tr>
<tr><td>Asset transfer</td></tr>
<tr><td colspan="2">Currency convertibility</td></tr>
<tr><td colspan="4">Change in taxation</td></tr>
<tr><td colspan="4">Social acceptance</td></tr>
<tr><td colspan="4">Change in regulatory or legal environment</td></tr>
<tr><td colspan="4">Enforceability of contracts, collateral and security</td></tr>
<tr><td rowspan="7">Macroeconomic and business</td><td>Prefunding</td><td colspan="3">Default of counterparty</td></tr>
<tr><td colspan="2" rowspan="3">Financing availability</td><td colspan="2">Refinancing risk</td></tr>
<tr><td colspan="2">Liquidity</td></tr>
<tr><td colspan="2">Volatility of demand/market risk</td></tr>
<tr><td colspan="4">Inflation</td></tr>
<tr><td colspan="4">Real interest rates</td></tr>
<tr><td colspan="4">Exchange rate fluctuation</td></tr>
<tr><td rowspan="6">Technical</td><td colspan="3">Governance and management of the project</td><td rowspan="5">Termination value different from expected</td></tr>
<tr><td colspan="3">Environmental</td></tr>
<tr><td>Project feasibility</td><td rowspan="2">Construction delays and cost overruns</td><td rowspan="2">Qualitative deficit of the physical structure/ service</td></tr>
<tr><td>Archaeological</td></tr>
<tr><td colspan="3">Technology and obsolescence</td></tr>
<tr><td colspan="4">Force majeure</td></tr>
</table>

Note: OECD (2015) provides a description of the taxonomy of infrastructure risks at the project level.
Source: OECD (2015).

Figure 7.3. Example of ESG risk analysis for infrastructure >

Environment	Social	Governance
• GHG emissions • Air quality • Energy management • Water and wastewater management • Waste and hazardous materials management • Ecological impacts • Physical impacts of climate change	• Health and safety • Employee engagement, diversity, and inclusion • Human rights and community relations • Customer privacy • Access and affordability • Product quality and safety	• Materials sourcing and efficiency • Business ethics • Supply chain management • Competitive behavior • Critical incident risk management

Source: Shroders (2019).

While there is increased investor interest in adopting ESG approaches, the linkage between ESG factors in infrastructure and infrastructure investment risks and returns is not well understood, and the literature is nascent (see Box 7.1). Some findings from the general ESG literature may be relevant; for instance, in regard to energy infrastructure, the shares of renewables over the past decade offered higher total returns relative to fossil fuels, with lower annualised volatility (a measure of investment risk) (IEA and Imperial College, 2020).[8]

Recent OECD discussions with asset managers[9] active in infrastructure investments, and creating infrastructure funds for institutional investors, revealed a consensus on the view that ESG factors are essential for effective risk management of infrastructure assets (especially to protect against downside risks), to preserve and enhance asset value over time (see also OECD, 2020a). It was regarded that consideration of ESG factors or other sustainability considerations in infrastructure is still underdeveloped relative to other asset classes. The environmental aspect is reportedly the most concrete, whereas "S" & "G" measures are less clearly defined. It was noted though that "S" and "G" components are already embedded in regulatory mechanisms governing infrastructure development. These discussions also revealed the limits on the management of ESG risks in infrastructure; as institutional investors often acquire assets after they are built (i.e. brownfield infrastructure), there may be limited scope for them to influence ESG factors, highlighting the importance of incorporating such factors upfront in infrastructure procurement decision-making and the need for investors to including these factors in investor due diligence.

Another key driver includes ***regulatory requirements*** related to ESG that have increased the adoption of ESG considerations in infrastructure investment. Funds are also adjusting to new regulations in some markets that seek to clarify the role of ESG in a fund's investment process. This is part of a broader policy and regulatory push to clarify and disclose climate-related risks in the financial sector, which provides an indirect push for asset owners (and asset managers, who may manage their investments) to consider climate and other ESG-related risk factors, given potential exposures through their investments.

Box 7.1. ESG and infrastructure investment performance

The impact of ESG factors on financial performance is a central issue in the debate around sustainable investment. The long-term nature of infrastructure investments implies a potential major impact of sustainability and resilience-related risks.

Some studies suggest ESG approaches tend to reduce risks and generate higher returns through an 'ESG factor' driving the performance of companies (see Amundi, 2019). For example, Fuerst (2015) regressed Global Real Estate Sustainability Benchmark (GRESB) scores on various REIT financial indicators such as ROA and ROE in order to test the link between sustainability and financial performance. The study found that there was a positive relationship between sustainability score and the profitability of real estate companies. The study attributed these results through gains in operating performance, efficiency, and lowering risk exposures.

While analysis in this Outlook finds mixed evidence on the impact of ESG performance on financial performance broadly (see Chapter 1), the long asset life cycles and investor timelines may expose infrastructure assets to particular ESG risks which are material to investors. However, data on infrastructure is often lacking and not comparable as it not being reported in a standardised format or audited by companies' auditors. Also, the same company can receive divergent ESG ratings, due to problems of inconsistency of criteria and misrepresentation through one single metric of the impact of multiple ESG factors.

As reporting is still immature, scoring has focused on firm's management approach and transparency of performance rather than direct performance. A recent study by EDHEC cross-references for the first time the ESG scores computed by GRESB Infrastructure and the financial metrics of the EDHEC infra universe, showing that ESG ratings are not positively or negatively correlated with returns, suggesting that the adoption of ESG investment approaches should not harm returns (no trade-offs) but also challenging the notion that ESG is a risk factor (EDHEC, 2020).

These regulations and policy initiatives have put added pressure on the investment community to improve ESG reporting and have also forced investors to consider long-term risks associated with ESG factors, including future regulations or policies that might impact their infrastructure assets. A growing number of investors concerned with the potential impact of sustainability on their long-term financial performance are involved in initiatives on voluntary disclosure of ESG practices.

A number of countries have put into place reporting requirements on disclosure of ESG practices by institutional investors, which may have implications for the application of ESG practices to infrastructure investments held within portfolios. For instance, Australia requires pension funds, insurance companies, and asset managers to disclose their ESG practices. France has introduced the most far-reaching requirements in terms of ESG reporting by institutional investors. Under Article 173-VI of the *Energy Transition Act*, asset managers, pension funds and insurance companies must provide information not only on how they integrate ESG factors in their investment and voting decisions but also on the climate risks they face and how their portfolio construction contributes to the transition to a low-carbon economy.

Furthermore, the adoption of ESG factors in infrastructure investment is enabling institutional investors with an impact orientation to screen and select projects, funds, and companies, and ***align their infrastructure investments with sustainability objectives***, consistent with return objectives. This alignment may be one of principle but it may also be motivated by a view on sectoral growth opportunities or as a way to avoid or manage certain types of risks, such asset stranding.

7.4. Frameworks and tools for ESG analysis for infrastructure

A number of infrastructure investors are turning to more directly measuring the impact of their investment portfolios for unlisted infrastructure projects. This is following similar trends seen for the use of ESG analysis for listed equity (see Chapters 1 and 4). ESG investment analysis strategies involve benchmark ESG performance, as well as the impact of ESG criteria on financial returns. While the main focus of this chapter is on institutional investors, standards adopted and developed by engineering firms and government agencies are also considered.[10]

Several international standards and tools have been developed in order to integrate sustainability and resilience aspects into infrastructure development and support ESG infrastructure asset analysis:

- **Standards and Frameworks related to ESG factors for Infrastructure**: International frameworks providing guidance on relevant criteria to be considered in ESG analysis for infrastructure investment (OECD, 2017; WWF, 2019).
- **Tools for Infrastructure:** defined broadly as checklists, guidelines software, and web-based platforms for analysing specified inputs (ESG data) in ESG infrastructure analysis. Outputs (rating, certification, or financial figure) can be qualitative or quantitative (LTIIA, 2020; WWF, 2019).

Several international standards and frameworks are used to determine ESG factors, covering a broad spectrum ranging from sustainable and resilient investment to SRI and impact investment. Among the most used are: the Sustainable Development Goals (SDGs), the IFC Performance Standards, Sustainable Accounting Standards Board (SASB), the International Organization for Standardization (ISO), the International Framework for Integrated Reporting (IR), the Global Reporting Initiative (GRI), and the UN-supported Principles for Responsible Investing (PRI), among others (see Annex 7.A.1).

While there has been growing recognition of the importance of measuring ESG factors in infrastructure, adoption of third-party ESG tools by investors has been limited, partly due to investor preference for internally developed methodologies for ESG analysis. However, as private markets do not have the same disclosure requirements as listed markets, institutional investors must rely significantly more on their asset managers and other service providers to track their exposure and performance. This has implications for the availability of information and explains the lack of evidence-based studies in this area.

In recent years, and building on the frameworks described above, a number of **tools** have been developed to support infrastructure investors and developers in the implementation and monitoring of ESG factors in investment analysis, with the aim of producing a rating, certification, or financial impact assessment (among others Sure, GRESB, Envision - see Table 7.1 below). A recent review by WWF (2019) makes the following distinctions:

- **Evaluation tools**: assessing the ESG performance of an asset; and/or an assessment of quantitative and qualitative ESG criteria, which may be reported as a set of information, and which typically results in a score or rating. Evaluation tools can be useful during the due diligence process, for benchmarking investments or projects, as a tool for reporting and stewardship, and for considering how a project addresses various ESG criteria across a portfolio.
- **Valuation tools**: quantifying the selected ESG criteria in a way that can be integrated into a financial model: assigning a monetary value to an ESG risk or benefit, which is then incorporated into a financial model. For example, ESG valuation may involve incorporating ESG metrics into a cost-benefit analysis, net present value calculations, or discounted cash flow models.

Table 7.1. ESG tools for infrastructure

Tool	Description	Evaluation/Valuation Output
SuRe (1) Standard for Sustainable and Resilient Infrastructure	A voluntary standard which integrates sustainability and resilience aspects into infrastructure development and upgrade. SuRe consists of 63 criteria divided into 14 themes spanning environmental, social and governance (ESG) aspects.	Evaluation output: certification
Envision (2)	A rating system for sustainable infrastructure. It provides a framework for evaluating and rating the community, environmental, and economic benefits of infrastructure projects during the planning and design phase, as well as when projects are finished.	Evaluation output: certification
CEEQUAL	International evidence-based sustainability assessment, rating and awards scheme for civil engineering.	Evaluation output: score/ rating
GRESB Infrastructure Assessment	GRESB Infrastructure provides systematic assessment, objective scoring, and peer benchmarking for environmental, social, and governance (ESG) performance of infrastructure companies and funds. It is specifically targeted towards institutional investors as it allows them to request ESG reporting from investments.	Evaluation output: rating
Rep Risk	RepRisk uses data science to perform due diligence on material ESG risks. They intentionally exclude company self-disclosures because of its unreliability and use what they call an "outside-in" approach.	Evaluation output: score/ rating
ISCA	A tool developed by ISCA in collaboration with the industry to drive and measure sustainability within infrastructure projects and assets – both to existing infrastructure and infrastructure in the planning stages.	Evaluation output: score/ rating
SAVi	SAVi is an assessment methodology that provides policy-makers and investors with a comprehensive analysis of how much their infrastructure projects and portfolios will cost throughout their life cycles, taking into account risks that are overlooked in a traditional valuation. SAVi also calculates the dollar value of externalities that result from infrastructure investment.	Valuation Output: Financial performance
TREDIS	TREDIS is a transportation economics suite that covers all modes of transport, incorporating wider economic benefits and employing a dynamic economic simulation. It is mostly used in the US and Canada, and is being expanded into Australia. It includes modules on travel costs, market access, benefit-cost analysis, economic adjustment analysis, a financial analysis, and freight and trade.	Valuation Output: Financial performance
AUTOCASE	Uses cost-benefit analysis to calculate triple bottom line metrics (social, financial, and environmental)	Valuation Output: Financial performance
Zofnass	A platform to understand sustainability externalities in infrastructure projects, so as to promote the implementation of sustainable strategies.	Valuation Output: Financial performance

1) http://www.gib-foundation.org/content/uploads/2017/01/SuRev0.3final.pdf\
2) https://sustainableinfrastructure.org/envision/
Source: LTIIA (2020), WWF (2019)

Despite the number of initiatives, several problems regarding the measurement of ESG factors in infrastructure persist (see also Chapter 1). Among the major issues are: a lack of a common definition and metric for measuring exposure to ESG risks in infrastructure; the heterogeneity of the infrastructure landscape; the lack of quality data and information required to perform analyses; the ability to quantify and monetise ESG criteria; transparency in valuation methodologies across the industry; investors' understanding and confidence in ESG valuation; and the costs of ESG analysis (LTIIA, 2020; WWF, 2019; Bennon M. and and R. Sharma, 2018; Garcia S. and T. Whittaker, 2019).

ESG scores might be inconsistent in terms of environment, social and governance weightings and inclusion. It will also be important to promote concrete alignment in sustainability expectations considering the multitude of stakeholders involved. The experience with responsible business conduct principles and standards can be useful in this regard.[11]

7.4.1. ESG classification for infrastructure

Analyses for understanding ESG-related risks and benefits vary among actors and between phases in the infrastructure process, sub-sectors and specific topics, asset or fund level, and impact on the asset or from the asset.

Current methods for ESG measurement and ESG-related analysis for infrastructure can also be categorised based on:

- The actors – ESG frameworks and tools are used to inform the decision-making of infrastructure investors, developers, procuring entities and civil society organisations
- The project phase – ESG frameworks and tools are adopted throughout infrastructure investment lifecycles
- The sectors, sub-sectors and specific topics – ESG frameworks and tools have been developed to address all classes of investments or specific sectors and sub-sectors in order to address their specificities (e.g. biodiversity and climate change matters)
- Asset or fund – analysis of ESG risks can be at project level or fund and portfolio level
- Impact on the asset or from the asset – infrastructure assets face several external (originated outside the asset) and internal (inherent to the asset) ESG factors

A number of institutions are involved in sustainability measurement throughout the value chain (see Figure 7.4).

Figure 7.4. Infrastructure investment value chain

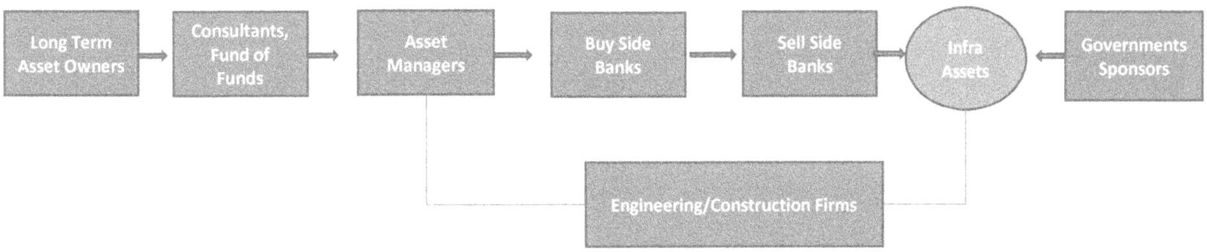

Source: Bennon M. and R. Sharma. (2018)

As project initiators, public sector actors (governments, procuring authorities and multilateral organisations) are more active in greenfield projects with assets being constructed for the first time and could be involved at the planning, development or construction stage. Taking into consideration externalities (negative and positive) resulting from a project, these actors are more likely to use valuation techniques to incorporate ESG criteria into their financial analyses. Developers, construction and engineering firms also active in greenfield projects are also accustomed to using sustainability standards in their project analysis.

Investors' use of infrastructure accounting or rating tools, however, covers management practices and performance indicators of assets already in operation or at the stage of being approved for construction. In fact, the majority of institutional investors such as pension funds insurers and SWFs invest predominantly in brownfield assets (i.e. existing assets that are already operational and have low capex requirements). Sustainability standards may be incorporated directly by asset owners or by asset managers or consultants reporting to asset owners, during due diligence and IRR analyses and NPV calculations.

In the development phase, ESG analyses are used to guide project planning and design. ESG metrics may be incorporated into feasibility studies and cost benefit analyses (CBAs) of procuring entities in deciding whether to initiate a project. The development phase can be further divided into planning, design and finance with different coverage by screening tools as reviewed recently by AECOM for sustainability, climate and resilience for infrastructure. The lack of due diligence has been an issue in project preparation with direct consequences on human rights, as analysed by OHCHR-HBF (2018).

With respect to emerging market investment, funds often partner with entities with a track-record of managing such risks, such as development finance institutions. For example, AllianzGI established one of the first International Finance Corporation (IFC) partnership funds through which AllianzGI invests in IFC-originated and managed infrastructure loan assets. Deals in some emerging economies may also need certain explicit covenants, such as demanding that all parties adhere to the minimum social and environmental standards set out in the IFC Performance Standards on Environmental and Social Sustainability and the Equator Principles.

Another important distinction for ESG analysis relates to impacts on the asset versus impacts from the asset (see WWF (2019) and AECOM (2017) for examples):

- ESG criteria with impacts on the asset include risks and benefits posed by the local or regional context in which the asset is being developed that either enable or inhibit the performance of the infrastructure asset (for example policy or regulatory context, social climate, or vulnerability to extreme weather events)
- ESG criteria related to impacts from the asset - externalities - include risks and benefits that the infrastructure asset generates on the external environment and community, which can in turn impact financial performance (impacts from the asset on biodiversity, health, or macroeconomic indicators such as employment that can impact long term cash flows of the infrastructure asset).

Box 7.2. Hydroelectric power station case study

Hydroelectric power may be considered one of the cleanest forms of energy accounting for the production of almost two-thirds of global renewable energy, according to the International Hydropower Association (IHA). However many big dam projects around the world have turned into ecological, economic and social disasters. This makes them good case studies for the application and use of ESG standards and tools. This case study provides an example of "best practice" according to the LTIIA ESG Handbook.

Case Study - 420 MW hydro dam project, Nachtigal - Cameroon

Since 2018, alongside Électricité de France (EDF), the Cameroonian State, the International Finance Corporation (IFC) and Africa 50, STOA has been investing in the construction of a large hydroelectric dam in Cameroon. The project, led by the Cameroonian company Nachtigal Hydro Power Company (NHPC), aims to develop the supply of electricity in the country. The objective is to build and operate a 420-megawatt hydroelectric dam in Nachtigal, a village located 65 kilometers from the capital Yaoundé.

When it is commissioned - planned for 2023 - the Nachtigal dam will be the largest dam developed on the African continent in project funding. It meets the demand for increased electricity in Cameroon while generating energy at a competitive cost. This low-carbon solution will also play a decisive role in the country's energy transition. Ultimately, nearly 850 kilotons of $CO2$ could be avoided each year on a national scale.

The environmental and social risks of the project are mitigated through an ambitious management system. This includes in particular a local economic development action plan and measures dedicated to biodiversity and social issues setting out IFC performance standards to protect but also avoid, reduce and compensate for the negative impacts of the project during the construction and development phases. With the support of IFC and specialised NGOs, NHPC trained its staff in the prevention of gender-based violence. In 2019, 29% of the company's employees are women, making it a flagship project on this subject in the world of infrastructure.

Source: LTIIA (2020).

7.5. Institutional investment in green investment and low-carbon infrastructure

The integration of ESG factors into investment decision-making and risk management, including for infrastructure investment, is part of a broader trend among institutional investors to adopt sustainable investment strategies, which also include divestment, corporate engagement, sustainability themed investment, and impact investing, among others. Sustainable investing assets stood at USD 30.7 trillion at the start of 2018, a 34% increase in two years, in certain regions it accounts for a sizeable share of professionally managed assets, from 18% in Japan to 63% in Australia and New Zealand (GSIA 2018).

Sustainable investments extend across the range of public and private asset classes commonly found in diversified investment portfolios. The latest Global Sustainable Investment Alliance (GSIA) report on sustainable assets shows that in 2018, 51% of total USD 31 trillion assets were allocated to public equities and 36% to fixed income with the remaining 13% in private markets in alternative asset classes such as real estate, private equity and infrastructure (Figure 7.5 and GSIA, 2018).[12] There are a variety of investors in sustainable investment with different objectives and mandates among the most active institutional investors such a pension funds and insurers. As Chapter 4 concludes, some investors examine ESG factors mainly via the risk management lens as an opportunity for higher financial returns, while others perceive ESG factors as non-financial objectives such as carbon emissions or other sustainability-performance targets that they wish to promote.

Figure 7.5. Global growth of sustainable investing strategies, 2016–2018

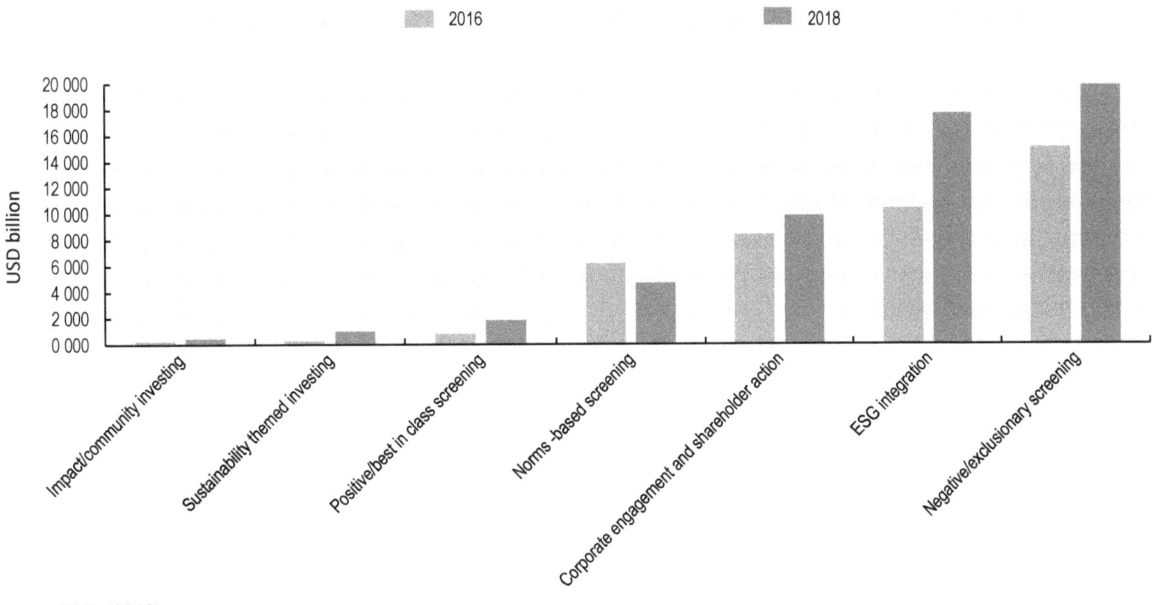

Source: GSIA (2018)

Corporate engagement and shareholder action is a popular and growing strategy among infrastructure investors in private markets. Infrastructure equity investors often have controlling stakes in the business, allowing significant scope in corporate engagement – limited though by the contractual nature of the services provided. Although a debt investor has less control over the operations of its assets compared to an equity investor, there are several ways debt can support equity to be more sustainable, including through setting conditions prior to funding and/or covenants related to the remediation of ESG risks. Projects may also need specific covenants related to environmental considerations, construction permitting, and post-closing remediation monitoring.

Relevant for infrastructure, the range of active strategies focused on sustainability as an investment outcome includes thematic and impact investing. Although starting from a low base they have known a huge growth in recent years with thematic investing accounting for USD 1 trillion in 2018, up from less than USD 280 billion in 2016 (GSIA 2018).[13] As noted in Chapter 4, environmental factor integration achieved via impact and thematic investing is relevant for infrastructure as it may include social infrastructure or renewable energy projects, green bonds and companies addressing environmental issues.

As the definition of infrastructure typically includes low-carbon projects, it is also important to understand current trends in investors' infrastructure portfolios related to sustainable and resilient investment. The OECD collects portfolio and infrastructure investment data through a survey of large pension funds (LPFs) and public pension reserve funds (PPRFs) (OECD, 2019a). These data include "green" and "social" investment and portfolio allocation to low-carbon infrastructure. The following sub-section reviews the investment trends in specific products, debt/equity instruments, or through specific mandates for green investment, with a brief analysis of the composition of infrastructure portfolios.[14] Green investment includes low-carbon infrastructure investment, which is also discussed in the survey.

7.5.1. Green investment

There are a variety of definitions of green investments, depending on investor standards. For the OECD survey of LPFs and PPRFs, examples of such investments include green equity indexes such as FTSE4Good, the S&P Global Eco Index, and the S&P Global Water Index; green bonds such as European Investment Bank climate awareness bonds, SEB Green Bonds, and Credit Suisse – World Bank/IFC Green Bonds; and alternative investments in real estate that are environmentally acceptable such as those that improve energy efficiency, reduce CO_2 emissions, or involve recycling (OECD, 2019a).

Funds have different approaches to green investments. For instance, while AIMCo (Canada) has no pre-determined target allocation for green investment, it tracks the percentage of its investments in renewable energy, its overall renewables exposure, and the climate change related impact of its investments. FFR (France) considers several green factors in its allocation decisions for both listed and non-listed investments, such as low-carbon indexes, environmental technology, infrastructure, clean technology, and the management of environmental issues. Furthermore, FRR targets a CO_2 emissions reduction of 50% in its listed equities mandates.

In 2019, sustainable debt issuance was nearly USD 450 billion, up from around USD 250 billion the year before, though it remains a fraction of overall debt issuance at just over 5% (IEA, 2020). New types of debt instruments are also linking financial performance to environmental outcomes. For example, interest rates for a USD 2.5 billion Enel bond issued in 2019 are tied to goals for renewables capacity and emissions levels. This overall growth was accompanied by an increase in the number of pension funds investing in green bonds and in the relative size of their allocations in, particular in Sweden, Belgium, and France.

Funds based in Austria, France, the Netherlands and Sweden reported sizeable allocations to green equities. PMT (the Netherlands) reported that approximately 30% of its portfolio in 2017 was green equities. The categorisation of its entire listed equity portfolio as "green" is the result of how it considers ESG factors in all of its investment decisions, including new investment strategies, product mandates, and investment proposals. France's ERAFP applies an ESG best-in-class approach to all equity mandates in 27.5% of its total portfolio. AP4 reported that 9.1% of its total portfolio was held in green equities, labelling this allocation as 'low-carbon' and 'ESG' strategies. For BCIMC, green equity refers to global equity securities whose ESG rating is high relative to sector peers.

Table 7.2. Detailed green investments of selected pension funds in 2017

As a % of total investment

Country head office	Name of the fund or institution	Total investments in 2017 (in USD m.)	Green investments (as a % of total investments)				
			Green equity	Green bonds	Alternative green asset classes (1)	Other green investments	Total green Investments
Australia	UniSuper Management Pty Ltd	48 694	4.2	0.3	0.7	..	5.2
Australia	Hostplus Superannuation Fund	22 640	..	..	..	1.5	1.5
Austria	VBV Pensionskasse AG	7 879	14.5	..	..	0.2	14.6
Belgium	EuroControl	1 888	4.3	4.7	..	..	9.0
Brazil	Banesprev	4 993	0.2	..	..	..	0.2
Brazil	Fundação Petrobras	21 681	..	..	..	0.3	0.3
Brazil	Previ	56 687			0.0	..	0.0
Brazil	Valia	6 701	3.7		0.2	..	4.0
Canada	AIMCo	82 613	0.4	0.0	..	..	0.5
Canada	Local Authorities Pension Plan	34 019	0.5	..	..	..	0.5
Canada	OTPP	147 750	..	..	0.9	..	0.9
Denmark	PFA Pension	76 949	0.5	..	1.1	..	1.6
Finland	Varma Mutual Pension Insurance Company (2)	54 347	17.0	0.7	..	..	17.7
France	FRR	43 724	18.1	0.6	0.2	..	18.9
Germany	BASF Pensionskasse	11 408	2.6	..	..	..	2.6
Iceland	Gildi Pension Fund	4 923	..	0.9	0.4	..	1.3
Iceland	Lifeyrissjodur Starfsmanna Rikisins	7 869	0.2	1.8	..	..	1.9
Japan	Pension Fund Association	109 053	..	0.1	..	..	0.1
Netherlands	PFZW	236 479	3.5	0.9	2.1	..	6.5
Netherlands	PME	55 887	36.2	0.4	0.9	..	37.5
Netherlands	PMT	83 377	33.0	0.3	0.2	..	33.6
Netherlands	Stichting Pensioenfonds ABP	545 464	1.1	1.0	1.2	4.4	7.7
New Zealand	New Zealand Superannuation Fund	26 837	..	..	..	6.2	6.2
Nigeria	RSA Fund	6 850	..	0.1	..	..	0.1
Norway	Government Pension Fund - Global	1 068 774	0.8	0.1	..	..	0.9
Romania	Azt Viitorul Tau	2 216	..	..	..	0.2	0.2
South Africa	GEPF	152 812	..	0.3	..	..	0.3
Spain	Endesa	2 092	..	0.6	..	..	0.6
Spain	Fonditel (3)	3 931	1.5	1.3	0.1	..	2.9
Spain	Santander	313	..	1.2	..	..	1.2
Sweden	Alecta	101 095	43.5	2.1	..	21.5	67.1
Sweden	AP1	40 511	..	0.5	..	..	0.5

Country head office	Name of the fund or institution	Total investments in 2017 (in USD m.)	Green investments (as a % of total investments)				
			Green equity	Green bonds	Alternative green asset classes (1)	Other green investments	Total green Investments
Sweden	AP2	42 000	1.6	1.5	5.8	3.4	12.5
Sweden	AP3	42 055	..	3.9	0.1	0.0	4.0
Sweden	AP4	43 453	13.4	1.3	..	..	14.7
Sweden	AP7	51 061	..	0.1	0.2	..	0.4
United Kingdom	USS (4)	87 060	..	..	0.1	..	0.1

Notes:".." means not available, or zero.
(1) Alternative green asset classes include hedge funds, natural resources, private equity, infrastructure, and inflation-linked bonds.
(2) All direct equity investments are "green", since investments are made under Varma's climate policy.
(3) Data refer to Fonditel's largest pension plan: Empleados de Telefónica de España.
(4) Data are as of March 2018.
Source: OECD calculations based on responses to OECD (2019a).

Beyond green bonds and green equity, some funds also reported holding alternative green investments, such as renewable energy and cleantech projects. AP2 (Sweden) reported a sizeable allocation to green investments, at 12.1% of its total portfolio, part of which included private equity investment in renewable energy/climate solutions. AP7 (Sweden) reported a small allocation to cleantech, which it defined as new environmentally improved business models and technical innovations that make it possible to use natural resources more efficiently and responsibly. The fund also reported that it was looking to increase its allocation to cleantech over the next couple of years.

Funds are paying increasing attention to European Union (EU) initiatives in relation to green investment. The EU taxonomy adopted in June 2020 aims to define which economic activities are sustainable, including socially and environmentally (OECD, 2020b). In addition, an EU regulation that entered into force in April 2020 defines two types of low-carbon benchmarks, the EU Paris Aligned and the EU Climate Transition, requiring ESG disclosures for benchmarks sold in the European Union.

7.5.2. Low-carbon infrastructure investment

As the renewable energy market continues to expand, a growing number of institutional investors have found that dedicated renewables funds are well-placed to meet their demands for ESG impact. For example, in April 2019, Norway's NOK 9 trillion (EUR 932 billion) sovereign wealth fund decided to invest up to 2% of the fund's value in unlisted renewable energy infrastructure.

Transportation and energy are the largest sectors in which the funds surveyed have made infrastructure allocations (see Figure 7.6). This indicates investor preference and the availability of opportunities. While there are differences across funds, corporate information suggests that pension funds are often attracted by the long-term tariff agreements in the transport and regulated utilities sector.

Renewable energy and social infrastructure are relatively new, although increasingly important, sectors in the portfolio of certain investors. While the majority of funds were not investing in renewables in 2015, the same sector represented 20% of the total infrastructure portfolio in 2017. Unlisted equity is only one medium through which funds may invest in renewables – it is likely that actual allocations to renewables are higher through investments in listed equity instruments and other channels.[15]

Figure 7.6. Infrastructure investment by sector, 2017

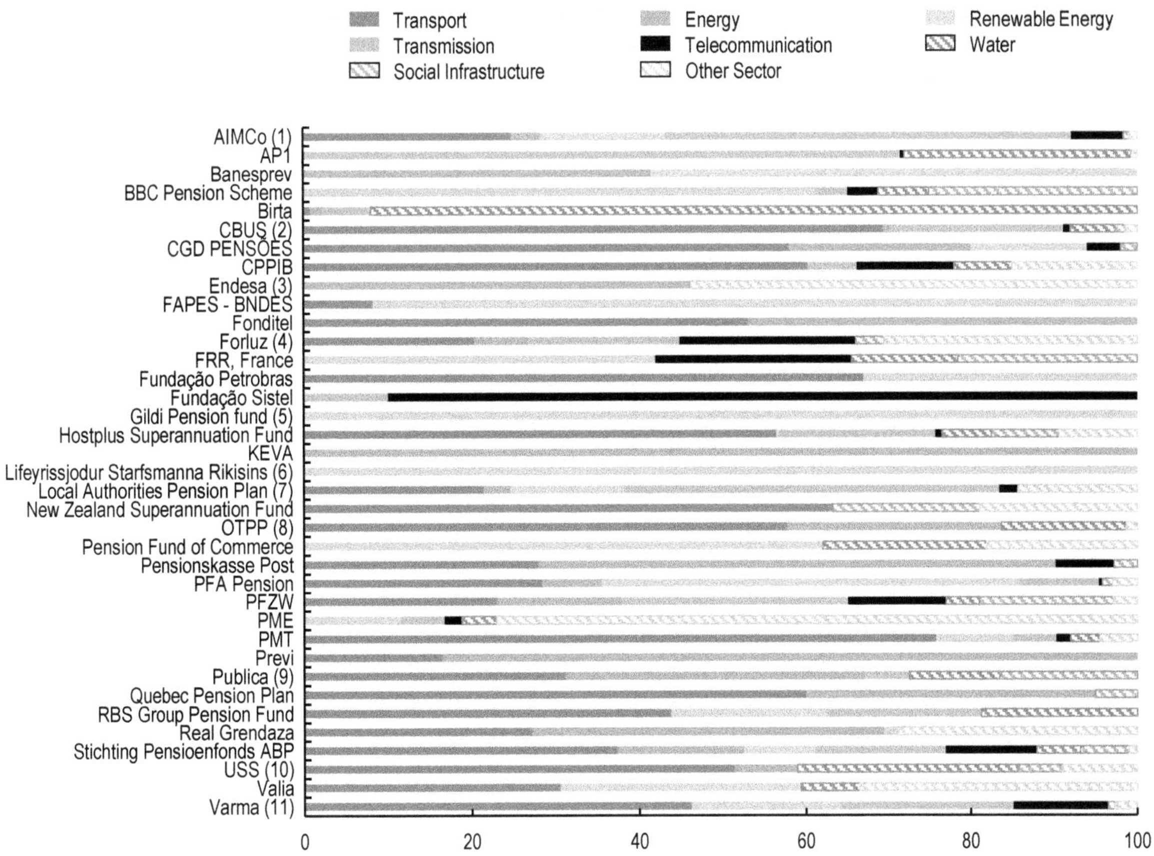

(1) AIMCo reported allocations for only a portion of the total portfolio.
(2) Includes land titles.
(3) Other includes multi-sector infrastructure.
(4) Other includes healthcare related investments; includes public and private infrastructure.
(5) Hydro and geothermal energy.
(6) Geothermal heat.
(7) Other includes timberlands, waste management.
(8) Energy includes generation and transmission.
(9) Allocations are for a loan portfolio.
(10) Data are as of March 2018.
(11) Allocations are as of December 2016.
Source: OECD calculations based on responses to the OECD Survey of large pension funds and public pension reserve funds.

In 2017, the average fund that reported the sectoral allocations of its unlisted infrastructure equity portfolio invested 28.6% of its portfolio in transportation, making this the largest sector. This was followed by renewable energy, with an average of 20% of the unlisted infrastructure equity portfolio. Two funds based in Iceland allocated 100% of their infrastructure allocation in geothermal energy and heat. Funds in the United Kingdom, including the BBC Pension Scheme and RBS Group Pension Fund, allocated sizeable allocations to renewables: RBS has financed onshore wind energy, while BBC has financed solar, onshore, and offshore wind investments. A number of Brazilian pension funds, including Banesprev, FAPES-BNDES, Petrobras, and Valia, also reported sizeable allocations to renewables.

As has been noted, investors have a strong preference for brownfield (operational) assets with proven abilities to generate cash flows. Some infrastructure assets offer cash flow stability and predictability over the long term, making them suitable for objectives related to diversification. Prospective risk and return are perceived to be higher for new greenfield assets and may require more due diligence on the part of the investor.

That being said, increased return appetite in relation to construction risk is pushing investors to acquire the expertise to be able to provide creditor oversight on new-build construction. For example PGGM has been investing in new projects through its partnership with Royal BAM in Holland. Lifeyrissjodur Starfsmanna Rikisins, based in Iceland, reported that 100% of its unlisted equity was invested in greenfield assets, likely linked to geothermal heat. Publica, based in Switzerland, reported allocating 93.1% in greenfield investment, which consisted of infrastructure loans, likely at construction stage.

Market development in infrastructure is offering new opportunities to investors. Beyond "core" infrastructure there is increasing interest among investors in what are considered to be value-added brownfield opportunities. These investments are focused on assets that need to be refurbished - either addressing operational or structural issues - or funding expansion. Expected returns on such projects already generating cash flows for the investors are higher than core projects. New fund structures try to align asset owners' long-term horizon with asset managers, to achieve specific ESG goals, including resilient urban infrastructure and energy transition (see Box 7.3).

Box 7.3. Investing in sustainable and resilient energy

Investment needs to meet the Paris Agreement include decarbonising industry and transport, building smart energy systems, and increasing access to affordable, clean energy. In the IEA Sustainable Development Scenario for example, spending on renewable power would need to double by the late 2030s (IEA Imperial (2020) and Bardalai A., Della Croce R., 2019). A study by McKinsey (2018) estimated that roughly USD 1.6 trillion of renewable power investments will be made available to institutional investors by 2030. Roughly 70% of that investment opportunity will be composed of unlisted assets that do not trade publicly.

Trends transforming traditional power and energy infrastructure systems are reshaping customer expectations and opening up new business models. The growth of renewable energy has significant technical implications in this area, particularly the need to adapt to intermittency. Funds active in the energy sector are trying to capture as much of the value chain as possible –as buying renewable energy assets together with storage.

Energy transition funds are adapting to these trends, focusing on the resiliency of the electricity system including the networks, biogas and the circular economy and energy efficiency. SUSI Partners was aiming in 2019 to first close on its EUR 1 billion SUSI Global Energy Transition Fund. An evergreen structure, this fund aims to invest in a diversified portfolio of around 20 construction and development-stage assets with a focus on infrastructure relevant for the energy transition.

7.6. Conclusions

Given the central role played by infrastructure in our economies and societies, and its broad economic, social, and environmental impacts, delivering quality infrastructure requires, amongst other things, gaining community support and the social licence to operate, highlighting the relevance of ESG factors for infrastructure investment. As institutional investors gain exposure to infrastructure through their portfolio investments, as providers of infrastructure financing, and start adopting ESG strategies for their investment portfolio(s), there is increasing recognition that ESG factors are relevant for infrastructure investments – in particular for the management of risks, to ensure downside protection and preserve if not enhance asset value over the holding period.

ESG approaches adopted by investors will vary depending on how the infrastructure investment is accessed, taking into account that the preferred route to infrastructure investment in the last decade has been through unlisted equity. In private markets, for pension funds and other institutional investors not capable of investing directly, hiring external consultants and asset managers to manage infrastructure investment has been the preferred way to access this asset class. Principal-agent issues between short-term private equity asset managers and long-term asset owners could cause disincentives to the adoption of ESG factors in the investment process.

The fact that infrastructure investment is often undertaken through private markets makes the adoption of ESG decision-making more challenging, as private markets do not have the same disclosure requirements as public markets. Given the often indirect nature of their infrastructure investments, through funds or managed separate accounts, institutional investors must rely significantly more on their asset managers and other service providers to track their exposure and performance. Hence asset managers play a key role in implementing and measuring ESG criteria in institutional investors' portfolios.

Despite broad recognition of the importance of ESG criteria and interest in incorporating these factors into infrastructure investment decision-making, the implementation of these criteria in asset valuation remains at an early stage. Several international standards and tools have been developed to integrate sustainability and resilience aspects into infrastructure development and support ESG infrastructure asset analysis. Current methods for ESG measurement and ESG-related analysis vary among stakeholders at different phases in the infrastructure process. Despite the number of initiatives, there seem to be several problems with the analysis of ESG factors in infrastructure. Among the major issues are: a lack of a common definition and metrics for measuring exposure to ESG in infrastructure; the lack of quality data and information required to perform analyses; the ability to quantify ESG criteria in financial terms; transparency in valuation methodologies across the industry; investors' understanding and confidence in ESG valuation; and the cost of ESG analysis.

From the perspective of government in many countries, implementation of quality infrastructure investment is a key priority, which requires, among other things, relevant ESG considerations to be taken into account in government procurement decisions, in the agreements governing public private partnerships for new projects, and in the conditions attached to budget facilities for infrastructure. Policy settings can also assist in overcoming key challenges or issues that impede proper private investor consideration of ESG factors in asset-level analysis of infrastructure, to the extent that the industry is unable to resolve the issues. Suggestions for government action have included better disclosure of private project-level data to investors, government sharing of its own project data, better government communication of priority ESG elements in infrastructure (see OECD 2020 and endnote 9), and clear, consistent guidance regarding ESG disclosures in financial markets more broadly.

A holistic framework aligning objective and definitions among stakeholders is needed. In order to differentiate among the effects of different ESG factors, investors and regulators need more granular data. This chapter highlights the need for work to understand the link between ESG and financial performance, especially on long-term effects and materiality and on asset allocation trends in private markets for infrastructure.

Given the shared interest in the effective management of ESG risks, so as to ensure positive social and economic outcomes for infrastructure investment, further progress could benefit from closer collaboration involving key stakeholders from private and public sectors, to enable a dialogue and identification of priority actions. As part this dialogue, understanding investor motivations, ESG approaches and methodologies used for infrastructure, and data requirements, accessibility, and limitations, would be valuable. Such collaboration could feature as part of broader current G20 and OECD efforts at public and private collaboration on infrastructure, undertaken with multilateral development banks, the GIH, and other stakeholders; indeed, ESG issues have already been identified as an important topic (see OECD, 2020a).

References

AECOM (2017), "Review of Screening Tools to Assess Sustainability and Climate Resilience of Infrastructure Development 2017-07-05", https://c402277.ssl.cf1.rackcdn.com/publications/1113/files/original/Review_of_Screening_Tools_Final_Report_SEP_2017.pdf.

Amundi (2019), The alpha and beta of ESG investing.

Bardalai A., Della Croce R (2019), Financing Low-Carbon Infrastructure, City UK and Imperial College, November 2019.

Bennon M. and R. Sharma, (2018), State of the Practice: Sustainability Standards for Infrastructure Investors, Investment Research Program, Global Projects Center, Stanford University.

Clark, G.L. and A.H.B. Monk (2017), Institutional Investors in Global Markets. Oxford: Oxford University Press.

EDHEC (2020), Infra300 equity index (local returns), First quarter 2020.

Fuerst, F. (2015), The Financial Rewards of Sustainability: A Global Performance Study of Real Estate Investment Trusts (June 16, 2015). Available at SSRN: https://ssrn.com/abstract=2619434 or http://dx.doi.org/10.2139/ssrn.2619434.

Garcia S. and T. Whittaker (2019), ESG Reporting and Financial Performance: the Case of Infrastructure, EDHEC Infrastructure.

GSIA (2018), Global Sustainable Investment Review 2018, The Global Sustainable Investment Alliance

IEA and Imperial College (2020), Energy Investing: Exploring Risk and Return in the Capital Markets, Imperial College, London.

IEA (2020), World Energy Investment 2020, International Energy Agency, https://www.iea.org/reports/world-energy-investment-2020.

IEA (2018), World Energy Outlook 2018, International Energy Agency, November 2018, https://www.iea.org/weo2018/.

Kirezci, E., I.R. Young, R. Ranasinghe. et al. (2020), Projections of global-scale extreme sea levels and resulting episodic coastal flooding over the 21st Century. Sci Rep 10, 11629 (2020), https://doi.org/10.1038/s41598-020-67736-6.

LTIIA (2020), ESG Handbook, Ernst & Young for the Long Term Infrastructure Investment Association, Paris.

McKinsey Global Energy Perspective (reference case 2019).

OECD (2020a), G20/OECD Report on the Collaboration with Institutional Investors and Asset Managers on Infrastructure: Investor proposals and the way forward, http://www.oecd.org/finance/g20-collaboration-with-institutional-investors-and-asset-managers-on-infrastructure.htm.

OECD (2020b - forthcoming), "Developing sustainable finance definitions and taxonomies".

OECD (2019a), Annual Survey of Large Pension Funds and Public Pension Reserve Funds.

OECD (2019b) Reference Note on Environmental and Social Considerations in Quality Infrastructure.

OECD (2019c), *Good Governance for Critical Infrastructure Resilience*, OECD Reviews of Risk Management Policies, OECD Publishing, Paris, https://doi.org/10.1787/02f0e5a0-en.

OECD (2018), Financing for Climate Future: Rethinking Infrastructure.

OECD (2017) Breaking Silos: Addressing the Information Gap and Developing Infrastructure as an Asset Class.

OECD (2015), Infrastructure Financing Instruments and Incentives: A Taxonomy.

OECD/IMF (2019), Reference Note on the Governance of Quality Infrastructure Investment.

OHCHR-HBF (2018), *The Other Infrastructure Gap: Sustainability: Human Rights and Environmental*

Dimensions, UN Office of the High Commissioner for Human Rights and Heinrich Boell Foundation.

Preqin (2020), 2020 Preqin Global Infrastructure Report.

Shroders (2019), ESG Policy Risk and Performance Impact Assessment Report: Infrastructure Finance.

Valenzuela, Sebastián, Nicolás M Somma, Andrés Scherman, and Arturo Arriagada (2016), "Social media in Latin America: deepening or bridging gaps in protest participation?" Online Information Review 40 (5):695-711.

Watkins, Graham, Hendrik Meller, Sven Mueller, Maria Cecilia Ramirez, Tomas Serebrisky, and Andreas Georgoulias (2017), Action Required: Lessons from Four Decades of Infrastructure Project Related Conflicts in Latin America and the Caribbean. Washington DC: Inter-American Development Bank and Zofnass Program Harvard.

WWF (2019), Valuing Sustainability in Infrastructure Investments: Market Status, Barriers and Opportunities: A Landscape Analysis, WWF Switzerland and Cadmus Group.

Annex 7.A. Standards and frameworks related to infrastructure and ESG factors

Standard	Type of Framework	Asset type	Certifying body
Equator Principles	Risk management framework	Infrastructure and large industrial projects	Member Equator Principles Financial Institutions (Standard Chartered, CIFI, Mizuho Bank, Bank of Montreal, FirstRand Limited, MUFG Bank, Commonwealth Bank of Australia, Wells Fargo, UK Export Finance, Nedbank)
UNEPFI – Property Investment	Investment framework	Real Estate	UNEP (United Nations Environment Programme) Finance Initiative
IFC Performance Standards on Environmental and Social Sustainability	Investment framework	Infrastructure	IFC (International Finance Corporation, World Bank Group)
UN-supported Principles for Responsible Investing (PRI)	Investment framework	Infrastructure	PRI Association Board
Sustainability Accounting Standards Board (SASB)	Accounting standard	Listed equity	Sustainability Accounting Standards Board Foundation
International Integrated Reporting Framework	Reporting framework	Listed equity	IIRC (International Integrated Reporting Council), a global coalition of regulators, investors, companies, standard setters, the accounting profession, academia, and NGOs.
Global Reporting Initiative (GRI)	Reporting framework	Corporations	Global Reporting Initiative

Source: OECD (2017), WWF (2019)

Notes

[1] Financial Times 31 July 2020, "Rise in coastal flooding poses threat to economies", Anna Gross: According to Professor Ian Young, infrastructure engineer at the University of Melbourne, "The sea-level

rise is now already baked in, the glaciers are melting and they aren't going to stop melting for hundreds of years. Even if we reduce our greenhouses gases today we'll still have significant flooding by 2100".

[2] As seen in previous chapters there is increasing evidence of market inefficiencies in pricing ESG risks.

[3] The OECD defines infrastructure as the system of public works in a country, state or region, including roads, utility lines and public building – in essence the tangible backbone of essential goods and services underpinning an economy. See: https://stats.oecd.org/glossary/detail.asp?ID=4511.

[4] The Inter-American Development Bank (2017) analysed 200 projects across six sectors in Latin America and the Caribbean that were strongly opposed by local communities and found that a lack of a multi-dimensional approach in project planning, design, and delivery was seriously detrimental for companies, investors, and national governments - 36 out of the 200 projects were cancelled; 162 faced delays; and 116 faced cost overruns.

[5] See Infrastructure Journal articles covering the period May–July 2020.

[6] The judgement, which sets a key legal precedent, said the government had wrongly ignored its international climate change commitments under the Paris Agreement.

[7] See also *Reference Note on Environmental and Social Considerations in Quality Infrastructure* (OECD, 2019b) and *Reference Note on the Governance of Quality Infrastructure Investment* (OECD/IMF, 2019), which provide reference material for the implementation of the G20 QII Principles. The forthcoming OECD *Compendium of Policy Good Practices for Quality Infrastructure Investment* (2020) provides a set of integrated and multidisciplinary good practices for policymakers and practitioners to use on a voluntary basis, and which promote a shared understanding of the elements needed to support QII in accordance with international standards. Complementing the Compendium, which is a policy guidance tool, an OECD *Implementation Handbook for Quality Infrastructure Investment* will be developed; it will provide an analytical and operational tool, focusing on selected major issues and challenges for QII, and providing implementation solutions through concrete examples and case studies.

[8] The IEA and Imperial College London are investigating the risk and return proposition available to investors in the energy sector through a series of special reports. The first study focuses on historical financial performance of fossil fuels versus renewable power in listed equity markets of select advanced economies. The methodology used in the report will be extended to other countries and unlisted (i.e. private market) investments in forthcoming work.

[9] From an OECD Dialogue with the Asset Management Industry on Sustainable Infrastructure, 25 October 2019.

[10] For more extensive reviews on methodologies used to measure or report on infrastructure sustainability, see LTIIA (2020), WWF (2019), Bennon M. and and R. Sharma (2018), AESCOM (2017) and IDB (2016).

[11] International responsible business conduct (RBC) principles and standards set out expectations for how businesses and investors should undertake risk-based due diligence to consider impacts on the people and the planet. More information is available at https://mneguidelines.oecd.org/Brochure-responsible-business-key-messages-from-international-instruments.pdf.

[12] The GSIA survey shows asset class allocation in Europe, the United States, Japan and Canada in 2018. Sustainable investments can also be found in hedge funds, cash or depository vehicles, commodities.

[13] For example, AllianzGI has a traditional infrastructure allocation in unlisted markets but also an infrastructure equity team that is dedicated to green energy assets. BlackRock currently manages a

USD 50 billion fund that supports the transition to a low-carbon economy, including renewable power infrastructure business, which invests in the private markets in wind and solar power, and green bond funds.

[14] This section benefits from data collected by the OECD for the period 2015-2017 and quantitative analysis. The focus is on two distinct pools of long-term savings: large pension funds (LPFs) and public pension reserve funds (PPRFs). In 2017, the OECD gathered, for the fourth year in a row, data on green and social investments by LPFs and PPRFs. Twenty-six and thirty-seven funds provided information about their green investments in the OECD surveys covering the period 2015- 2017.These data included information on investments that funds have made in specific products, debt/equity instruments, or through specific mandates for social impact and/or green investment. Not all funds included in the survey reported that they actively implement ESG frameworks in their investment processes as In 2017, twenty-six LPFs stated that they were not active in green finance. The sample although subject to bias towards more active investors is still significant to represent current trends and market evolution in recent years.

[15] In the OECD survey, infrastructure investment is calculated as a % of total assets of funds investing in infrastructure. Infrastructure investment is calculated as a % of total assets of all funds in the survey, excluding the ones stemming from publicly available reports.

www.ingramcontent.com/pod-product-compliance
Ingram Content Group UK Ltd.
Pitfield, Milton Keynes, MK11 3LW, UK
UKHW051501290926
15471UKWH00008B/1349